George Wilson

The Financial Philosophy

Or, the principles of the science of money. With observations on the present situation.

George Wilson

The Financial Philosophy
Or, the principles of the science of money. With observations on the present situation.

ISBN/EAN: 9783337071813

Printed in Europe, USA, Canada, Australia, Japan

Cover: Foto ©Suzi / pixelio.de

More available books at **www.hansebooks.com**

ROBERT STEPHEN HAWKER

THE
VICAR OF MORWENSTOW

BEING A LIFE OF

ROBERT STEPHEN HAWKER, M.A.

BY

S. BARING-GOULD, M.A.

NEW AND REVISED EDITION

METHUEN & CO.
36 ESSEX STREET, W.C.
LONDON
1899

Homme étrange, original et supérieur, mais qui, dès l'enfance, portait en soi un germe de folie, et qui à la fin devint fou tout à fait ; esprit admirable et mal équilibré, en qui les sensations, les émotions et les images étaient trop fortes ; à la fois aveugle et perspicace, véritable poëte et poëte malade, qui au lieu des choses, voyait ses rêves, vivait dans un roman et mourut sous le cauchemar qu'il s'était forgé ; incapable de se maîtriser et de se conduire, prenant ses résolutions pour des actes, ses velléités pour des résolutions, et le rôle qu'il se donnait pour le caractère qu'il croyait avoir ; en tout disproportionné au train courant du monde, se heurtant, se blessant, se salissant à toutes les bornes du chemin ; ayant commis des extravagances, des injustices, et néanmoins gardant jusqu'au bout la sensibilité délicate et profonde, l'humanité, l'attendrissement, le don des larmes, la faculté d'aimer, la passion de la justice, le sentiment religieux, l'enthousiasme, comme autant de racines vivaces où fermente toujours la séve généreuse pendant que la tige et les rameaux avortent, se déforment ou se flétrissent sous l'inclémence de l'air.—H. TAINE.

CONTENTS

CHAPTER I

PAGE

Birth of Mr. Hawker—Dr. Hawker of Charles Church—The Amended Hymn—Robert S. Hawker runs away from School—Boyish Pranks—At Cheltenham—Publishes his *Tendrils*—At Oxford—Marries—The Stowe Ghost—Robert Hawker and Mr. Jeune at Boscastle—The Mazed Pigs—Nanny Heale and the Potatoes—*Records of the Western Shore*—The Bude Mermaid—Takes his Degree—Comes with his Wife to Morwenstow - - - - - - - - 1

CHAPTER II

Ordination—The Black Pig "Gyp"—Writes to the Bishop—His Father appointed to Stratton—He is given Morwenstow—The Waldron Lantern—St. Morwenna—The Children of Brychan—St. Modwenna of Burton-on-Trent—The North Cornish Coast—Tintagel—Stowe—Sir Bevil Grenville—Mr. Hawker's Discovery of the Grenville Letters—Those that remain—Antony Payne the Giant—Letters of Lady Grace—Of Lord Lansdown—Cornish Dramatic Power—Mr. Hicks of Bodmin - - - - - - 20

CONTENTS

CHAPTER III

PAGE

Description of Morwenstow—The Anerithmon Gelasma—Source of the Tamar—Tonacombe—Morwenstow Church—Norman Chevron Moulding—Chancel—Altar—Shooting Rubbish—The Manning Bed—The Yellow Poncho—The Vicarage—Mr. Tom Knight—The Stag Robin Hood—Visitors—Silent Tower of Bottreaux—The Pet of Boscastle - - - - 47

CHAPTER IV

Mr. Hawker's Politics—Election of 1857—His Zeal for the Labourers—"The Poor Man and his Parish Church"—Letter to a Landlord—Death of his Man Tape—Kindness to the Poor—Verses over his Door—Reckless Charity—Hospitality—A Breakdown—His Eccentric Dress—The Devil and his Barn—His Ecclesiastical Vestments—Ceremonial—The Nine Cats—The Church Garden—Kindness to Animals—The Rooks and Jackdaws—The Well of St. John—Letter to a Young Man entering the University 78

CHAPTER V

The Inhabitants of Morwenstow in 1834—Cruel Coppinger—Whips the Parson of Kilkhampton—Gives Tom Tape a Ride—Tristam Pentire—Parminter and his Dog Satan—The Gauger's Pocket—Wrecking—The Wrecker and the Ravens—The Loss of the *Margaret Quail*—The Wreck of the *Ben Coolan*—"A Croon on Hennacliff"—Letters concerning Wrecks—The Donkeys and the Copper Ore—The Ship *Morwenna*—Flotsam and Jetsam—Wrecks on 14th Nov., 1875—Bodies in Poundstock Church—The Loss of the *Caledonia*—The Wreck of the *Phœnix* and of the *Alonzo* - - - - - - - - - - 105

CONTENTS

CHAPTER VI

Wellcombe—Mr. Hawker Postman to Wellcombe—The Miss Kitties—Advertisement of Roger Giles—Superstitions—The Evil Eye—The Spiritual Ether—The Vicar's Pigs Bewitched—Horse killed by a Witch—He finds a lost Hen—A Lecture against Witchcraft—Its Failure—An Encounter with the Pixies—Curious Picture of a Pixie Revel—The Fairy Ring—Antony Cleverdon and the Mermaids - - - 148

CHAPTER VII.

Condition of the Church last Century—Parson Radford—The Death of a Pluralist—Opposition Mr. Hawker met with—The Bryanites—Hunting the Devil—Bill Martin's Prayer-meeting—Mr. Pengelly and the Candle-end—Cheated by a Tramp—Mr. Hawker and the Dissenters—Mr. B——'s Pew—A Special Providence over the Church—His Prayer when threatened with the Loss of St. John's Well—Objection to Hysterical Religion—Mr. Vincent's Hat—Regard felt for him by old Pupils—"He did not Appreciate Me"—Modryb Marya—A Parable—A Carol—Love of Children—Angels—A Sermon, "Here am I" - - 167

CHAPTER VIII

The Vicar of Morwenstow as a Poet—His Epigrams—The "Carol of the Pruss"—"Down with the Church"—The "Quest of the Sangreal"—Editions of his Poems—Ballads—The "Song of the Western Men"—The "Cornish Mother's Lament"—"A Thought"—Churchyards - - - - - - - 202

CHAPTER IX

Restoration of Morwenstow Church—The Shingle Roof—The First Ruridecanal Synod—The Weekly Offer-

tory—Correspondence with Mr. Walter—On Alms—
Harvest Thanksgiving—The School—Mr. Hawker
belonged to no Party—His Eastern Proclivities—
Theological Ideas—Baptism—Original Sin—The
Eucharist—His Preaching—Some Sermons - - 218

CHAPTER X

The First Mrs. Hawker—Her Influence over her Husband
—Anxiety about her Health—His Fits of Depression
—Letter on the Death of Sir Thomas Acland—Reads
Novels to his Wife—His Visions—Mysticism—Death
of his Wife—Unhappy Condition—Burning of his
Papers—Meets with his Second Wife—The Unburied
Dead—Birth of his Child—Ruinous Condition of his
Church—Goes to London—Resumes Opium-eating
—Sickness—Goes to Boscastle—To Plymouth—His
Death and Funeral—Conclusion - - - - 241

LIFE OF ROBERT STEPHEN HAWKER

CHAPTER I

Birth of Mr. Hawker—Dr. Hawker of Charles Church—The Amended Hymn—Robert S. Hawker runs away from School—Boyish Pranks—At Cheltenham—Publishes his *Tendrils*—At Oxford—Marries—The Stowe Ghost—Robert Hawker and Mr. Jeune at Boscastle—The Mazed Pigs—Nanny Heale and the Potatoes—*Records of the Western Shore*—The Bude Mermaid—Takes his Degree—Comes with his Wife to Morwenstow.

ROBERT STEPHEN HAWKER was born at Stoke Damerel on 3rd December, 1804, and was baptised there in the parish church. His father, Mr. Jacob Stephen Hawker, was at that time a medical man, practising at Plymouth. He afterwards was ordained to Altarnun, and spent thirty years as curate and then vicar of Stratton in Cornwall, where he died in 1845. Mr. J. S. Hawker was the son of the famous Dr. Hawker, incumbent of Charles Church in Plymouth, author of *Morning and Evening Portions*, a man as remarkable for his abilities as he was for his piety.

Young Robert was committed to his grandfather to be educated. The doctor, after the death of his wife, lived in Plymouth with his daughter, a widow, Mrs. Hodgson, at whose expense Robert was educated.

The profuse generosity, the deep religiousness, and the eccentricity of the doctor, had their effect on the boy, and traced in his opening mind and forming character deep lines, which were never effaced. Dr. Hawker had a heart always open to appeals of poverty, and in his kindness he believed every story of distress which was told him, and hastened to relieve it without inquiring closely whether it were true or not; nor did he stop to consider whether his own pocket could afford the generosity to which his heart prompted him. His wife, as long as she lived, found it a difficult matter to keep house. In winter, if he came across a poor family without sufficient coverings on their beds, he would speed home, pull the blankets off his own bed, and run with them over his arm to the house where they were needed.

He had an immense following of pious ladies, who were sometimes troublesome to him. "I see what it is," said the doctor in one of his sermons: "you ladies think to reach heaven by hanging on to my coat-tails. I will trounce you all: I will wear a spencer."

In Charles Church the evening service always closed with the singing of the hymn, "Lord, dismiss us with Thy blessing," composed by Dr. Hawker himself. His grandson did not know the authorship of the hymn: he came to the doctor one day with a paper in his hand, and said: "Grandfather, I don't altogether like that hymn, 'Lord, dismiss us with

Thy blessing': I think it might be improved in metre and language, and would be better if made somewhat longer".

"Oh, indeed!" said Dr. Hawker, getting red; "and pray, Robert, what emendations commend themselves to your precocious wisdom?"

"This is my improved version," said the boy, and read as follows :—

> 'Lord, dismiss us with Thy blessing,
>   High and low, and rich and poor:
> May we all, Thy fear possessing,
>   Go in peace, and sin no more!
>
> Lord, requite not as we merit;
>   Thy displeasure all must fear:
> As of old, so let Thy Spirit
>   Still the dove's resemblance bear.
>
> May that Spirit dwell within us!
>   May its love our refuge be!
> So shall no temptation win us
>   From the path that leads to Thee.
>
> So when these our lips shall wither,
>   So when fails each earthly tone,
> May we sing once more together
>   Hymns of glory round Thy throne!'

"Now, listen to the old version, grandfather :—

> 'Lord, dismiss us with Thy blessing;
>   Fill our hearts with joy and peace;
> Let us each Thy love possessing,
>   Triumph in redeeming grace.
>   Oh, refresh us,
>   Travelling through this wilderness!

> Thanks we give, and adoration,
> For the Gospel's joyous sound;
> May the founts of Thy salvation
> In our hearts and lives abound!
> May Thy presence
> With us evermore be found!'

"This one is crude and flat; don't you think so, grandfather?"

"Crude and flat, sir! Young puppy, it is *mine!* I wrote that hymn."

"Oh! I beg your pardon, grandfather; I did not know that: it is a very nice hymn indeed; but—but *grace* is a bad rhyme for *peace*, and one naturally wishes to put grease in its place. Your hymn may be good"—and, as he went out of the door—"but mine is better."

Robert was sent to a boarding-school by his grandfather; where, I do not know, nor does it much matter, for he stayed there only one night. He arrived in the evening, and was delivered over by the doctor to a very godly but close-fisted master. Robert did not approve of being sent supperless to bed, still less did he approve of the bed and bedroom in which he was placed.

Next morning the dominie was shaving at his window, when he saw his pupil, with his portmanteau on his back, striding across the lawn, with reckless indifference to the flower-beds, singing at the top of his voice, "Lord, dismiss us with Thy blessing." He shouted after him from the window, but Robert was deaf. The boy flung his portmanteau over the hedge, jumped after it, and was seen no more at that school.

He was then put with the Rev. Mr. Laffer, at

Liskeard. Mr. Laffer was the son of a yeoman at Altarnun: he afterwards became incumbent of St. Gennys. At this time he was head master of the Liskeard Grammar School. There Robert Hawker was happy. He spent his holidays either with his father at Stratton, or with his grandfather and aunt at Plymouth. At Stratton he was the torment of an old fellow who kept a shop in High Street, where he sold groceries, crockery and drapery. One day he slipped into the house when the old man was out, and found a piece of mutton roasting before the fire. Robert took it off the crook, hung it up in the shop, and placed a bundle of dips before the fire, to roast in its place.

He would dive into the shop, catch hold of the end of thread that curled out of the tin in which the shopkeeper kept the ball of twine with which he tied up his parcels, and race with it in his hand down the street, then up a lane and down another, till he had uncoiled it all, and laced Stratton in a cobweb of twine, tripping up people as they went along the streets. The old fellow had not the wits to cut the thread, but held on like grim death to the tin, whilst the ball bounced and uncoiled within it, swearing at the plague of a boy, and wishing him "back to skule again."

"I doan't care whether I ring the bells on the king's birthday," said the parish clerk, another victim of the boy's pranks; "but if I never touch the ropes again, I'll give a peal when Robert goes to skule, and leaves Stratton folks in peace."

As may well be believed, the mischievous, high-spirited boy played tricks on his brothers and sisters.

The clerk was accustomed to read in church, "I am an alien unto my mother's children," pronouncing "alien" as "a lion." "Ah!" said Mrs. Hawker, "that means Robert: he is verily a lion unto his mother's children."

"I do not know how it is," said his brother one day: "when I go out with Robert nutting, he gets all the nuts; and when I go out rabbiting, he gets all the rabbits; and when we go out fishing together, he catches all the fish."

"Come with me fishing to-morrow, Claud," said Robert, "and see if you don't have luck."

Next day he surreptitiously fastened a red herring to his brother's hook, playing on his brother the trick Cleopatra had played on Anthony; and, when it was drawn out of the water, "There!" exclaimed Robert, "you are twice as lucky as I am. My fish are all raw; and yours is ready cleaned, smoked and salted."

The old vicarage at Stratton is now pulled down: it stood at the east end of the chancel, and the garden has been thrown into the burial-ground.

At Stratton he got one night into the stable of the surgeon, hogged the mane, and painted the coat of his horse like a zebra with white and black oil paint. Then he sent a message to the doctor, as if from a great house at a distance, requiring his immediate attendance. The doctor was obliged to saddle and gallop off the horse in the condition in which he found it, thinking that there was not time for him to stay till the coat was cleaned of paint.

His pranks at Plymouth led at last to his grandfather refusing to have him any longer in his house.

Robert held in aversion the good pious ladies, who swarmed round the doctor. It was the time of sedan-chairs; and trains of old spinsters and dowagers were wont to fill the street in their boxes between bearers, on the occasion of missionary teas, Dorcas meetings, and private expositions of the Word. Robert used to open the house door, and make a sign to the bearers to stop. A row of a dozen or more sedans were thus arrested in the street. Then the boy would go to each sedan in order, open the window, and, thrusting his head in, kiss the fair but venerable occupant, and then start back in mock dismay, exclaiming: "A thousand pardons! I thought you were my mother. I am sorry. How could I have made such a mistake, you are so much older?"

Sometimes, with the gravest face, he would tell the bearers that the lady was to be conveyed to the Dockyard, or the Arsenal, or to the Hoe; and she would find herself deposited among anchors and ropes, or cannon-balls, or on the windy height overlooking the bay, instead of at the doctor's door.

Two old ladies, spinster sisters, Robert believed were setting their caps at the doctor, then a widower. He took an inveterate dislike to them, and their insinuating, oily manner with his grandfather; and he worried them out of Plymouth.

He did it thus. One day he called on a certain leading physician in Plymouth, and told him that Miss Hephzibah Jenkins had slipped on a piece of orange peel, broken her leg, and needed his instant attention. He arrived out of breath with running, very red; and, it being known that the Misses

Jenkins were intimate friends of Dr. Hawker, the physician went off at once to the lady, with splints and bandages.

Next day another medical man was sent to see Miss Sidonia Jenkins. Every day a fresh surgeon or physician arrived to bind up legs and arms and heads, or revive the ladies from extreme prostration, pleurisy, inflammation of the lungs, heart-complaint, etc., till every medical man in Plymouth, Stonehouse and Devonport had been to the house of the spinsters. When these were exhausted, an undertaker was sent to measure the old ladies for their coffins; and next day a hearse drew up at their door to convey them to their graves, which had been dug according to order in the St. Andrew's churchyard.

This was more than the ladies could bear. They shut up the house and left Plymouth. But this was also the end of Robert's stay with his grandfather. The good doctor had endured a great deal, but he would not put up with this; and Robert was sent to Stratton, to his father.

When the boy left school at Liskeard, he was articled to a lawyer, Mr. Jacobson, at Plymouth, a wealthy man in good practice, first cousin to his mother; but this sort of profession did not at all approve itself to Robert's taste, and he remained with Mr. Jacobson a few months only. Whether he then turned his thoughts towards going into holy orders, cannot be told; but he persuaded his aunt, Mrs. Hodgson, to send him to Cheltenham Grammar School.

The boy had great abilities, and a passionate love

of books, but wanted application. He read a great deal, but his reading was desultory. He was, however, a good classic scholar. To mathematics he took a positive dislike, and never could master a proposition in Euclid. At Cheltenham he wrote some poems, and published them in a little book entitled *Tendrils, by Reuben*. They appeared in 1821, when he was seventeen years old.

From Cheltenham, Robert S. Hawker went to Oxford, 1823, and entered at Pembroke; but his father was only a poor curate, and unable to maintain him at the university. Robert was determined to finish his course there. He could not command the purse of his aunt, Mrs. Hodgson, who was dead; and when he retired to Stratton for his long vacation in 1824, his father told him that it was impossible for him to send him back to the university.

But Robert Hawker had made up his mind that finish his career at college he would. The difficulty was got over in a manner somewhat novel.

There lived at Whitstone, near Holsworthy, four Miss I'ans, daughters of Colonel I'ans. They had been left with an annuity of £200 apiece, as well as lands and a handsome place. At the time when Mr. Jacob Hawker announced to his son that a return to Oxford was impossible, the four ladies were at Efford, near Bude, an old manor house leased from Sir Thomas Acland. Directly that Robert Hawker learnt his father's decision, without waiting to put on his hat, he ran from Stratton to Bude, arrived hot and blown at Efford, and proposed to Miss Charlotte I'ans to become his wife. The lady was then aged forty-one, one year older than his mother; she was his godmother, and had taught him his letters.

Miss Charlotte I'ans accepted him; and they were married in November, when he was twenty. Robert S. Hawker and his wife spent their honeymoon at Morwenstow, in Combe Cottage. During that time he was visited by Sir William Call and his brother George. They dined with him, and told ghost-stories. Sir William professed his utter disbelief in spectral appearances, in spite of the most convincing, properly authenticated cases adduced by Mr. Hawker. It was late when the two gentlemen rose to leave. Their course lay down the steep hill by old Stowe. The moment that they were gone Robert got a sheet and an old iron spoon which he had dug up in the garden, and which bore on it the date 1702. He slipped a tinder-box and a bottle of choice brandy, which had belonged to Colonel I'ans, into his pocket, and ran by a short cut to a spot where the road was overshadowed by trees, at the bottom of the Stowe hill, which he knew the two young men must pass. He had time to throw the sheet over himself, strike a light, fill the great iron spoon with salt and brandy, and ignite it, before Sir William and his brother came up.

In the dense darkness of the wood, beside the road, they suddenly saw a ghastly figure, illumined by a lambent blue flame which danced in the air before it. They stood rooted to the spot, petrified with fear. Slowly the apparition stole towards them. They were too frightened to cry out and run. Suddenly, with an unearthly howl, the spectre plunged something metallic into the breast of Sir William Call's yellow nankeen waistcoat, the livid flame fell around him in drops, and all vanished.

When he came to himself Sir William found an iron spoon in his bosom. He and his brother, much alarmed, and not knowing what to think of what they had seen, returned to Combe. They knocked at the door. Hawker put his head with nightcap on out of the bedroom-window and asked who were disturbing his rest. They begged to be admitted: they had something of importance to communicate. He came down stairs in a dressing-gown, and introduced them to his parlour. There the iron spoon was examined. "It is very ancient," said Sir William: "the date on it is 1702—just the time when Stowe was pulled down."

"It smells very strong of brandy," said George Call.

Robert Hawker's twinkling eye and twitching mouth revealed the rest.

"'Pon my word," said Sir William Call, "you nearly killed me; and, what is more serious, nearly made me believe in spirits."

"Ah!" added Robert dryly, "you probably did believe in them when they ran in a river of flame over your yellow nankeen waistcoat."

The marriage with Charlotte I'ans took place on 6th November, 1824. On Hawker's return to Oxford with his wife after the Christmas vacation (and he took her there, riding behind him on a pillion), he was obliged, on account of being married, to migrate from Pembroke to Magdalen Hall. About this time he made acquaintance with Jeune and Jacobson, the former afterwards Bishop of Peterborough, the latter Bishop of Chester. Jeune, and afterwards Jacobson, came down into Cornwall to pay him a visit in the long vacation of 1825; and Mr. Jeune acted as groomsman at the marriage of Miss Hawker to Mr. Kingdon. It was on the occasion of this visit of Mr. Jeune to Robert Hawker that they went over together to Boscastle, and there performed the prank described in *Footprints of Former Men in Cornwall.* The two young men put up in the little inn of Joan Treworgy, entitled The Ship. The inn still exists; but it is rebuilt, and has become more magnificent in its accommodation and charges.

"We proceeded to confer about beds for the night, and, not without misgivings, inquired if she could supply a couple of those indispensable places of repose. A demur ensued. All the gentry in the town, she declared, were accustomed to sleep two in a bed; and the officers that travelled the country, and stopped at her house, would mostly do the same: but, however, if we commanded two beds for only two people, two we must have; only, although they were both in the same room, we must certainly pay for two, and sixpence apiece was her regular price. We assented, and then went on to entreat that we might dine. She graciously agreed; but to all questions as to our fare her sole response was, 'Meat—meat and taties. Some call 'em,' she added, in a scornful tone, 'purtaties; but we always says taties here.' The specific differences between beef, mutton, veal, etc., seemed to be utterly or artfully ignored;

and to every frenzied inquiry her calm, inexorable reply was, 'Meat—nice wholesome meat and taties.'

"In due time we sat down in that happy ignorance as to the nature of our viands which a French cook is said to desire; and, although we both made a not unsatisfactory meal, it is a wretched truth that by no effort could we ascertain what it was that was roasted for us that day by widow Treworgy, and which we consumed. Was it a piece of Boscastle baby? as I suggested to my companion. The question caused him to rush out to inquire again; but he came back baffled and shouting, 'Meat and taties.' There was not a vestige of bone, nor any outline that could indentify the joint; and the not unsavoury taste was something like tender veal. It was not till years afterwards that light was thrown on our mysterious dinner that day by a passage which I accidently turned up in an ancient history of Cornwall. Therein I read, 'that the silly people of Bouscastle and Boussiney do catch in the summer seas divers young soyles (seals), which, doubtful if they be fish or flesh, conynge housewives will nevertheless roast, and do make thereof savory meat.'"

Very early next morning, before any one else was awake, Hawker and Jeune left the inn, and, going to all the pig-sties of the place, released their occupants. They then stole back to their beds.

"We fastened the door, and listened for results. The outcries and yells were fearful. By-and-by human voices began to mingle with the tumult: there were shouts of inquiry and surprise, then sounds of expostulation and entreaty, and again 'a storm of hate and wrath and wakening fear.' At last the tumult reached the ears of our hostess, Joan Treworgy. We heard her puff and blow, and call for Jim. At last, after waiting a prudent time, we thought it best to call aloud for shaving-water, and to inquire with astonishment into the cause of that horrible disturbance which had roused us from our morning sleep. This brought the widow in hot haste to our door. 'Why, they do say, captain,' was her doleful response, 'that all the pegs up-town have a-rebelled, and they've a-been, and let one the wother out, and they be all a-gwain to sea, hug-a-mug, bang!'"

Some years after, when Mr. Jeune was Dean of Magdalen Hall, Mr. Hawker went up to take his M.A. degree. The dean on that occasion was, according to custom, leading a gentleman-commoner of the same college, a very corpulent man, to the vice-chancellor, to present him for his degree, with a Latin speech. Hawker was waiting his turn. The place was crowded, and the fat gentleman-commoner was got with difficulty through the throng to the place. Hawker leaned towards the dean as he was leading and endeavouring to guide this unwieldy candidate, who hung back, and got hitched in the crowd, and said in a low tone:—

"Why, your peg's surely mazed, maister."

When the crowd gave way, and the dean reached the vice-chancellor's chair, he was in spasms of uncontrollable laughter.

At Oxford Mr. Robert Hawker made acquaintance with Macbride, afterwards head of the college; and the friendship lasted through life.

In after years, when Jeune, Jacobson and Macbride were heads of colleges, Robert S. Hawker went up to Oxford in his cassock and gown. The cassock was then not worn, as it sometimes is now, except by heads of colleges and professors. Mr. Hawker was therefore singular in his cassock. He was outside St. Mary's one day, with Drs. Jeune, Jacobson and Macbride, when a friend, looking at him in his gown and cassock, said: "Why, Hawker, one would think you wanted to be taken for a head."

"About the last thing I should like to be taken for, as heads go," was his ready reply, with a roguish glance at his three companions.

Mr. Hawker has related another of his mischievous tricks when an undergraduate. There was a poor old woman named Nanny Heale, who passed for a witch. Her cottage was an old decayed hut, roofed with turf. One night Robert Hawker got on the roof, and looking down the chimney, saw her crouching over her turf fire, watching with dim eyes an iron crock, or round vessel, filled with potatoes, that were simmering in the heat. This utensil was suspended by its swing handle to an iron bar that went across the chimney. Hawker let a rope, with an iron hook at the end, slowly and noiselessly down the chimney, and, unnoted by poor Nanny's blinking sight, caught the handle of the caldron; and it, with its mealy contents, began to ascend the chimney slowly and majestically.

Nanny, thoroughly aroused by this unnatural proceeding of her old iron vessel, peered despairingly after it, and shouted at the top of her voice:—

"Massy 'pon my sinful soul! art gawn off—taties and all?"

The vessel was quietly grasped, and carried down in hot haste, and planted upright outside the cottage door. A knock, given on purpose, summoned the inmate, who hurried out, and stumbled over, as she afterwards interpreted the event, her penitent crock.

"So, then," was her joyful greeting,—"so, then! theer't come back to holt, then! Ay, 'tis a-cold out o' doors."

Good came out of evil: for her story, which she rehearsed again and again, with all the energy and persuasion of truth, reached the ears of the parochial authorities; and they, thinking that old Nanny's wits had failed her, gave an additional shilling a week to her allowance.

Hawker's vacations were spent at Whitstone, or at Ivy Cottage, near Bude. At Whitstone he built himself a bark shanty in the wood, and set up a life-sized carved wooden figure, which he had procured in Oxford, at the door, to keep it. The figure he called "Moses." It has long since disappeared.

In this hut he was wont to read. His meals were brought out there to him. His intervals of work were spent in composing ballads on Cornish legends, afterwards published at Oxford in his *Records of the Western Shore*, 1832. They have all been reprinted in later editions of his poems. One of these, his "Song of the Western Men," was adapted to the really ancient burden :—

> And shall they scorn Tre, Pol and Pen,
> And shall Trelawny die?
> Here's twenty thousand Cornish men
> Will know the reason why!

These verses have so much of the antique flavour, that Sir Walter Scott, in one of his prefaces to a later edition of the *Border Minstrelsy*, refers to them as a "remarkable example of the lingering of the true ballad spirit in a remote district"; and Mr. Hawker possessed a letter from Lord Macaulay in which he admitted that, until undeceived by the writer, he had always supposed the whole song to be of the time of the Bishops' trial.

At Ivy Cottage he had formed for himself a perch on the edge of the cliff, where he could be alone with his books, his thoughts, and, as he would say with solemnity, "with God."

Perhaps few thought then how deep were the religious impressions in the joyous heart, full of exuberant spirits, of the young Oxford student. All people knew of him was, that he was remarkable for his beauty, for his brightness of manner, his overflowing merriment, and love of playing tricks. But there was a deep undercurrent of religious feeling setting steadily in one direction, which was the main governing stream of his life. Gradually this emerges into sight, and becomes recognised. Then it was known to few except his wife and her sisters.

Of this period of his life, it is chiefly his many jests which have lingered on in the recollection of his friends and relations.

One absurd hoax that he played on the superstitious people of Bude must not be omitted.

At full moon in the July of 1825 or 1826, he swam or rowed out to a rock at some little distance from the shore, plaited seaweed into a wig, which he threw over his head, so that it hung in lank streamers half-way down his back, enveloped his legs in an oilskin wrap, and, otherwise naked, sat on the rock, flashing the moonbeams about from a hand-mirror, and sang and screamed till attention was arrested. Some people passing along the cliff heard and saw him, and ran into Bude, saying that a mermaid with a fish's tail was sitting on a rock, combing her hair, and singing.

A number of people ran out on the rocks and along the beach, and listened awestruck to the singing and disconsolate wailing of the mermaid. Presently she dived off the rock, and disappeared.

Next night crowds of people assembled to look out for the mermaid; and in due time she reappeared, and sent the moon flashing in their faces from her glass. Telescopes were brought to bear on her; but she sang on unmoved, braiding her tresses, and uttering remarkable sounds, unlike the singing of mortal throats which have been practised in do-re-mi.

This went on for several nights; the crowd growing greater, people arriving from Stratton, Kilkhampton, and all the villages round, till Robert Hawker got very hoarse with his nightly singing, and rather tired of sitting so long in the cold. He therefore wound up the performance one night with an unmistakable "God save the King," then plunged into the waves, and the mermaid never again revisited the "sounding shores of Bude."

Miss Fanny I'ans was a late riser. Her brother-in-law, to break her of this bad habit, was wont to throw open her window early in the morning, and turn in a troop of setters, whose barking, yelping and frantic efforts to get out of the room again, effectually banished sleep from the eyes of the fair but somewhat aged occupant.

Efford Farm had been sub-let to a farmer, who broke the lease by ploughing up and growing crops on land which it had been stipulated should be kept in grass.

Sir Thomas Acland behaved with great generosity in the matter. He might have reclaimed the farm without making compensation to the ladies; but he allowed them £300 a year as long as they lived, took the farm away, and re-leased it to a more trusty tenant.

Mr. Robert Stephen Hawker obtained the Newdegate in 1827:[1] he took his degree of B.A. in 1828, and then went with his wife to Morwenstow, a place for which even then he had contracted a peculiar love, and there read for holy orders.

> Welcome, wild rock and lonely shore!
> Where round my days dark seas shall roar,
> And thy grey fane, Morwenna, stand
> The beacon of the Eternal Land.

[1] The poem, "Pompeii," has been reprinted in his *Echoes of Old Cornwall, Ecclesia*, etc.

CHAPTER II

Ordination—The Black Pig, "Gyp"—Writes to the Bishop—His Father appointed to Stratton—He is given Morwenstow—The Waddon Lantern—St. Morwenna—The Children of Brychan—St. Modwenna of Burton-on-Trent—The North Cornish Coast—Tintagel—Stowe—Sir Bevil Grenville—Mr. Hawker's discovery of the Grenville Letters—Those that remain—Antony Payne the Giant—Letters of Lady Grace—Of Lord Lansdown—Cornish Dramatic Power—Mr. Hicks of Bodmin.

ROBERT STEPHEN HAWKER was ordained deacon in 1829, when he was twenty-five years old, by the Bishop of Exeter, to the curacy of North Tamerton, of which the Rev. Mr. Kingdon was non-resident incumbent. He threw two cottages into one, and added a veranda and rooms, and made himself a comfortable house, which he called Trebarrow. He was ordained priest in 1831, by the Bishop of Bath and Wells. He took his M.A. degree in 1836. He had a favourite rough pony which he rode, and a black pig of Berkshire breed, well cared for, washed and curry-combed, which ran beside him when he went out for walks and paid visits. Indeed, the pig followed him into ladies' drawing-rooms, not always to their satisfaction. The pig was called Gyp, and was intelligent and obedient. If Mr. Hawker saw that those whom he visited were annoyed at the intrusion of the pig, he would order it forth; and the black creature slunk out of the door with its tail out of curl.

It was whilst Mr. Hawker was at Tamerton that Henry Phillpotts was appointed Bishop of Exeter. There was some unpleasant feeling aroused in the diocese at the mode of his appointment; and the bishop sent a pastoral letter to his clergy to state his intentions and explain away what caused unpleasantness. Mr. Hawker wrote the bishop an answer of such a nature that it began a friendship which subsisted between them till the death of Dr. Phillpotts. Whilst Mr. Hawker was curate of Tamerton, on one or two occasions the friends of the labouring dead requested that the burial hour might be that at which the deceased was accustomed "to leave work." The request touched his poetical instinct, and he wrote the lines:—

> Sunset should be the time, they said,
> To close their brother's narrow bed.
> 'Tis at that pleasant hour of day
> The labourer treads his homeward way.
> His work is o'er, his toil is done;
> And therefore at the set of sun,
> To wait the wages of the dead,
> We laid our hireling in his bed.

In 1834 died the non-resident vicar of Stratton, and the Bishop of Exeter offered to obtain the living for Mr. Robert Stephen Hawker; but he refused it, as his father was curate of Stratton, and he felt how unbecoming it would be for him to assume the position of vicar where his father had been, and still was, curate. In his letter to the bishop he urged his father's long service at Stratton; and Dr. Phillpotts, at his request, obtained the presentation for Mr. Jacob Stephen Hawker to the vicarage of Stratton.

The very next piece of preferment that fell vacant was Morwenstow, whose vicar, the Rev. Mr. Young, died in 1834. Mr. Young had been non-resident, and had lived at Torrington, the parish being served by a succession of curates, some of them also non-resident. The vicarage house, which stood west of the tower near a gate out of the churchyard, was let to the clerk, and inhabited by him and his wife. The first curate was Mr. Badcock, who lived at Week St. Mary, some fourteen miles distant. He rode over for Sunday duty. Next came a M. Savant, a Frenchman ordained deacon in the English Church, but never priest. He was a dapper dandy, very careful of his ecclesiastical costume, in knee-breeches and black silk stockings. He lodged at Marsland. Parson Davis of Kilkhampton came over to Morwenstow to celebrate the holy communion. The Frenchman was succeeded by Mr. Bryant, who lived at Flexbury, in the parish of Poughill; the next to him was Mr. Thomas, a man who ingratiated himself with the farmers—a cheery person, fond of a good story, and interested in husbandry, " but not much of the clerical in him," as an old Morwenstow man describes him. Whilst Mr. Thomas was curate, the vicar, Parson Young, died. A petition from the farmers and householders of Morwenstow to the bishop was got up, to request him to appoint Mr. Thomas. The curate, so runs the tale, went to Exeter to present the paper with their signatures, and urge his claims in person.

"My lord," said he, "the Dissenters have all signed the petition: they are all in favour of me. Not one has declined to attach his name; even the Wesleyan minister wishes to see me vicar of Morwenstow."

"Then, my good sir," said Dr. Phillpotts, "it is very clear that you are not the man for me. I wish you a good-morning." And he wrote off to Robert Stephen Hawker, offering him the incumbency of Morwenstow.

There was probably not a living in the whole diocese, perhaps not one in England, which could have been more acceptable to Mr. Hawker. As his sister tells me, "Robert always loved Morwenstow: from a boy he loved it, and, when he could, went to live there."

He at once accepted the preferment, and went into residence. There had not been a resident vicar since the Rev. Oliver Rose*,[1] who lived at Eastaway, in the parish. This Rev. Oliver Rose had a brother-in-law, Mr. Edward Waddon of Stanbury; and the cronies used to meet and dine alternately at each other's house. As they grew merry over their port, the old gentlemen uproariously applauded any novel joke or story by rattling their glasses on the table. Having laughed at each other's venerable anecdotes for the last twenty years, the introduction of a new tale or witticism was hailed with the utmost enthusiasm. This enthusiasm reached such a pitch, that,

---

[1] Throughout this memoir, wherever an asterisk accompanies a name it is for the purpose of showing that the real name has not been given, either at the request of descendants, or because relatives are still alive.

in their applause of each other's sallies, they occasionally broke their wine-glasses.

The vicar of Morwenstow, when Mr. Waddon snapped off the foot of his glass, would put the foot and a fragment in his pocket, and treasure it; for each wine-glass broken was to him a testimony to the brilliancy of his jokes, and also a reminder to him of them for future use.

In time he had accumulated a considerable number of broken wine-glasses, and he had them fitted together to form an enormous lantern; and thenceforth, when he went to dine at Stanbury, this testimony to his triumphs was borne lighted before him.

The lantern fell into the hands of Mr. Hawker, and he presented it to the lineal descendant of Mr. E. Waddon, as a family relic. It is still in existence, and duly honoured. It is of oak, with the fragments of wine-glasses let in with great ingenuity in the patterns of keys, hearts, etc., about the roof, the sides being composed of the circular feet of the glasses.

On looking at the map of Cornwall, one is surprised to see it studded with the names of saints, of whom one knows nothing, and these names of a peculiarly un-English sound. The fact is, that Cornwall was, like Ireland, a land of saints in the fifth and sixth centuries. These were either native Cornish, or were Irish or Welsh saints who migrated thither to seek on the desolate moors or wild, uninhabited coasts of Cornwall, solitary places, where they might live to God, and fight demons, like the hermits of Egypt. Cornwall was the Thebaid of the Welsh.

Little or nothing is known of the vast majority

of these saints. They have left their names and their cells and holy-wells behind them, but nothing more.

> They had their lodges in the wilderness,
> Or built their cells beside the shadowy sea;
> And there they dwelt with angels like a dream.
> So they unclosed the volume of the Book,
> And filled the fields of the Evangelist
> With thoughts as sweet as flowers![1]

The legends of a few local saints survive, but of very few. Such is that of St. Melor "with the golden hand," probably some old British deity who has bequeathed his myth to an historical personage. St. Padarn, St. Cadoc, St. Petrock, have their histories well known, as they belong to Wales. But there are other saints, emigrants from Wales, who settled on the north-west coast, of whom but little is known.

What little can be collected concerning St. Morwenna, who had her cell at Morwenstow, I proceed to give.

In the fifth century there lived in Brecknock an Irish invader, Brychan by name, who died in 450. According to Welsh accounts, he had twenty-four sons and twenty-five daughters, in all forty-nine children. Statements, however, vary, of which this is the largest. The smallest number attributed to him is twenty-four; and, as his grandchildren may have been included in the longer list, this may account for the discrepancy. He is said to have had three wives—Ewrbrawst, Rhybrawst and Peresgri

---

[1] "The Cornish Fathers," in Mr. Hawker's *Echoes of Old Cornwall*, 1846.

—though it is not said that they were living at the same time. The fact seems to have been that all the Hy Brychan or family are regarded as brothers and sisters.

The names of the sons and daughters and grandchildren of Brychan are given in the *Cognacio Brychani*, and in the Bonnedd-y-Saint; and a critical examination of the lists is given by Dr. Rees in his *Essay on the Welsh Saints*. In the "Young Woman's Window" at St. Neots, near Liskeard, in Cornwall, is fifteenth-century glass, which represents Brychan with his offspring, twenty-four in number, all of whom have been confessors or martyrs in Devon and Cornwall. The following are named: 1. St. John, or Ive, who gave his name to the Church of St. Ive; 2. Endelient, who gave his name to Endelion; 3. Menfre, to St. Miniver; 4. Teth, to St. Teath; 5. Mabina, to St. Mabyn; 6. Merewenna, to Marham Church near Bude; 7. Wenna, to St. Wenn; 8. Yse, to St. Issey; 9. Morwenna, to Morwenstow; 10. Cleder, to St. Clether; 11. Kerie, to Egloskerry; 12. Helic, to Egloshayle; 13. Adwen, to Advent; 14. Lanent, to Lelant. Leland, in his *Itinerary*, adds Nectan, Dilic, Wensenna, Wessen, Juliana,[1] Wymp, Wenheder, Jona, Kananc, and Kerhender.

A few, but not many of these can be identified with those attributed to Brychan by the Welsh genealogists. Morwenna is most probably the Welsh Mwynen, in Latin Monyina, daughter of Brynach Wyddel by Corth, one of the daughters of

[1] St. Juliot, who has left her name near Boscastle.

Brychan; and her sisters Gwennan and Gwenlliu are probably the Wenna and Wenheder of Leland's list.

St. Morwenna was therefore apparently the granddaughter of Brychan. Her father, Brynach Wyddel, is the St. Branock of Braunton near Ilfracombe. He also founded churches in Carmarthen and Pembroke.

In Cornwall, as in Wales, churches were called after the saints who founded cells there. Morwenna, we may safely conclude, like so many of her brothers, sisters, cousins, uncles and aunts, migrated to Cornwall. St. Nectan, who may have been her brother, and who certainly was a near relation, established himself, we may conjecture, at St. Neighton's Kieve, at which time probably Morwenna had her cell at Marham Church. St. Nectan afterwards established himself on Hartland Point from which, in clear weather, and before a storm, the distant coast of his native Wales was visible; and perhaps at the same time Morwenna erected her cell on the cliff above the Atlantic, which has since borne her name. There she died. Leland, in his *Collectanea*, quoting an ancient MS. book of places where the bodies of saints rest, says that St. Morwenna lies at Morwenstow: " In villa, quæ Modwenstow dicitur, S. Mudwenna quiescit."

It will be seen from this extract that Leland confounded Morwenna with Modwenna; and Mr. Hawker, following Leland and Butler, did the same. In the year before he died I had a correspondence with him on this point.

There exists a late life of St. Modwenna by one Concubran, an Irish writer of the end of the thirteenth and beginning of the fourteenth century. There is also an Irish life of a Monynna of Newry, in Ireland, who received the veil from the hands of St. Patrick, and died about A.D. 518.

Concubran had this life, and knowing of the fame of the saintly abbess Modwenna of Burton-on-Trent, he supposed the two saints were the same, and wove the Irish legend of Monynna with the English life of Modwenna, and made out of them a life which is a tissue of anachronisms. He represents St. Modwenna as contemporary with Pope Cœlestine I. (423-432), St. Patrick (died 465), St. Ibar (died 500), St. Columba (died 597), St. Kevin (died 618), and King Alfrid of Northumbria (died 705).

St. Modwenna, or Moninna, founded a convent at Fochard Brighde, near Faugher, in the county of Louth, about the year 630; and 150 virgins placed themselves under her rule. But one night, an uproarious wedding having disturbed the rest and fluttered the hearts of her nuns, and threatened to turn their heads, Modwenna deemed it prudent to remove the excitable damsels to some more remote spot, where no weddings took place, nor convivial songs were heard; and she pitched upon Killsleve-Cuilin, in the county of Armagh, where she erected a monastery. One of her maidens was named Athea, another Orbile. She had a brother, a holy abbot, named Ronan.

In Concubran's *Life of St. Modwenna*, we are told that about this time Alfrid, son of the King of

England, came to Ireland. This is certainly Alfrid, the illegitimate son of Oswy, who, on the accession of Egfrid (A.D. 670), fled to Ireland, and remained there studying, as Bede tells us, for some while. The Irish king, according to Concubran, was Conall. But this is a mistake. Conall, nephew of Donald II., reigned from 642 to 658. Seachnach was king in 670, but was killed the following year, and was succeeded by Finnachta, who reigned till 695. When Alfrid was about to return to Northumbria, the Irish king wanted to make him a present, but, having nothing in his treasury, bade a kinsman go and rob some church or convent, and give the spoils to the Northumbrian prince. The noble fell on all the lands of the convent of Moninna, and pillaged them and the church. Then the saint, with great boldness, took ship, crossed over to England, went to Northumbria, and found the Prince Alfrid at Whitby (A.D. 685), and demanded redress. The king—for Alfrid was now on the throne—promised to repay all, and placed Moninna in the famous double monastery of Whitby founded by St. Hilda in 658. His own sister, Elfleda, was there ; and he committed her to St. Modwenna, to be instructed by her in the way of life. Elfleda was then aged thirty-one. Three years after she succeeded to the place of St. Hilda, and was second Abbess of Whitby. Then St. Modwenna returned to Ireland, and visited her foundations there. After a while she made a pilgrimage to Rome, and in passing through England founded a religious house at Burton-on-Trent, and left in it some of her nuns. I need not follow her history farther.

Concubran tells some odd stories of St. Modwenna. One day she and her nuns went to visit St. Bridget —regardless, be it remembered, of the gap of two centuries which intervened. A girl in the company took an onion away with her lest she should be hungry on the road. On reaching the Liffey, the river was found to be too swollen to be crossed. "There is something wrong," said Modwenna: "let us examine our consciences and cast away the accursed thing."

"The accursed thing is this onion," said the maiden, producing the bulb.

"Take it back to Bridget," said Modwenna; and, when the onion had been restored, the Liffey subsided.

Bridget sent a silver chalice to Modwenna. She threw it into the river, and the waves washed it to its destination.

One night Modwenna said to her assembled nuns: "My sisters, we must all cleanse our consciences, for our prayers stick in the roof of the chapel, and cannot break out."

Then one of the nuns said: "It is my fault. I complained to a knight of my acquaintance of the cold I felt; and he told me I was too scantily clothed. He was moved to such pity of me, that he gave me some warm lamb's-wool underclothing, and I have that on now." The garment was removed and destroyed; and the prayers got out of the roof and flew to heaven.[1]

---

[1] "Dixit S. Movenna: Melius, ut illi subtulares imponantur in profundissimum branum (? barathrum) pro quibus nunc absentiam sentimus Angelorum! Vocata itaque una ex sororibus Brigna et aliis cum ea ex sororibus, dixit eis: Ite! Illos subtulares in aliquo profundo abscondite."

One night, shortly before her death, before the grey dawn broke, a couple of lay sisters came to her cell. As they approached, they saw two silver swans rise in the air, and sail away. They immediately concluded that these were angels come to bear off the soul of the abbess.

Her body was laid at Burton-on-Trent, and was long an object of pilgrimage. But the fact that for a short while St. Modwenna instructed the sister of Alfrid, "son of the King of England," has led some writers into strange mistakes. Capgrave supposes him to be Alfred the Great, son of Ethelwolf, and that the sister was Edith of Polesworth, who died in 954. And Dugdale followed Capgrave. Mr. Hawker, following Alban Butler, who accepted the account of Dugdale and Capgrave, made the blunder greater by fusing St. Morwenna of Cornwall, who, as has been shown, lived in the fifth century, with Modwenna, who lived at the end of the seventh century, and made her the instructress of St. Edith of Polesworth, who died in the tenth century, in the year 954. And Modwenna, as has been stated, was confounded by Concubran with Monynna of Newry, who died at the beginning of the sixth century.

On unravelling this tangle in 1874, I wrote to Mr. Hawker of Morwenstow, and told him that the east window of his church represented Morwenna of Cornwall teaching Edith of Polesworth, and that it was an anachronism and mistake altogether, as it was not Edith who was educated by the saintly Modwenna, and the abbess Modwenna was not the virgin Morwenna. I told him also that St. Modwenna was buried at Burton-on-Trent.

I received this answer:—

"What! Morwenna not lie in the holy place at Morwenstow! Of that you will never persuade me —no, never. I know that she lies there. I have seen her, and she has told me as much; and at her feet ere long I hope to lay my old bones."

In the little glen of Morwenstow, 350 feet above the Atlantic, St. Morwenna had her cell, and gave origin to the church and parish of Morwenstow. As she lay a-dying, says a legend according to Hawker, her brother Nectan came to her from Hartland.

"Raise me in thy arms, brother," she said, "that my eyes may rest on my native Wales." And so she died on Morwenstow cliff, looking out across the Severn Sea to the faint blue line of the Welsh mountains. St. Nectan had a cell at Wellcombe, as also at Hartland, for both of these churches bear his name.

The coast from Tintagel to Hartland is almost unrivalled for grandeur. The restless Atlantic is ever thundering on this iron-walled coast. The roar can be heard ten miles inland; flakes of foam are picked up after a storm at Holsworthy. To me, when staying three miles inland, it has seemed the roar of a hungry caged beast, ravening at its bars for food.

The swell comes unbroken from Labrador, to hurl itself against this coast, and to be shivered into foam on its iron cuirass.

"Twice," said a friend who dwelt near this coast,

"twice in the sixteen years that I have spent here has the sea been calm enough to reflect a passing sail."

This Atlantic has none of the tameness of the German Ocean, that plays on the low flat shores of Essex; none of the witchery of the green crystal that breaks over the white sands of Babbicombe and Torquay: it is emphatically "the cruel sea," fierce, insatiate, hungering for human lives and stately vessels, that it may cast them up mumbled and mangled after having robbed them of life and treasure.

It is a rainy coast. It is said in Devon, and the same is true here:—

> The west wind comes, and brings us rain;
> The east wind blows it back again;
> The south wind brings us rainy weather;
> The north wind, cold and rain together.
> When the sun in red doth set,
> The next day surely will be wet;
> But, if the sun should set in grey,
> The next will be a rainy day.
> When buds the ash before the oak,
> Then that year there'll be a soak;
> But, should the oak precede the ash,
> Why then expect a rainy splash.

The moist air from the ocean condenses over the land, and envelops it in fine fog or rain. But when the sky is clear, with only floating clouds drifting along it, the sunlight and shadows that fall over the landscape through the vaporous air are exquisite in their delicacy of colour; the sun-gleams soft as primrose, the shadows pure cobalt, tenderly laid on as the bloom on the cheek of a plum.

As the tall cliffs on this wild coast lose themselves in mist, so does history, which attaches itself to many a spot along it, stand indistinct and weird in its veil of legend. Kings and saints of whom little authentic is known, whose very dates are uncertain, have given their names to castle and crag and church.

Tintagel Rock is crowned with the ruins of the stronghold of Duke Gorlois, whose wife became the mother of the renowned Arthur, by Uther Pendragon. We have the tale in *Geoffry of Monmouth*. There, in the home of the shrieking sea-mews, Arthur uttered his first feeble cries. It is a scene well suited to be the cradle of the hero of British myth—a tremendous crag standing out of the sea, which has bored a tunnel through it, and races in and clashes in subterranean passages under the crumbling walls which sheltered Arthur.

The crag is cut off from the mainland by a chasm once spanned by a drawbridge, but now widened by storm so as to threaten to convert Tintagel into an island.

Near Boscastle rises Pentargon, "Arthur's Head," a noble black sheer precipice, forming one horn of a little bay into which a waterfall plunges from a green combe.

But there are other names besides those of Arthur, Uther Pendragon, Morwenna, Juliot and Nectan, which are associated with this coast.

At Stowe, in the parish of Kilkhampton, adjoining Morwenstow, lived Sir Bevil Grenville, the Bayard of old Cornwall, "sans peur et sans reproche," who fought and conquered at Stratton, and fell at Lansdown. Sir Bevil nearly ruined himself for the cause of his king, Charles I.

One of Mr. Hawker's most spirited ballads is—

THE GATE SONG OF STOWE.

Arise! and away! for the king and the law;
   Farewell to the couch and the pillow:
With spear in the rest, and with rein in the hand,
   Let us rush on the foe like a billow.

Call the hind from the plough, and the herd from the fold;
   Bid the wassailer cease from his revel;
And ride for old Stowe when the banner's unfurled
   For the cause of King Charles and Sir Bevil.

Trevanion is up, and Godolphin is nigh,
   And Harris of Hayne's o'er the river;
From Lundy to Looe, "One and all!" is the cry,
   And "the king and Sir Bevil for ever!"

Ay! by Tre, Pol and Pen, ye may know Cornishmen
   'Mid the names and the nobles of Devon;
But if truth to the king be a signal, why, then,
   Ye can find out the Grenville in heaven.

Ride! ride with red spear! there is death in delay:
   'Tis a race for dear life with the devil!
If dark Cromwell prevail, and the king must give way,
   This earth is no place for Sir Bevil.

So at Stamford he fought, and at Lansdown he fell:
   But vain were the visions he cherished;
For the great Cornish heart that the king loved so well,
   In the grave of the Grenville it perished.

One day, if indeed we may trust the story, Mrs. Hawker, the first wife of the vicar of Morwenstow, when lunching at Stowe in the farmhouse, noticed that a letter in old handwriting was wrapped round the mutton-bone that was brought on the table. Moved by curiosity, she took the paper off, and showed it to Mr. Hawker. On examination it was found that the letter bore the signature of Sir Bevil Grenville. Mr. Hawker at once instituted inquiries, and found a large chest full of letters of different members of the Grenville family in the sixteenth and seventeenth centuries. He at once communicated with Lord Carteret, owner of Stowe, and the papers were removed; but by some unfortunate accident they were lost. The only ones saved were a packet extracted from the chest by Mr. Davies, rector of Kilkhampton, previous to their being sent away from Stowe. These were copied by Miss Manning of Eastaway, in Morwenstow; and her transcript, together with some of her originals—I fear not all—is now in the possession of Ezekiel Rous, Esq., of Bideford.[1]

In his *Footprints of Former Men*, Mr. Hawker has printed a letter from Antony Payne, the gigantic serving-man of Sir Bevil, written after the battle of Lansdown, to Lady Grace Grenville, giving an account of the death of her husband. This was probably one of the letters in the collection found by Mr. Hawker, and so sadly lost.

This Antony Payne was a remarkable man. He measured seven feet two inches without his shoes when aged twenty-one, when he was taken into the

[1] I do not myself believe in the story of the finding of the papers by Mrs. Hawker.

establishment at Stowe. He afterwards added two inches to his height. It is said that one Christmas Eve the fire languished in the hall at Stowe. A boy with an ass had been sent to the woods for logs, but had loitered on his way. Lady Grace lost patience. Then Antony started in quest of the dilatory lad, and re-entered the hall shortly after, bearing the loaded animal on his back. He threw down his burden at the hearth-side, shouting, 'Ass and fardel! Ass and fardel for my lady's Yule!"

On another occasion he rode into Stratton with Sir Bevil. An uproar proceeded from the little inn-yard, and Sir Bevil bade his giant find out what was the cause of the disturbance. Antony speedily returned with a man under each arm, whom he had arrested in the act of fighting.

"Here are the kittens," said the giant; and he held them under his arms whilst his master chastised them with his riding-whip.

After the battle of Stamford Hill, Sir Bevil returned for the night to Stowe; but his giant remained with some other soldiers to bury the dead. He had caused trenches to be dug to hold ten bodies side by side, and in these trenches he and his followers deposited the slain. On one occasion they had laid nine corpses in their places; and Payne was bringing another, tucked under his arm like one of the "kittens," when all at once the supposed dead man began to kick and plead for life. "Surely you won't bury me, Mr. Payne, before I am dead?"—"I tell thee, man," was the grim reply, "our trench was dug for ten, and there's nine in it already: thou must take thy place."—"But I bean't dead, I say; I haven't done living yet: be massyful, Mr. Payne; don't ye hurry a poor fellow into the earth before his time." —"I won't hurry thee: thou canst die at thy leisure." Payne's purpose was, however, kinder than his speech. He carried the suppliant to his own cottage, and left him to the care of his wife. The man lived, and his descendants are among the principal inhabitants of Stratton at this day.

I make no apology for transcribing from the original letters a very few of the most interesting and touching, some for whose escape we cannot feel too thankful. The following beautiful letter is from Lady Grace Grenville to her husband.

The superscription is :—

FOR MY BEST FRIEND, SIR BEVILL GRENVILE.

MY EVER DEAREST,—I have received yours from Salisbury, and am glad to hear you came so farr well, with poore Jack. Ye shall be sure of my prairs, which is the best service I can doe you. I canott perceave whither you had receaved mine by Tom, or no, but I believe by this time you have mett that and another since by the post. Truly I have been out of frame ever since you went, not with a cough, but in another kinde, much indisposd. However, I have striven with it, and was at Church last Sunday, but not the former. I have been vexed with diverse demands made of money than I could satisfie, but I instantly paid what you sent, and have intreated Mr. Rous his patience a while longer, as you directed. It grieves me to think how chargeable your family is, considering your occasion. It hath this many yeares troubled me to think to what passe it must come at last, if it run on after this course. How many times what hath appeared hopefull, and yet proved contrary in the conclusion, hath befalen us, I am loth to urge, because tis farr from my desire to disturbe your thoughts; but this sore is not to be curd with silence, or patience either, and while you are loth to discourse or thinke of that you can take little comfort to see how bad it is, and I was unwilling to strike on that string which sounds harsh in your eare (the matter still grows worse, though). I can never putt it out of my thoughts, and that makes me often times seeme dreaming to you, when you expect I should sometimes observe more complement with my frends, or be more active in matters of curiousity in our House, which doubtlesse you would have been better pleasd with had I been capable to have performd it, and I believe though I had a naturall dullnes in me, it would never so much have appeard to my prejudice, but twas increasd by a continuance of sundry disasters, which I still mett with, yet never till this yeare, but I had some strength to encounter them, and truly now I am soe cleane overcome, as tis in vaine to deny a truth. It seems to me now tis high time to be sensible that God is displeased, having had many sad remembrances in our estate and childrene late, yet God spard us in our children long, and when I strive to follow your advice in moderating my grieffe (which I praise God) I have thus farr been able to doe as not to repine at God's will, though I have a tender sence of griefe which hangs on me still, and I think it as dangerous and improper to forgett it, for I cannott but think it was a neer touched correction, sent from God to check me for my many neglects of my duty to God. It was the tenth and last plague God smote the Egyptians with, the death of their first borne, before he utterly destroyed them, they persisting in their disobedience notwithstanding all their former punishments. This apprehension makes me both tremble and humbly beseech Him to withdraw His punishments from us, and to give us grace to know and amend whatever is amisse. Now I have powrd out my sad thoughts which in your absence doth most oppresse me, and tis my weakness hardly to be able to say thus much unto you, how brimfull soever my heart be, though oftentimes I heartely wish I could open my heart truly unto you when tis overchargd. But the least thought it may not be pleasing to you will at all times restraine me. Consider me rightly, I beseech you, and excuse, I pray, the liberty I take with my pen in this kinde. And now at last I must thanke you for wishing me to lay aside all feare, and depend on the Almighty, who can only helpe us; for His mercy I daily pray, and your welfare, and our poore boys; so I conclude, and am ever your faithfully and only   GRACE GRENVILE.

STOW, *Nov.* 23, 1641.

I sent yours to Mr. Prust, but this from him came after mine was gone last weeke. Ching is gone to Cheddar. I looke for Bawden, but as yet is not come. Sir Rob. Bassett is dead.

I heard from my cosen Grace Weekes, who writes that Mr. Luttrell says if you and he could meete the liking between the young people, he will not stand for money you shall finde. Parson Weekes wishes you would call with him, and that he might entice you to take the castle in your way downe. She sayes they enquire in the most courteous manner that can be imagind. Deare love, thinke how to farther this what you can.

The following is an earlier letter by many years, written when Grace was a wife of six years' standing.

SWEET MR. GRENVILE,—I cannott let Mr. Oliver passe without a line, though it be only to give you thankes for yours, which I have receaved. I will in all things observe your directions as neer as I can, and because I have not time to say much now I will write againe to-morrow . . . [something torn away], and think you shall receave advertizment concerning us much as you desyre. I cannot say I am well, neither have I bin so since I saw you, but, however, I will pray for your health, and good successe in all businesses, and pray be so kinde as to love her who takes no comfort in anything but you, and will remayne yours ever and only   GRACE GRENVILE.

FRYDAY NIGHT, *Nov.* 13, 1629.

The superscription of this letter is:—

"To my ever dearest and best Friend, Mr. Bevill Grenvile, at the Rainbow, in Fleet Street."

THE GRENVILLE LETTERS

Lady Grace was the daughter of Sir George Smith of Exeter, Kt.: she was born in 1598, and married Sir Bevil Grenville in 1620. He died in 1643, on the battlefield of Lansdown, near Bath; and she followed him to the grave in 1647. Her portrait is at Haynes, "ætatis suæ 36, 1634". One of Sir Bevil is in the possession of Lord John Thynne; another with date 1636, "ætatis suæ 40," is in the possession of Rev. W. W. Martyn of Tonacombe, in Morwenstow.

There are other letters of the Grenvilles in the bundle from which I have selected these. One from John Grenville to his brother, giving a curious picture of London life in the seventeenth century, narrating how he quarrelled with a certain barber Wells, and came very nigh to pulling off noses;[1] one from Jane, wife of John Grenville, Earl of Bath, to her husband "for thy deare selfe," beginning, "My deare Heart," and telling how:—

I am now without any man in the house, my father being gone, and Jacke is drunk all day and leyes out of nights, and if I do but tell him of it he will be gone presantly; therefore, for God's sake, make haste up, for I am so parpetually ill that I am not fit to bee anny longgar left in this condission. My poore motther hath now so much bisnese that I do not knowe how long she will be abble to tary with mee, and if that should happen, which God forbid it should at any time, much more now, what dost thou thinke I should do? I want the things thou prommysed to send me very much, which, being to long to put in a lettar, I have geven my brother a not of. My deare, consider how nere I am my time, and many women comming this yeare before thar time. . . . Thou mayst now

[1] To Beville Grenville, Esq., dated July 18, 1621.

thinke how impassiontly I am till I see thee agane, thinking every day a hondared yeare; my affecksion being so gret that I wounder how I have stayd till the outmoust time. I will saye no more now, hopping to see thee every day, but that I am, and ever will bee, thy most affectionate and faithful wife and sarvant, JANE GRENVILE.

Thy babe bayrs thy blessing.

This letter is dated only June 17, without year. It is always pleasant to meet with the beating of a warm human heart. A third letter I venture to transcribe here, from George Lord Lansdown,[1] grandson of Sir Bevil, to his nephew, Bevil Grenville.

DEAR NEPHEW,—I approve very well of your resolution of dedicating yourself to the service of God. You could not chuse a better master, provided you have so sufficiently searched your heart and examined your reins, as to be persuaded you can serve Him well. In so doing, you may secure to yourself many blessings in this world, as well as sure hope in the next.

There is one thing which I perceive you have not yet thoroughly purged yourself from; which is, flattery. You have bestowed so much of it upon me in your last letter, that I hope you have no more left, and that you meant it only to take your leave of such flights, which, however well meant, oftener put a man out of countenance than oblige him. You are now to be a searcher after truth, and I shall hereafter take it more kindly to be justly reproved by you than to be undeservedly complimented.

I would not have you misunderstand me, as if I recommended to you a sour Presbyterian severity. That is yet more to be avoided: advice, like physick, must be so sweetned and

---

[1] George Lord Lansdown was son of Bernard Grenville, son of Sir Bevil. Bernard, who died 1701, had three sons, Bevil, George and Barnard; and Barnard had two sons, Barnard and Bevil, and Mary, a daughter, who married Dr. Delany. Bevil, the son of Barnard, is the nephew to whom this letter is addressed.

prepared as to be made palatable, or Nature may be apt to revolt against it.

Be always sincere, but at the same time be always polite. Be humble without descending from your character, and reprove and correct without ofending good manners. To be a Cynick is as bad as to be a Sycophant: you are not to lay aside the gentleman with the sword, nor put on the gown to hide your birth and good breeding, but to adorn it.

Such has been the malice of the wicked, that pride, avarice, and ambition have been charged upon the Clergy in all ages, in all countrys, and equally in all religions. What they are most obliged to combat against in the pulpits they are most accused of encouraging in their conduct. Let your example confirm your doctrine, and let no man ever have it in his power to reproach you with practising contrary to what you preach.

You had an unckle, the late Dean of Durham,[1] whose memory I shall ever revere. Make him your example. Sanctity sat so easy, so unaffected, and so gracefull upon him, that in him we beheld the very beauty of Holiness. He was as chearful as familiar, as condescending in his conversation, as he was strict, regular, and exemplary in his piety; as well-bred and accomplished as a courtier, and as reverend and venerable as an Apostle; he was indeed Apostolical in everything, for he left all to follow his Lord and Master. May you resemble him; may he revive in you; may his spirit descend upon you, as Elijah's on Elisha; and may the great God of heaven, in guiding, directing, and strengthening your pious resolutions, pour down the choicest of his blessings upon you!

LANSDOWN.

The old house at Stowe was converted into farm buildings, and a new red brick mansion, square, containing a court in the middle, was built in 1660 by John, Earl of Bath. He died in 1701; and his son,

---

[1] Denys Grenville, Dean of Durham (born February, 1636), was son of Sir Bevil. He was a nonjuror, and so lost his deanery: he retired to Rouen in Normandy, and there died, greatly respected.

Charles, shot himself accidentally when going from London to Kilkhampton to his father's funeral, leaving a son, William Henry, third Earl of Bath, seven years of age when his father died. Thus, as was said, at the same time there were three Earls of Bath above ground. William Henry died at the age of seventeen, in 1711; and then the Grenville property was divided between the sisters of Charles, second Earl of Bath— Jane, who married Sir William Gower, ancestor of the Dukes of Sutherland; and Grace, who at the age of eight married George, afterwards first Lord Carteret, then aged eleven.

The letters of this little pair to one another, when the husband was at school and she at Haynes, exist in the possession of Lord John Thynne.

Stowe House was pulled down. Within the memory of one man, grass grew and was mown in the meadow where sprang up Stowe House, and grew and was mown in the meadow where Stowe had been.

A few crumbling walls only mark the site of the old home of the Grenvilles.[1]

The Cornish people in former days were passionately fond of theatrical performances. In numerous parts of Cornwall there exist green dells or depressions in the surface of the ground, situated generally on a moor. These depressions have been assisted by the hand of man to form rude theatres: the slopes were terraced for seats, and on fine summer days, at the "revels" of the locality, were occupied by crowds of spectators, whilst village actors performed on the

---

[1] A picture of old Stowe is in the possession of Lord John Thynne; another in that of Rev. W. W. Martyn of Lifton and Tonacombe.

turf stage.[1] Originally the pieces acted were sacred, curious mysteries, of which specimens remain, relating to the creation, or the legendary history of St. Meriadoc, or the passion of the Saviour, the prototypes of the Ammergau Passions-spiel. These in later times gave way to secular pieces, not always very choice in subject, and with the broadest of jokes in the speeches of the performers; not worse, perhaps, than are to be found in Shakspeare, and which were tolerated in the days of Elizabeth. These dramatical performances were in full vigour when Wesley preached in Cornwall. He seized on these rude green theatres, and harangued from their turfy platforms to wondering and agitated crowds, which thronged the grassy slopes.

The Cornish people became Methodists, and play-going became sinful. The doom of these dramas was sealed when the place of their performances was turned into an arena for revivals. The camp-meeting supplanted the drama.

But, though these plays are things of the past, the dramatic instinct survives among the Cornish people. There is scarce a parish in which some are not to be found who are actors by nature. For telling a story, with power of speech, expression and gesture, they have not their equals in England among un-professionals.

One of the most brilliant *raconteurs* of our times was Mr. Hicks, Mayor of Bodmin.

Some years ago a member sauntering into the Cos-

---

[1] There is one such not far from Morwenstow, in the parish of Kilkhampton.

mopolitan Club would find a ring of listeners gathered about a chair. In that ring he would recognise the faces of Thackeray, Dickens, and other literary celebrities, wiping away the tears which streamed from their eyes between each explosion of laughter. He would ask, in surprise, what was the attraction.

"Only the little fat Cornishman from Bodmin telling a story."[1]

His tales were works of art, wrought out with admirable skill, every point sharpened, every detail considered, and the whole told with such expression and action as could not be surpassed. His "Rabbit and Onions" has been essayed by many since his voice has been hushed; but the copies are pale, and the outlines blurred.

The subject of this memoir had inherited the Cornish love of story-telling, and the power of telling stories with dramatic force. But he had not the skill of Mr. Hicks in telling a long story, and keeping his hearers thrilling throughout the recital, breathless lest they should lose a word. Mr. Hawker contented himself with brief anecdotes, but those he told to perfection.

I shall, in the course of my narrative, give a specimen or two of stories told by common Cornish peasants. Alas, that I cannot reproduce the twinkling eye, the droll working countenances, and the agitated hands, all assistants in the story-telling!

---

[1] He was formerly governor of the lunatic asylum at Bodmin, and afterwards clerk of the Board of Guardians, and in turn Mayor of Bodmin. Being very fat, he had himself once announced at dinner as "The Corporation of Bodmin." A memoir of Mr. Hicks, and a collection of his stories has been written by Mr. W. Collier, and published by Luke, Plymouth.

CHAPTER III

Description of **Morwenstow**—The Anerithmon Gelasma—Source of the Tamar—Tonacombe—Morwenstow Church—Norman Chevron-Moulding—Chancel—Altar—Shooting Rubbish—The Manning Bed—The Yellow Poncho—The Vicarage—Mr. Tom Knight—**The Stag**, Robin Hood—Visitors—The Silent Tower of Bottreaux—The **Pet of Boscastle.**

A WRITER in *The Standard* gives this description of Morwenstow: " No railway has as yet come near Morwenstow, and none will probably ever approach it nearer than Bude. The coast is iron-bound. Strangely contorted schists and sandstones stretch away northward in an almost unbroken line of rocky wall to the point of Hartland; and to the south-west a bulwark of cliffs, of very similar character, extends to and beyond Tintagel, whose rude walls are sometimes seen projected against the sunset in the far distance. The coast scenery is of the grandest description, with its spires of splintered rock, its ledges of green turf, inaccessible, but tempting from the rare plants which nestle in the crevices, its seal-haunted caverns, its wild birds (among which the red-legged chough can hardly be reckoned any longer, so much has it of late years lessened in numbers),[1] the miles of sparkling blue sea over which

---

[1] This is inaccurate. There is scarce a cliff along this coast which has not its pair of choughs building in it. On the day on which this was written,

the eye ranges from the summits ablaze and fragrant with furze and heather; and here and there the little coves of yellow sand, bound in by towering blackened walls, haunts which seem specially designed for the sea-elves—

> Who chase the ebbing Neptune, and do fly him
> When he comes back.

"Even in bright weather, and in summer—in spite of the beauty and quiet of the scene, and in spite, too, of the long, deep valleys, filled with wood, which, in the parish of Morwenstow especially, descend quite to the sea, and give an impression of extreme stillness and seclusion—no one can wander along the summit of the cliffs without a consciousness that he is looking on a giant, at rest indeed for a time, but more full of strength and more really terrible than any of the Cormorans or the Goemagots who have left their footprints and their strongholds on the hills of Cornwall. The sea and the coast here are, in truth, pitiless; and, before the construction of the haven at Bude, a vessel had no chance whatever of escape which approached within a certain distance of the rocks. Such a shipwreck as is described in Galt's story of *The Entail*—when persons standing on the cliff, without the smallest power to help, could see the vessel driven onward, could watch every motion on its deck, and at last see it dashed to pieces close under their feet—has more than once been

---

I went out on Morwenstow cliff, and saw two red-legged choughs flying above me. A friend tells me he has counted six or seven together on Bude sands. The choughs are, however, becoming scarce, being driven away by the jackdaws.

observed from the coast of Morwenstow by Mr. Hawker himself. No winter passes without much loss of life. The little churchyards along the coast are filled with sad records; and in that of Morwenstow the crews of many a tall vessel have been laid to rest by the care of the vicar himself, who organised a special band of searchers for employment after a great storm."[1]

The road to Morwenstow from civilisation passes between narrow hedges, every bush on which is bent from the sea. Not a tree is visible. The whole country, doubtless, a century ago was moor and fen. At Chapel is a plantation; but every tree crouches shrivelled, and turns its arms imploringly inland. The leaves are burnt and sear soon after they have expanded.

The glorious blue Atlantic is before one, with only Lundy Isle breaking the continuity of the horizon line. In very clear weather, and before a storm, far away in faintest blue, the Welsh coast can be seen to the north-west.

Suddenly the road dips down a combe; and Morwenstow tower, grey-stoned, pinnacled, stands up against the blue ocean, with a grove of stunted sycamores on the north of the church. Some way below, deep down in the glen, are seen the roofs and fantastic chimneys of the vicarage. The quaint lyche-gate and ruined cottage beside it, the venerable church, the steep slopes of the hills blazing with gorse or red with heather, and the background of sparkling blue sea half-way up the sky—from such

[1] *Standard*, 1st September, 1875.

a height above the shore is it looked upon—form a picture, once seen, never to be forgotten.

The bottom of the glen is filled with wood, stunted, indeed, but pleasant to see after the treeless desolation of the high land around.

A path leads from church and vicarage upon Morwenstow cliffs. On the other side of the combe rises Hennacliffe to the height of 450 feet above the sea, a magnificent face of splintered and contorted schist, with alternating friable slaty beds.

Half-way down Morwenstow cliff, only to be reached by a narrow and scarcely distinguishable path, is the well of St. Morwenna. Mr. Hawker repaired it; but about twenty years ago the spring worked itself a way through another stratum of slate, and sprang out of the sheer cliff some feet lower down, and falls in a miniature cascade, a silver thread of water, over a ledge of schist into the sea.

On a green spot, across which now run cart-tracks, in the side of the glen, stood originally, according to Mr. Hawker, a chapel to St. Morwenna, visited by those who sought her sacred well. The green patch forms a rough parallelogram, and bears faint traces of having been levelled out of the slope. No stone remains on another of the ancient chapel.

From the cliff an unrivalled view can be had of the Atlantic, from Lundy Isle to Padstow point. Tintagel Rock, with its ancient castle, stands out boldly, as the horn of a vast sweep against glittering water, lit by a passing gleam behind. Gulls, rocks, choughs, wheel and scream around the crag, now fluttering a little way above the head, and then diving down towards the sea, which roars and foams several hundreds of feet below.

The beach is inaccessible save at one point, where a path has been cut down the side of a steep gorse-covered slope, and through slides of ruined slate rock, to a bay, into which the Tonacombe Brook precipitates itself in a broken fall of foam.

The little coves with blue-grey floors wreathed with sea-foam; the splintered and contorted rock; the curved strata, which here bend over like exposed ribs of a mighty mammoth; the sharp skerries that run out into the sea to torment it into eddies of froth and spray—are of rare wildness and beauty.

It is impossible to stand on these cliffs, and not cite the ἀνήριθμον γέλασμα, παμμῆτόρ τε γῆ of the poet.

If this were quoted in the ears of the vicar of Morwenstow, he would stop, lay his hand on one's arm and say—

"How do you translate that?"

"'The many-twinkling smile of ocean.'"

"I thought so. So does every one else. But it is wrong," with emphasis—"utterly wrong. Listen to me. Prometheus is bound, held backwards, with brazen fetters binding him to the rock. He cannot see the waters, cannot note their smiles. He gazes up into the sky above him. But he hears. Notice how Æschylus describes the sounds that reach his ears, not the sights. Above, indeed, is the 'divine æther'; he is looking into that, and he hears the fanning of the 'swift-winged breezes,' and the murmur and splash of the 'fountains of rivers'; and then comes the passage which I translate, 'The loud laugh of ocean waves.'"

A little way down the side of the hill that descends in gorse banks and broken rock and clean precipice to one of the largest and grandest of the caves, is a hut made of fragments of wrecked ships thrown up on this shore. The sides are formed of curved ribs of vessels, and the entrance ornamented with carved work from a figure-head. This hut was made by Mr. Hawker himself; and in it he would sit, sheltered from storm, and look forth over the wild sea, dreaming, composing poetry, or watching ships scudding before the gale dangerously near the coast.

It was in this hut that most of his great poem, "The Quest of the Sangreal," was composed.

A friend says: "I often visited him whilst this poem was in process of composition, and sat with him in this hut as he recited it. I shall never forget one wild evening, when the sun had gone down before our eyes as a ball of red-hot iron into the deep. He had completed 'The Quest of the Sangreal,' and he repeated it from memory to me. He had a marvellous power of recitation, and with his voice, action and pathos, threw a life into the words which vanishes in print. I cannot forget the close of the poem, with the throbbing sea before me, and Tintagel looming out of the water to the south:—

> He ceased, and all around was dreamy night;
> There stood Dundagel, throned; and the great sea
> Lay, a strong vassal at his master's gate,
> And, like a drunken giant, sobbed in sleep.

THE TAMAR AND TORRIDGE

On a rushy knoll, in a moor in the parish of Morwenstow, rises the Tamar,[1] and from the same mount flows the Torridge.

> Fount of a rushing river! wild flowers wreathe
>   The home where thy first waters sunlight claim;
> The lark sits hushed beside thee while I breathe,
>   Sweet Tamar spring! the music of thy name.
>
> On through thy goodly channel, on! to the sea!
>   Pass amid heathery vale, tall rock, fair bough;
> But never more with footstep pure and free,
>   Or face so meek with happiness as now.
>
> Fair is the future scenery of thy days,
>   Thy course domestic, and thy paths of pride:
> Depths that give back the soft-eyed violet's gaze,
>   Shores where tall navies march to meet the tide.
>
> . . . .
>
> Yet false the vision, and untrue the dream,
>   That lures thee from thy native wilds to stray:
> A thousand griefs will mingle with thy stream,
>   Unnumbered hearts will sigh these waves away.
>
> Scenes fierce with men, thy seaward current laves;
>   Harsh multitudes will throng thy gentle brink;
> Back with the grieving concourse of thy waves,
>   Home to the waters of thy childhood, shrink.
>
> Thou heedest not! thy dream is of the shore,
>   Thy heart is quick with life; on! to the sea!
> How will the voice of thy far streams implore
>   Again amid these peaceful weeds to be!
>
> My soul! my soul! a happier choice be thine,—
>   Thine the hushed valley and the lonely sod;
> False dream, far vision, hollow hope, resign,
>   Fast by our Tamar spring, alone with God!

---

[1] Tamar in Cornish is Taw-mawr, the great water; Tavy is Taw-vach, the lesser water.

In the parish of Morwenstow is one very interesting old house, Tonacombe, or, as it was originally called, Tidnacombe. It belonged originally to the Jourdains, passed to the Kempthornes, the Waddons, and from thence to the Martyns. The present proprietor is the Rev. W. Waddon Martyn, rector of Lifton.

It is an ancient mansion of the sixteenth century, quite perfect and untouched, very small and plain, but in its way a gem, and well deserving a visit. It is low, crouching to the ground like the trees of the district, as for shelter, or as a ptarmigan cowering from the hawk, with wings spread over her young. A low gate, with porter's lodge at the side, leads into a small yard, into which look the windows of the hall. The hall goes to the roof with open timbers; it is small—thirty feet long—but perfect in its way, with minstrel's gallery, large open fireplace with andirons, and adorned with antlers, old weapons and banners bearing the arms of the Jourdains, Kempthornes, Waddons and Martyns. The hall gives access to a dark panelled parlour, with peculiar and handsome brass andirons in the old fireplace, looking out through a latticed window into the old walled garden, or Paradise.

It is curious that Mr. Kingsley, when writing *Westward Ho!* should have overlooked Tonacombe, and laid some of his scenes at Chapel in the same parish, where there never was an old house nor were any traditions. Probably he did not know of the existence of this charming old mansion. The minstrel's gallery was divided off from the hall, and converted into a bedroom; but Mr. Hawker pointed out its original destination to the owner, and he at once threw down the lath-and-plaster partition, and restored the hall to its original proportions.[1] The hall was also flat-ceiled across; but the vicar of Morwenstow discovered the oaken roof above the ceiling, and persuaded Mr. Martyn to expose it to view. A narrow slit in the wall from the bedroom of the lady of the house allowed her to command a view of her lord at his carousals, and listen to his sallies.

Morwenstow Church stands on the steep slope of a hill.

> My Saxon shrine! the only ground
>   Wherein this weary heart hath rest;
> What years the birds of God have found
>   Along thy walls their sacred nest.
> The storm, the blast, the tempest shock,
>   Have beat upon those walls in vain:
> She stands! a daughter of the rock,
>   The changeless God's eternal fane.
>
> Firm was their faith, the ancient bands,
>   The wise of heart in wood and stone,
> Who reared with stern and trusty hands
>   These dark grey towers of days unknown.

---

[1] Tonacombe was panelled by John Kempthorne, who died in 1591. The panelling remains in three of the rooms, and the initials J. K. and K. K. (Katherine Kempthorne) appear in each. The date is also given, 1578, on the panelling. In the large parlour on two shields are the arms of Ley quartered with those of Jordan and Kempthorne impaling Courtenay and Redvers. Prince, in his *Worthies of Devon*, gives a notice of Sir John Kempthorne, Kt., who put up this panelling. He is buried in the Morwenstow Church, where there is an interesting incised stone to his memory under the altar. His wife, Katherine Kempthorne, daughter of Sir Piers Courtenay of Ugbrook, is also buried there.

They filled these aisles with many a thought;
  They bade each nook some truth reveal;
The pillared arch its legend brought;
  A doctrine came with roof and wall.

Huge, mighty, massive, hard and strong,
  Were the choice stones they lifted then;
The vision of their hope was long,—
  They knew their God, those faithful men.
They pitched no tent for change or death,
  No home to last man's shadowy day:
There, there, the everlasting breath
  Would breathe whole centuries away.

It is a church of very great interest, consisting of nave, chancel and two aisles. The arcade of the north aisle is remarkably fine, and of two dates. Two semicircular arches are richly carved with Norman zigzag and billet: one is plain, eventually intended to be carved like the other two. The remaining two arches are transition early English pointed and plain. At the spring of the sculptured arches, in the spandrels, are very spirited projecting heads: one of a ram is remarkably well modelled. The vicar, who mused over his church, and sought a signification in everything, believed that this represented the ram caught in a thicket by the horns, and was symbolical of Christ, the true sacrifice. Another projecting head is spirited—the mouth is contorted with mocking laughter: this, he asserted, was the head of Arius. Another head, with the tongue lolling out, was a heretic deriding the sacred mysteries.

But his most singular fancy was with respect to the chevron ornamentation on the arcade. When first I visited the church, I exclaimed at the beauty of the zigzag moulding.

"Zigzag! zigzag!" echoed the vicar scornfully. "Do you not see that it is near the font that this ornament occurs? It is the ripple of the lake of Genesareth, the Spirit breathing upon the waters of baptism. Look without the Church—there is the restless old ocean thundering with all his waves: you can hear the roar even here. Look within— all is calm: here plays over the baptismal pool only the Dove who fans it into ripples with His healing wings."

The font is remarkably rude, an uncouth, misshapen block of stone from the shore, scooped out, its only ornamentation being a cable twisted round it, rudely carved. The font is probably of the tenth century.

The entrance door to the nave is of very fine Norman work in three orders, but defaced by the removal of the outer order, which has been converted into the door of the porch. Mr. Hawker, observing that the porch door was Norman, concluded that his church possessed a unique specimen of a Norman porch; but it was pointed out to him that his door was nothing but the outer order of that into the church, removed from its place; and then he determined, as soon as he could collect sufficient money, to restore the church, to pull down the porch, and replace the Norman doorway in its original condition.

The church is dedicated to St. John the Baptist. A little stream runs through the graveyard, and rushes down the hill to the porch door, where it is diverted, and carried off to water the glebe. This, he thought, was brought through the churchyard for symbolic reasons, to typify Jordan, near which the Baptist ministered. The descent into the church is by three steps. "Every church dedicated to John the Baptiser," he said in one of his sermons, "is thus arranged. We go down into them, as those who were about to be baptised of John went down into the water. The Spirit that appeared when Christ descended into Jordan hovers here, over that font, over you, over me, and ever will hover here as long as a stone of Morwenna's church stands on this green slope, and a priest of God ministers in it." The south arcade of the nave is much posterior to that on the north side. One of the capitals bears the inscription :—

THIS WAS MADE ANNO MVCLX$_4$ (1564).

Another capital bears :—

THIS IS THE HOUSE OF THE LORD.

It has been put up inverted. The arcade is rich and good for the date.

Of the same date are the carved oak benches. A few only are earlier, and bear the symbols of the transfixed heart on the spear, the nails and cross. These Mr. Hawker found laid as flooring under the pews, their faces planed. The rest bear, on shields, sea-monsters. There was a fine oak screen very much earlier in style than the benches. When Mr. Hawker arrived at Morwenstow, the clerk said to him: "Please, your honor, I have done you a very gude turn. I've just been and cut down and burned a rubbishing old screen that hid the chancel."

"You had much better have burnt yourself!" he exclaimed. "Show me what remains."

Only a few fragments of the richly sculptured and gilt cornice, and one piece of tracery, remained. The cornice represents doves flying amidst oak-leaves and vine-branches, and a fox running after them. The date not later than 1535, when a screen in the same style and character was erected at Broadwood Widger.[1]

Mr. Hawker collected every fragment, and put the pieces together with bits of modern and poor carved wood, and cast-iron tracery, and constructed therewith a not ineffective rood-screen.

Outside the screen is an early incised cross in the floor, turned with feet to the west, marking the grave of a priest. "The flock lie with their feet to the east, looking for the rising of the day-star. But the pastor always rests with his head to the east, and feet westward, that at the resurrection day, when all rise, he may be facing those for whom he must give an account to the Maker and Judge of all, and may say with the prophet: Behold, I and the children whom the Lord hath given me."

The chancel was originally lighted by lancets, which have, however, been blocked up and plastered

---

[1] The date is on a scroll, which is in a hand descending from the clouds, upon one of the bench-ends. Benches and screens are of the same date. The Morwenstow screen has been removed at the recent miserable "restoration." The wreckers are not extinct in Cornwall, they call themselves architects and fall on and ravage churches.

over. The floor he kept strewn with southernwood and thyme, "for angels to smell to."

The east wall was falling, and in 1849 was rebuilt, and a stained window by Warrington inserted, given by the late Lord Clinton. It represents St. Morwenna teaching Editha, daughter of Ethelwolf,[1] between St. Peter and St. Paul. The window is very poor and coarse in drawing and in colour. The ancient piscina in the wall is of early English date.

Mr. Hawker discovered under the pavement in the church, when reseating it, the base of a small pillar, Norman in style, with a hole in it for a rivet which attached to it the slender column it supported. This he supposed was a piscina drain, and accordingly set it up in the recess beside his altar.

Mr. Hawker used an old stable, very decayed, on the north side of the chancel, as his vestry, and descended by a stair from it to the church. Floor and roof and stair are now in the last stage of decay.

His altar was of wood, and low. He had on it a clumsy wooden cross, without figure, vases with bouquets of flowers, and two Cornish serpentine candlesticks.

There was an embroidered frontal on his altar, given him in 1843, and used for all seasons alike. Considering the veneration in which Mr. Hawker held holy things and places, a little more tidiness might

---

[1] This, as has been already shown, is an error; he confounded St. Morwenna of Cornwall with St. Modwenna of Burton-on-Trent. At the "restoration" frescoes were discovered throughout the church; all but one were wantonly destroyed.

have been expected; but his altar was never very clean, the top having strewn over it the burnt ends of matches with which he had lighted his candles. It had also on it a large magnifying glass, like those often on drawing-room tables, to assist in the examination of photographs. For a long time Mr. Hawker used to say matins, litany and communion-service standing at his altar; but in later years his curates introduced a reading-desk within the chancel near the screen. A deal kitchen-table likewise served for the furnishing of the chancel. On this he would put his mufflers and devotional books.

The untidy condition of the church affected one of his curates, a man of a somewhat domineering character, to such an extent that one day he swept up all the rubbish he could find in the church, old decorations of the previous Christmas, decayed southernwood and roses of the foregoing midsummer festivity, pages of old Bibles, prayer-books and manuscript scraps of poetry, match-ends, candle-ends, etc.; and, having filled a barrow with all these sundries, he wheeled it down to the vicarage door, rang the bell, and asked for Mr. Hawker. The vicar came into the porch.

"This is the rubbish I have found in your church."

"Not all," said Mr. Hawker. "Complete the pile by seating yourself on the top, and I will see to the whole being shot speedily."

In the chancel is a vine, carved in wood, which creeps thence all along the church—an emblem, according to him, of the Christian life.

> Hearken! there is in old Morwenna's shrine,—
>   A lonely sanctuary of the Saxon days,
>   Reared by the Severn Sea for prayer and praise —
> Amid the carved work of the roof, a vine.
>   Its root is where the eastern sunbeams fal
>   First in the chancel; then along the wall
> Slowly it travels on, a leafy line,
>   With here and there a cluster, and anon
>   More and more grapes, until the growth hath gone
> Through arch and aisle. Hearken! and heed the sign.
>   See at the altar-side the steadfast root,
>   Mark well the branches, count the summer fruit:
> So let a meek and faithful heart be thine,
> And gather from that tree a parable divine.

Formerly, whilst saying service he kept his chancel screen shut, and was invisible to his congregation; but his curates afterwards insisted on the gate being left open. The chancel is very dark.

Access to his pulpit was obtained through a narrow opening in the screen just sixteen inches wide, and it was a struggle for him to get through the aperture. After a while he abandoned the attempt, and had steps into the pulpit erected outside the screen.

Above the screen he set up in late years a large cross painted blue with five gold stars on it, the cross of the heavens in the southern hemisphere. Near the pulpit he erected a curious piece of wood-carving, gilt and coloured, which he brought with him from Tamerton. It represents a castle attacked by a dragon with two heads. From the mouth of a beardless face issues a dove, which is represented flying towards the castle. This, he said, was an allegory. The castle is the Church assailed by Satan, the old dragon, through his twofold power, temporal and spiritual. But the Holy Spirit proceeding from the Son flies to the defence of the Church. On the other side of the castle was originally a bearded head, and a dove issuing in a similar manner from it; but it has been broken away. This represented the Paraclete proceeding from the Father as from the Son.

In the churchyard of Morwenstow is a granite tomb bearing the following inscription:—

> Here Liet John Maning of ..
> Who Died Without Issue ...
> I am Beried in
> the vi Daie of Av
> gvst 1601.

John Manning of Stanbury, in Morwenstow, lived in the sixteenth century. He married Christiana Kempthorne. About six weeks after their marriage the husband was gored by a bull in a field between Tonacombe and Stanbury. His young bride died of grief within the year, and was buried in this altar tomb beside him.

The bed of this ill-fated pair, with their names carved on the head-board, was found by Mr. Hawker in one of the farms in the parish. He was very anxious to get possession of it. He begged it, and when refused offered money, but to no avail: the farmer would not part with it. After trying persuasion, entreaty, and offering large sums in vain, he had recourse to another expedient.

The vicar said to the farmer: "Does it ever strike

you, S——, when lying in that bed, as you do of a night, how many corpses have preceded you? There was first of all poor John Manning, all dead and bloody, in 1601, his side ripped up by a bull's horns, just where you lie so snug of a night. Then there was his bride, Christiana, lying there, where your wife sleeps, sobbing away her life, dying of a broken heart. Just you think, John, when you lie there, of that poor lone woman, how her tears dribbled all night long over the pillow on which your wife's head rests. And one morning, when they came to look at her, SHE WAS DEAD. That was two hundred and fifty years ago. What a lot of corpses have occupied that bed, where you and your wife lie, since then! Think of it, John, of a night, and tell your wife to do the same. I dare say the dead flesh has struck a chill into the bed, that the feel of it makes you creep all over at times at dead of night. Doesn't it, John? Two hundred and fifty years ago! That is about five generations—five men washed and laid out, their chins tied up on your pillow, John, and their dead eyes looking up at your ceiling; and five wives dead and laid out there too, and measured for their coffins, just where your wife sleeps so warm. And then, John, consider, it's most likely some of these farmers were married again, so we may say there were at least six or seven female corpses, let alone dead babies, in that bed. Why, John, there have been at least fourteen corpses in that bed, including John Manning bleeding to death, and Christiana weeping her life away. Think of that of a night. You will find it conducive to good."

"Parson," said the farmer aghast, "I can never sleep in that bed no more. You may take it, and welcome."

So Mr. Hawker got the Manning bed, and set it up in the room that commanded the tomb in the churchyard; "so that the bed may look at the grave, and the grave at the bed," as he expressed it.

The writer in *The Standard*, already quoted, thus describes his first acquaintance with the vicar of Morwenstow:—

It was on a solemn occasion that we first saw Morwenstow. The sea was still surly and troubled, with wild lights breaking over it, and torn clouds driving through the sky. Up from the shore, along a narrow path between jagged rocks and steep banks tufted with thrift, came the vicar, wearing cassock and surplice, and conducting a sad procession, which bore along with it the bodies of two seamen flung up the same morning on the sands. The office used by Mr. Hawker at such times had been arranged by himself—not without reference to certain peculiarities, which, as he conceived, were features of the primitive Cornish Church, the same which had had its bishops and its traditions long before the conference of Augustine with its leaders under the great oak by the Severn. Indeed, at one time he carried his adhesion to these Cornish traditions to some unusual lengths. There was, we remember, a peculiar yellow vestment, in which he appeared much like a Lama of Thibet, which he wore in his house and about his parish, and which he insisted was an exact copy of a priestly robe worn by St. Padarn and St. Teilo. We have seen him in this attire proceeding through the lanes on the back of a well-groomed mule—the only fitting beast, as he remarked, for a Churchman.

We have here one instance out of many of the manner in which the vicar delighted in hoaxing visitors.

The yellow vestment in question was a **poncho**. It came into use in the following manner:—

Mr. Martyn, a neighbour, was in conversation one day with Mr. Hawker, when the latter complained that he could not get a greatcoat to his fancy.

"Why not wear a poncho?" asked Mr. Martyn.

"Poncho! what is that?" inquired the vicar.

"Nothing but a blanket with a hole in the middle."

"Do you put your legs through the hole, and tie the four corners over your head?"

"No," answered Mr. Martyn. "I will fetch you my poncho, and you can try it on." The poncho was brought: it was a dark blue one, and the vicar was delighted with it. There was no trouble in putting it on. It suited his fancy amazingly; and next time he went to Bideford he bought a yellowish-brown blanket, and had a hole cut in the middle, through which to thrust his head.

"I wouldn't wear your livery, Martyn," said he, "nor your political colours, so I have got a yellow poncho."

Those who knew him well can picture to themselves the sly twinkle in his eye as he informed his credulous visitor that he was invested in the habit of St. Padarn and St. Teilo.

After a few years at Morwenstow in a hired house, the vicar set to work to build himself a vicarage near the church. He chose a spot where he saw lambs take shelter from storm; not so much because he thought the spot a "lew" one (that is, a sheltered one), as from the fancy that the refuge of the lambs should typify the vicarage, the sheltering-place of his flock.

Whilst he was building it Mr. Daniel King came over to see him, and was shown the house in course of erection. Mr. Daniel King and Mr. Hawker were not very cordial friends.

"Ha!" said Mr. King, "you know the proverb—'Fools build houses for wise men to live in.'"

"Yes," answered the vicar promptly; "and I know another — 'Wise men make proverbs, and fools quote them.'"

He had the chimneys of the vicarage built to resemble the towers of churches with which he had had to do: one was like Tamerton, another like Magdalen Hall, a third resembled Wellcombe, a fourth Morwenstow.

When Archdeacon, afterwards Bishop, Wilberforce came into the neighbourhood to advocate the cause of the Society for the Propagation of the Gospel, he met Mr. Hawker.

"Look here," said Archdeacon Wilberforce, "I have to speak at the meeting at Stratton to-night, and I am told that there is a certain Mr. Knight[*] who will be on the platform, and is a wearyful speaker. I have not much time to spare. Is it possible by a hint to reduce him to reasonable limits?"

"Not in the least: he is impervious to hints."

"Can he not be prevented from rising to address the meeting?"

"That is impossible: he is irrepressible."

"Then what is to be done?"

"Leave him to me, and he will not trouble you."

At the S.P.G. meeting a crowd had gathered to hear the eloquent speaker. Mr. Tom Knight was on the platform, waiting his opportunity to rise.

"Oh, Knight!" said Mr. Hawker in a whisper, "the archdeacon has left his watch behind, and mine is also at home; will you lend yours for timing the speeches?"

With some hesitation Mr. Knight pulled his gold repeater, with bunch of seals attached, from his fob, and gave it to the vicar of Morwenstow.

Presently Mr. Knight was on his legs to make a speech. Now, the old gentleman was accustomed, when addressing a public audience, to swing his bunch of seals round and round in his left hand. Directly he began his oration, his hand went instinctively to his fob in quest of the bunch: it was not there. He stammered, and felt again, floundered in his speech, and, after a few feeble efforts to recover himself, and find his bunch of seals, sat down, red and melting and angry.

Mr. Hawker had a pair of stags which he called Robin Hood and Maid Marian, given to him by the late Sir Thomas Acland, from his park at Killerton. These he kept in the long open combe in front of the house, through which a stream dashes onwards to the sea. One day the same Mr. Knight proceeded too curiously to approach Robin Hood, when the deer ran at him and butted him down. The clergyman shrieked with fear, and the stag would have struck him with his antlers had not the vicar rushed to the rescue. Being an immensely strong man, he caught Robin by the horns, and drew his head back, and held him fast whilst the frightened man crawled away.

"I was myself in some difficulty," said Mr. Hawker, when telling the story. "The stag would have turned on me when I let go, and I did not quite see my way to escape; but that wretched man did nothing but yell for his wig and hat, which had come off and were under the deer's feet; as if my life were of no account beside his foxy old wig and battered beaver."

Dr. Phillpotts, the late Bishop of Exeter, not long after this occurred, came to Morwenstow to visit Mr. Hawker. Whilst being shown the landscape from the garden, the bishop's eye rested on Robin Hood.

"Why! that stag which butted and tossed Mr. Knight is still suffered to live! It might have killed him."

"No great loss, my lord," said Mr. Hawker. "He is very Low Church."

Early next morning loud cries for assistance penetrated the vicar's bedroom. Looking from his window, he beheld the bishop struggling with Robin Hood, who, like his fellow of Sherwood, seems to have had little respect for episcopal dignity. Robin had taken a fancy to the bishop's apron, and, gently approaching, had secured one corner in his mouth.

There is a story of a Scottish curate, who, when Jenny Geddes seized him by his "prelatical" gown as he was passing into the pulpit, quietly loosed the strings, and allowed Jenny and the gown to fall backward together. There was no such luck for the bishop. He sought in vain to unfasten the apron, which descended farther and farther into Robin's throat, until the vicar, coming to the rescue, restored the apron to daylight, and sent the "masterful thief" about his business.

Mr. Hawker accompanied the late Bishop of Exeter on his first visit to Tintagel, and delighted in telling how the scene, then far more out of the world than it can now be considered, impressed the powerful mind of Dr. Phillpotts. He stood alone for some time on the extreme edge of the castle cliff, while the sun went down before him in the tumbling, foaming Atlantic a blaze of splendour, flaking the rocks and ruined walls with orange and carmine; and as he turned away he muttered the line from *Zanga*:—

> I like this rocking of the battlements.

Another visitor to Morwenstow was the Poet Laureate; he presented himself at the door, and sent in his card, and was received with cordiality and hospitality by the vicar, who, however, was not sure that the stranger was the poet. After lunch they walked together on the cliffs, and Mr. Hawker pointed to the Tonacombe Brook forming a cascade into the sea.

"Falling like a broken purpose," he observed.

"You are quoting my lines," said the Poet Laureate.

"And thus it was," as Mr. Hawker said when relating the incident, "that I learned whom I was entertaining." He flattered himself that it was he who had introduced the Arthurian cycle of legends to Tennyson's notice.

Charles Kingsley also owed to Mr. Hawker his first introduction to scenery which he afterwards rendered famous. Stowe and Chapel, places which figured so largely in *Westward Ho!* were explored by them together; and the vicar of Morwenstow was struck, as every one must have been struck who accompanied Mr. Kingsley under similar circumstances, by the wonderful insight and skill which seized at once on the most characteristic features of the scene, and found at the instant the fitting words in which to describe them.

Mr. Hawker, for his own part, not only did this for his own corner of Cornwall, but threw into his prose and his poetry the peculiar feeling of the district, the subtle aroma which, in less skilful hands, is apt to vanish altogether.

His ballads found their way into numerous publications without his name being appended to them, and sometimes were fathered on other writers. In a letter to T. Carnsew, Esq., dated 2nd January, 1858, he says as much.

My Dear Sir,—A happy New Year to yours and you, and many of them! as we say in the West. The kind interest you have taken in young Blight's book[1] induces me to send you the royal reply to my letter. Through Col. Phipps to the Queen I sent a simple statement of the case, and asked leave for the youth to be allowed to dedicate his forthcoming book to the Duke of Cornwall. I did not, between ourselves, expect to succeed, because no such thing has hitherto been permitted, and also because I was utterly unknown, thank God, at Court. But it has been always my fate to build other people's houses. For others I usually succeed; for myself, always fail. Let me tell you one strange thing. Every year of my life for full ten years I have had to write to some publisher, editor or author, to claim the paternity of a legend or a ballad or a page of prose,

---

[1] *Ancient Crosses in Cornwall*, by J. T. Blight. Penzance, 1858.

which others have been attempting to foist on the public as their own. Last year I had to rescue a legendary ballad—" The Sisters of Glennecten "—from the claims of a Mr. H. of Exeter College.[1] Yesterday I wrote for the January number of *Blackwood*, wherein I see published " The Bells of Bottreaux," a name and legend which, if any one should claim, I say with Jack Cade, " He lies, for I invented it myself!"

" The Silent Tower of Bottreaux " is one of his best ballads. To the poem he appends the following note:[2] " The rugged heights that line the seashore in the neighbourhood of Tintagel Castle and Church are crested with towers. Among these, that of Bottreaux Castle, or, as it is now written, Boscastle, is without bells. The silence of this wild and lonely churchyard on festive or solemn occasions is not a little striking. On inquiring as to the cause, the legend related in the text was told me, as a matter of implicit belief in those parts."

THE SILENT TOWER OF BOTTREAUX.

Tintagel bells ring o'er the tide:
The boy leans on his vessel's side;
He hears that sound, and dreams of home
Soothe the wild orphan of the foam.
 " Come to thy God in time!"
 Thus saith their pealing chime:
 " Youth, manhood, old age, past,
 Come to thy God at last!"

---

[1] The mysterious sisters really lived and died in North Devon. Mr. Hawker transplanted the story to St. Knighton's Kieve. Any attempt in prose or verse to associate these sisters with Glennectan he afterwards resented as a literary theft.

[2] *Ecclesia:* a volume of poems. Oxford, 1840. Really, the church of Forrabury on the height above Boscastle, which is a hamlet in the parish of Forrabury.

THE SILENT TOWER OF BOTTREAUX

But why are Bottreaux's echoes still?
Her tower stands proudly on the hill:
Yet the strange chough that home hath found,
The lamb lies sleeping on the ground.
 "Come to thy God in time!"
 Should be her answering chime.
 "Come to thy God at last!"
 Should echo on the blast.

The ship rode down with courses free,
The daughter of a distant sea:
Her sheet was loose, her anchor stored,
The merry Bottreaux bells on board.
 "Come to thy God in time!"
 Rang out Tintagel chime.
 "Youth, manhood, old age, past,
 Come to thy God at last!"

The pilot heard his native bells
Hang on the breeze in fitful swells.
"Thank God!" with reverent brow he cried:
"We make the shore with evening's tide."
 "Come to thy God in time!"
 It was his marriage-chime.
 Youth, manhood, old age, past,
 His bell must ring at last.

Thank God, thou whining knave, on land!
But thank at sea, the steersman's hand,
The captain's voice above the gale,
Thank the good ship and ready sail.
 "Come to thy God in time!"
 Sad grew the boding chime,
 "Come to thy God at last!"
 Boomed heavy on the blast.

Up rose that sea, as if it heard
The mighty Master's signal word.
What thrills the captain's whitening lip?
The death-groans of his sinking ship!

"Come to thy God in time!"
Swung deep the funeral chime.
"Grace, mercy, kindness, past,
Come to thy God at last!"

Long did the rescued pilot tell,
When grey hairs o'er his forehead fell,—
While those around would hear and weep,—
That fearful judgment of the deep.
"Come to thy God in time!"
He read his native chime:
Youth, manhood, old age, past,
His bell rung out at last!

Still, when the storm of Bottreaux's waves
Is wakening in his weedy caves,
Those bells that sullen surges hide
Peal their deep notes beneath the tide.
"Come to thy God in time!"
Thus saith the ocean chime:
"Storm, billow, whirlwind, past,
Come to thy God at last!"

I may be allowed, as this is a gossiping book, here to tell a story of Boscastle, which came to my ears when staying there a few years ago, and which is true.

There lived at Boscastle, within twenty years, an old seafaring man whom we will call Daddy Tregellas—his real name has escaped me. A widow in the village died, leaving a fair young daughter of eighteen, very delicate and consumptive, without a home or relation. Daddy Tregellas had known the widow and felt great pity for the orphan, but how to help her he did not see. After much turning the matter over in his mind he thought the only way in which he could make her a home and provide her with comforts without giving the gossips occasion to talk, was by marrying her. And married accordingly they were. The Boscastle people to this day tell of the tenderness of the old man for his young, delicate wife; it was that of a father for a daughter, —how he watched the carnation spots on her cheek with intense anxiety and listened with anguish to her cough; how he walked out with her on the cliffs, wrapping shawls round her; and sat in church with his eyes fixed on her whilst she sang, listened or prayed. The beautiful girl was his idol, his pet.

She languished in spite of all his care. He nursed her through her illness like a mother, with his rough, brown hand as gentle as that of a woman. She died propped up in bed, with her chestnut hair flowing over his blue sailor's jersey, as he held her head on his breast.

When he had laid his pet in Forrabury churchyard the light of his life was extinguished. The old man wandered about the cliffs all day, in sunshine and in storm, growing more hollow-cheeked and dull-eyed, his thin hair lank, his back bowed, speaking to no one and breaking slowly but surely.

But Mr. Avery, the shipbuilder, about this time laid the keel of a little vessel, and she was reared in Boscastle haven. The new ship interested the old man, and when the figurehead was set up he fancied he traced in it a likeness to his dead wife.

"It is—it is the Pet," faltered the old man.

The owner heard the exclamation and said: "So shall it be. She shall be called *The Pet*."

And now the old love, which had wound itself round the wife, began to attach itself to the little vessel. Every day the old man was on the quay watching the growth of *The Pet*; he could not bear her out of his sight. When *The Pet* was ready to be launched Mr. Avery offered Tregellas the position of captain to her. The old man's joy was full; he took the command and sailed for Bristol for coals.

One stormy day, when a furious west wind was driving upon the land and bowling mountains of green water against the coast, it was noised that a vessel was visible scudding before the wind in dangerous proximity to the shore. The signal-rock was speedily crowded with anxious watchers. The coastguardsman observed her attentively with his glass and said: "It is *The Pet*. The hatchways are all closed."

Eyes watched her bounding through the waves, now on the summit of a huge green billow, now deep in its trough, till she was lost to sight in the rain and spondrift.

That was the last seen of *The Pet*; she, with old Daddy Tregellas and all on board, went to the bottom in that dreadful storm.

Boscastle is a hamlet of quaint, gabled, weather-beaten cottages, inhabited by sailors, clinging to the steep sides of the hills that dip rapidly to the harbour, a mere cleft in the rocks, in shape like an S.

The entrance is between huge precipices of black rock, one of them scooped out into a well; it is the resort of countless gulls, which breed along the ledges. The harbour is masked by an islet of rock covered by a meagre crop of sea-grass and thrift.

Mr. Claud Hawker, the brother of the subject of this memoir, resided till his death at Penally in Boscastle.

CHAPTER IV

Mr. Hawker's Politics—Election of 1857—His Zeal for the Labourers—"The Poor Man and his Parish Church"—Letter to a Landlord—Death of his Man, Tape—Kindness to the Poor—Verses over his Door—Reckless Charity—Hospitality—A Breakdown—His Eccentric Dress—The Devil and his Barn—His Ecclesiastical Vestments—Ceremonial—The Nine Cats—The Church Garden—Kindness to Animals—The Rooks and Jackdaws—The Well of St. John—Letter to a Young Man entering the University.

MR. HAWKER in politics, as far as he had any, was a Liberal; and in 1857 he voted for Mr. Robartes, afterwards Lord Robartes.

MARCH 26, 1857. *My Dear Sir,*—Your mangold is remarkably fine. I must, of course, visit Stratton, to vote for Robartes; and I do wish I could be told how far a few votes would throw out Kendall by helping Carew, then I would give the latter one. If I can contrive to call at Flexbury, I will; but Mrs. Hawker is so worried by bad eyes that she will not risk the roads. Last time we were annoyed by some rascals, who came after the carriage, shouting, "Kendall and protection!" It will be a dark infamy for Cornwall if Nick, the traitor to every party, should get in. Tom S—— has been out to-day, blustering for Nick, but, when asked what party he belonged to, could not tell. How should he? A note from M—— to-night, dated Bude, informs me that he is there. I am glad to find that, though not yet registered as a Cornish voter, his heart and wishes are for Robartes. It will always be to me a source of pride, that I was the first, or well-nigh, I think, the only clergyman in this deanery who voted for a Free-trade candidate. Yours, my dear sir, faithfully,

R. S. HAWKER.

J. CARNSEW, Esq.

... I cannot conclude without a word about the mighty theme of elections. When Carew's address arrived, and I read it to Mrs. Hawker, her remark was: "It doesn't ring well." Nor did it. There were sneaky symptoms about it. S—— writes that "sinister influence, apart from political, has been brought to bear against Carew." We save a breakfast by this; for Mrs. Hawker had announced her intention to give one, as she did last time, to Mr. Robartes' voters; and I save what is to me important—a ride. When I was in Oxford, there was a well-known old man, Dr. Crowe, public officer, etc. He had risen from small beginnings, and therefore he was a man of mind. Somewhat rough, and so much the better, as old wine is. Him the young, thoughtless fellows delighted to tease after dinner in the common-room, over their wine at New College. (N.B.—The rumour used to run, that, when the fellows of the college retired from the hall, the butler went before, with a warming-pan, which he passed over the seat of every stuffed chair, that the reverend fogies might not catch cold as they sat down.) Well, one day, said a junior to old Crowe: "Do you know, Dr. C., what has happened to Jem Ward?"—"No, not I. Is he hanged?"—"Oh, no! they say he is member of Parliament."—"Well, what of that?"—"Oh, but consider what a thing for a fellow like that to get into the House of Commons—such a *blackguard!*"—"And pray, young man, where should a blackguard go, but into the House of Commons, eh?"

Good-night, dear sir, good-night. Yours faithfully,

R. S. HAWKER.

But Mr. Hawker's sympathies were by no means bound up with one party. He was as enthusiastic in 1873 for the return of a Conservative member for

Exeter, as he had been in 1857 for that of a Free-trade candidate for East Cornwall.

> MORWENSTOW, Dec. 11, 1873. *My dear Mr. and Mrs. Mills*,—The good tidings of your success in Exeter has only just arrived in our house; and I make haste to congratulate you, and to express our hearty sympathy with Mr. Mills' great triumph. Only yesterday Mr. M—— was here, and we were discussing the probabilities and chances of the majority. I had heard from Powderham Castle that the contest would be severe, and the run close; but every good man's wishes and sympathies were with Mr. Mills. I hope that God will bless and succour him, and make his election an avenue of good and usefulness to his kind, which I am sure you both will value beyond the mere honour and rank. Our men heard guns last night, but could not decide whether the sound came from Bude or Lundy. But to-day I heard there were great and natural rejoicings around your Efford home. How you must have exulted also at your husband's strong position in London, and at the School Board! He must have been very deeply appreciated there, and will, of course, succeed to the chairmanship of his district. You will be sorry to hear that Mr. R——[1] has disappointed us, and will not be back again until after Christmas. So, although I am so weak that I can hardly stagger up to the church, and I incur deadly risk, I must go through my duty on Sunday. Our dutiful love to you both. I am, yours ever faithfully,
>
> R. S. HAWKER.

It was his intense sympathy with the poor that constituted the Radicalism in Mr. Hawker's opinions. A thorough-going Radical he was not, for he was filled with the most devoted veneration for the Crown and Constitution; but his tender heart bled for the labourer, whom he regarded as the sufferer through

---

[1] A clergyman on whom he had calculated for his assistance in his services.

protection, and he fired up at what he regarded as an injustice. When he broke forth into words, it was with the eloquence and energy of a prophet. What can be more vigorous and vehement than the following paper, which he wrote in 1861 ?

There are in Morwenstow about six thousand acres of arable land, rented by seventy farmers; forty large, and thirty small.

There are less than sixty able-bodied labourers, and twenty-five half-men, at roads, etc.

With this proportion of one labourer to a hundred acres, there can be no lack of *employ*.

The rate of wages is eight shillings a week, paid, not in money, but by truck of corn.

A fixed agreement of a hundred and thirty-five pounds of corn, or eighteen gallons (commonly called seven scores), is allotted to each man in lieu of fourteen shillings, be the market price what it will.

A man with a wife and three or four children will consume the above quantity of corn in fourteen days.

Therefore, such a man, receiving for his fortnight's work fourteen shillings' worth of corn, will only leave in his master's hand one shilling a week, which one shilling usually is paid for house-rent.

Now, this inevitable outlay for the loaf and for the rent will leave—for fuel, for shoes, for clothing, for groceries, for tools, for club . . . *nil* · ol. os. od.

But, but. But in the year 1860-61, the fourteen shillings paid for that corn will only yield in flour and meal ten shillings and sixpence, the millers being judges.

"If a man have only a wife and two children to house and feed, his surplus money above his bread and rent will be one shilling (?) a week beyond the above example." *But, but,* in the recited list of exigencies, will that suffice ?

It was from a knowledge of the state of the parish, that I assented to the collection, of which I enclose a statement.

Two farmers only had the audacity to allege that the effort was uncalled for; and a labourer of one of these must have gone barefooted to his work the whole winter, had not the money for a pair of shoes been advanced to him by the victim of the parish.

It appears to be a notion entertained by a chief patron of all our charities, that the wages and the treatment of the labourers in Kilkhampton are more favourable than in Morwenstow. *But, but, but* ——

What is the weekly wage?

How paid?

If in corn, at what price?

And are there contracts in other respects?

These are not questions which I want to be answered, but only questions for your own private consideration.

A letter narrating the success of this appeal is in my hands, and may find a place here.

FEB. 21, 1861. *My dear Sir*,—I have postponed replying to your last letter until I could acquaint you with the progress or result of the subscriptions to the poor. Lord J. Thynne has given five pounds; Mr. Dayman, three pounds; Messrs. Cann and Harris, churchwardens, one pound each; other parishioners, about three or four pounds. So that we shall divide twenty-five pounds and upwards among the really destitute. I am much obliged to you for your readiness to allow my influence to count with that of others in the parish; but the reference in my letter to the churchwardens was to the past, and not altogether to the future. Be this as it may, when Moses languishes, manna falls, thank God!

You will be sorry to hear that Mrs. H—— is very ill. Her attack is so full of peril, and demands such incessant medical succour, that Capt. H—— resolved on removing her while she could be moved to London, to the charge of her accustomed doctor; and thither they went last Monday. Our loss is deep. It was indeed a gift from God to have a thorough lady and gentleman in the parish to appreciate the utterance of truth, and the effects of duty: it was indeed a happiness, and it is now gone. Mrs. H—— had taken great trouble with our choir. Every Thursday evening she has allowed them to come to learn the musical scale, and they were fast learning to read and sing the notes.

We have been visited of late by the new kind of hurricane, the κύκλων, or whirl. It is just as fierce and strong as the old storm; but the scene of its onslaught is rigidly local: indeed, we might almost call them parochial. They had theirs at Kilkhampton two days before Mr. T——'s christening. The Poughill rush was the week after the vicar brought home his wife. A pinnacle was snapped off there, and the wall of the church rent. At Kilkhampton the damage done was in the immediate vicinity of the church. We had ours last night, but the church did not suffer harm, although two-thirds of the roof are rotten, and the pinnacles overhang. Lent is always the demon's time, and the strength of evil. A woman who is just come in tells me that the new chimney in the kitchen at Tidnacombe was blown down last night, and is now lying on the roof in fragments. Yours faithfully,

R. S. Hawker.

The energy with which he upheld the cause of the labourer was one cause of some unreasonable resentment against him being felt by the farmers; and this explains his expression "the victim of the parish," in reference to himself in his appeal.

The same intense sympathy with the poor and the down-trodden breaks out in his ballad, "The Poor Man and his Parish Church," of which I insert a few verses:—

> The poor have hands and feet and eyes,
>   Flesh, and a feeling mind:
> They breathe the breath of mortal sighs,
>   They are of human kind;
> They weep such tears as others shed,
>   And now and then they smile;

For sweet to them is that poor bread
   They win with honest toil.

The poor men have their wedding-day,
   And children climb their knee:
They have not many friends, for they
   Are in such misery.
They sell their youth, their skill, their pains,
   For hire in hill and glen:
The very blood within their veins,
   It flows for other men.

They should have roofs to call their own
   When they grow old and bent—
Meek houses built of dark grey stone,
   Worn labourer's monument.
There should they dwell beneath the thatch,
   With threshold calm and free:
No stranger's hand should lift the latch
   To mark their poverty.

Fast by the church these walls should stand,
   Her aisles in youth they trod:
They have no home in all the land
   Like that old house of God!
There, there, the sacrament was shed
   That gave them heavenly birth,
And lifted up the poor man's head
   With princes of the earth.

There in the chancel's voice of praise
   Their simple vows were poured,
And angels looked with equal gaze
   On Lazarus and his Lord.
There, too, at last, they calmly sleep,
   Where hallowed blossoms bloom;
And eyes as fond and faithful weep
   As o'er the rich man's tomb.

    .   .   .   .

"THE POOR MAN AND HIS PARISH CHURCH"

I know not why; but when they tell
   Of houses fair and wide,
Where troops of poor men go to dwell
   In chambers side by side,
I dream of an old cottage door,
   With garlands overgrown,
And wish the children of the poor
   Had flowers to call their own.

And when they vaunt that in these walls
   They have their worship-day,
Where the stern signal coldly calls
   The prisoned poor to pray,
I think upon an ancient home
   Beside the churchyard wall,
Where roses round the porch would roam,
   And gentle jasmines fall.

I see the old man of my lay,
   His grey head bowed and bare:
He kneels by our dear wall to pray,
   The sunlight in his hair.
Well! they may strive, as wise men will,
   To work with wit and gold:
I think my own dear Cornwall still
   Was happier of old.

Oh, for the poor man's church again,
   With one roof over all,
Where the true hearts of Cornishmen
   Might beat beside the wall!
The altars where, in holier days,
   Our fathers were forgiven,
Who went with meek and faithful ways,
   Through the old aisles, to heaven!

A letter to one of the landlords in his parish shows how vehemently Mr. Hawker could urge the claims of one of the farmers.

Morwenstow, May 21, 1867. *My dear Mr. Martyn,—* Just as I was about to write to you on other matters, your advertisement for the letting of your lands reached me. It is not, of course, my duty to express any opinion between landlord and tenant, or to give utterance to my sympathy with any one candidate over another; yet there is a matter on which I am sure you will forgive me if I venture to touch. It is on the tenancy of your farm of Ruxmoore by Cann. He has been my churchwarden during the whole of his last term. He and his have been the most faithful adherents to the church of their baptism in my whole parish; and he has been to me so sincere and attached a friend in his station of life, that he without Ruxmoore, or Ruxmoore without the Canns, would be to me an utterly inconceivable regret. It was I who first introduced him to the choice of your family, twenty-eight years agone; and throughout the whole of that time he has been, in his humble way, entirely faithful to me and to you. I do not imagine that you intend to exclude him from your farm, but I venture to hope that you will put me in possession confidentially of your wishes in regard to his future tenancy. Do you mean that he shall tender as before? and does your valuation of his part of your land ascend? He is not aware that I write to you hereon; and, if you are disinclined to answer my questions, I hope you will allow me to record my hearty hope and trust that you will give him the preference over other new and local candidates, in or out of Morwenstow. I have firm confidence in the justice and mercy of your heart. But you must not infer that Cann alone of all your tenants is, or has been, the object of my special regard. . . . In Wellcombe, B——, whom you remember, no doubt, by name, is one of my regular communicants. And now the very kind and generous sympathy which Mrs. Martyn and yourself have shown towards my school demands a detail of our success.

The children on the day-school books amount to sixty-three. The inspectors (diocesan) pronounce it to be the most satisfactory school in their district. I always visit and instruct the children in person once a week. Mrs. Hawker has had a singing class of boys and girls weekly at the vicarage. But this duty and the harmonium in church are now undertaken by Mrs. T——, for a reason that will readily suggest itself to your mind. But why should I hesitate to avow to old friends that we expect another guest at the vicarage? How I hope that God may grant us a boy, that I may utter the words of the fathers of holy time, "My son, my son!"

MORWENSTOW, Jan. 22, 1857. *My dear Sir*,—It is no longer possible to nourish the project which I have all along, every week and day, intended to essay, *viz.*, a journey down to Flexbury Hall. We have continually talked of it, more than once fixed the day, but we have been as singularly prevented as if some evil spirit had it at heart to hinder our purpose. And these obstacles have very often been occurrences full of pain, domestic or personal. You have no doubt heard of the frightful accident to poor old George Tape, my caretaker and very excellent servant. He lived all his early life with old Mr. Shearm, here in the old Vicarage House; was sexton twenty-five years; worked with me from 1835 to 1851; then visited Australia as a gold-digger; returned about two years agone with enough to live on, aided by a little work, and came back to be again my hind at Michaelmas last. He was, therefore, a long-accustomed face, almost as one of my own family. You will, therefore, understand the shock when we heard a man rushing up stairs to our little sitting-room with the tale of fear; and on going down, I found poor George seated in a chair, with the hand crushed into pulp below the wrist, and dangling by the naked sinews. I made a rude tourniquet, in haste, of a silk handkerchief and short stick, and so the hemorrhage was stopped. We got him home. I was with him nearly all night, and the next day till he died; but the amputation I could not witness. We found two fingers and other pieces of flesh among the barley afterwards. . . . I remain yours, my dear sir, very faithfully,

R. S. HAWKER.

T. CARNSEW, Esq.

The generosity of the vicar to the poor knew no

bounds. It was not always discreet, but his compassionate heart could not listen to a tale of suffering unaffected; nay, more, the very idea that others were in want impelled him to seek them out at all times, to relieve their need.

On cold winter nights, if he felt the frost to be very keen, the idea would enter his head that such and such persons had not above one blanket on their beds, or that they had gone, without anything to warm their vitals, to the chill damp attics where they slept. Then he would stamp about the house, collecting warm clothing and blankets, bottles of wine, and any food he could find in the larder, and laden with them, attended by a servant, go forth on his rambles, and knock up the cottagers, that he might put extra blankets on their beds, or cheer them with port wine and cold pie.

The following graphic description of one of these night missions is given in the words of an old workman named Vinson.

It was a very cold night in the winter of 1874-75, about half-past nine: he called me into the house, and said: "The poor folk up at Shop will all perish this very night of cold. John Ode is ill, and cannot go: can you get there alive?"

"If you please, sir, I will, if you'll allow me," I said.

"Take them these four bottles of brandy," he says; and he brought up four bottles with never so much as the corks drawed. "Now," says he, "what will you have yourself?" And I says, "Gin, if you plase, sir," I says. And he poured me out gin and water; and then he gi'ed me a lemonade bottle of gin for me to put in my side-pocket. "That'll keep you alive," he says, "before you come back." So he fulled me up before I started, and sent me off to Shop, to four old people's houses, with a bottle of brandy for each. And then he says: "There's two shillings for yourself; and you keep pulling at that bottle, and you'll keep yourself alive afore you come back." So I went there, and delivered the bottles; and I'd had enough before I started to bring me home again, so I didn't uncork my bottle of gin.

And it isn't once, it's scores o' times, he's looked out o' window, after I've going home at night, and **shouted to me**: "Here, stay! come back, Vinson," and he's gone into the larder, and cut off great pieces of meat, and sent me with them, and p'raps brandy or wine, to some poor soul; and he always gi'ed me a shilling, either then **or** next day, for myself, besides meat **and** drink.

"They are crushed down, my poor people," he would say with energy, stamping about his room—"ground down with poverty, with a wretched wage, the hateful truck system, **till they are** degraded in mind and body." It was a common saying of his, "If I eat and drink, and see my poor hunger and thirst, I am not a minister of Christ, but a lion that lurketh in his den to ravish the poor."

The monetary value of the living was £365. He wrote up over the porch of his vicarage—

> A house, a glebe, a pound a day,
> A pleasant place to watch and pray:
> Be true to Church, be kind to poor,
> O minister, for evermore!

Of his overflowing kindness to the shipwrecked, mention shall be made in another chapter. The many sufferers whom he rescued from the water, housed, fed, nursed and clothed, and sent away with liberal gifts, always spoke of his charity with warmth and gratitude. In no one instance would he accept compensation for the deeds of charity which he performed. He received letters of thanks for his services to the shipwrecked from shipowners in Norway, Denmark, France, Scotland and Cornwall, who had lost vessels on this fatal coast, as well as from the Consuls of the several nations.

Like his grandfather, Dr. Hawker, he was ready to give away everything he had; and he was at times in straitened circumstances, owing to the open house he kept, and the profusion with which he gave away to the necessitous.

This inconsiderate generosity sometimes did harm to those who received it. One instance will suffice.

The vicar of Morwenstow had, some years ago, a servant, whom we will call Stanlake: the man may be still alive, and therefore his real name had better not be given to the world.

One day Mr. Hawker ordered his carriage to drive to Bideford, some twenty miles distant. The weather was raw and cold. He was likely to be absent all day, as he was going on to Barnstaple by train to consult his doctor. His compassion was roused by the thought of Stanlake having forty miles of drive in the cold, and a day of lounging about in the raw December air; and just as he stepped into the carriage he produced a bottle of whisky, and gave it to Stanlake.

Mr. Hawker was himself a most abstemious man: he drank only water, and never touched wine, spirits, or beer.

On the way to Bideford, at Hoops, thinking the coachman looked blue with cold, the vicar ordered him a glass of hot brandy and water. When he reached Bideford station he said: " Now, Stanlake, I shall be back by the half-past four train: mind you meet me with the carriage."

"All right, sir."

But Mr. Hawker did not arrive by the half-past four train.

Up till that hour Stanlake had kept sober, he had not touched his bottle of whisky; but finding that his master did not arrive, and that time hung heavily on his hands, he retired to the stable, uncorked the bottle, and drank it off.

At six o'clock Mr. Hawker arrived at Bideford. There was no carriage at the station to meet him. He hurried to the inn where he put up, and ordered his conveyance. He was told that his man was incapable.

"Send him to me, send him here," he thundered, pacing the coffee-room in great excitement.

"Please, sir, he is under a heap of straw and hay in a loose box in the stable dead drunk."

"Make him come."

After some delay the information was brought him, that, when Mr. Stanlake after great efforts had been reared upon his legs he had fallen over again.

"Put the horses to. I can drive as well as Stanlake. I will drive home myself; and do you shove that drunken boor head and crop into the carriage."

The phaeton was brought to the door: the vicar mounted the box, the drunken servant was tumbled inside, the door shut on him, and off they started for a long night drive with no moon in the sky, and frosty stars looking down on the wintry earth.

Half-way between Bideford and Morwenstow, in

descending a hill the pole-strap broke; the carriage ran forward on the horses' heels; they plunged, and the pole drove into the hedge; with a jerk one of the carriage springs gave way.

Mr. Hawker, afraid to get off the box without some one being at hand to hold the horses' heads, shouted lustily for help. No one came.

"Stanlake, wake up! Get out!"

A snore from inside was the only answer. Mr. Hawker knocked the glasses with his whip handle, and shouted yet louder: "You drunken scoundrel, get out and hold the horses!"

"We won't go home till morning, till daylight doth appear," chanted the tipsy man in bad tune from within.

After some time a labourer, seeing from a distance the stationary carriage lamps, and wondering what they were, arrived on the scene. By his assistance the carriage was brought sideways to the hill, the horses were taken out, a piece of rope procured to mend the harness and tie up the broken spring; and Mr. Hawker, remounting the box, drove forward, and reached Morwenstow vicarage about one o'clock at night.

In the morning Stanlake appeared in the library, very downcast.

"Go away," said the vicar in a voice of thunder. "I dismiss you forthwith. Here are your wages. I will not even look at you. Let me never see your face again. You brought me into a pretty predicament last night."

Two days after he met the man again. In the

meantime his wrath had abated, and he began to think that he had acted harshly with his servant. "Forgive us our trespasses as we forgive them that trespass against us," ran in his head.

"Stanlake," said he, "you played me a hateful trick the other night. I hope you are sorry for it."

"I'se very sorry, your honour, but you gave me the whiskey."

"You think you won't do it again?"

"I'se very sure I won't, if you give me no more."

"Then, Stanlake, I will overlook it. You may remain in my service."

Not many weeks after, the vicar sent Stanlake to Boscastle, and, thinking he would be cold, gave him again a bottle of whisky. Of course, once more the man got drunk. This time the vicar did not overlook it; but which of the two was really to blame?

Mr. Robert Stephen Hawker was a man of the most unbounded hospitality. Every one who visited Morwenstow met with a warm welcome: everything his larder and dairy contained was produced in the most lavish profusion. The best that his house could afford was freely given. On one occasion, when about to be visited by a nephew and his wife, he sent all the way to Tavistock, about thirty miles, for a leg and shoulder of Dartmoor mutton. If he saw friends coming along the loop drive which descended to his vicarage, he would run to the door, with a sunny smile of greeting, and both hands extended in welcome, and draw them in to break his bread and partake of his salt. Sometimes his larder was empty, he had fed so many visitors; and he would say sorrowfully:

"There is nothing but ham and eggs: I give thee all, I can no more." And visitors were most numerous in summer. In one of his letters he speaks of having entertained 150 in a summer.

His drawing-room on a summer afternoon was often so crowded with visitors from Bude, Clovelly, Bideford, Stratton and elsewhere, come to tea, that it was difficult to move in it.

"Look here, my dear," he would say to a young wife, "I will tell you how to make tea. Fill the pot with leaves to the top, and pour the water into the cracks." His tea was always the best Lapsing Souchong from Twining's.

He was a wretched carver. He talked and laughed, and hacked the meat at the same time, cutting here, there and anywhere, in search of the tenderest pieces for his guests.

"One day that we went over to call on him unexpectedly," says a friend, "he made us stay for lunch. He was in the greatest excitement and delight at our visit, and in the flurry decanted a bottle of brandy and filled our wine-glasses with it, mistaking it for sherry. The joint was a fore-quarter of lamb. It puzzled him extremely. At last, losing all patience, he grasped the leg-bone with one hand, the shoulder with the fork driven up to the hilt through it, and tore it by main force asunder."

Another friend describes a "high tea" at his house. A whole covey of partridges was brought on table. He drove his fork into the breast of each, then severed the legs by cutting through the back, and so helped each person to the whole breast and wings. The birds had not been cooked by an experienced hand, and properly trussed. The whole covey lay on their backs with their legs in the air, presenting the drollest appearance when the cover—large enough for a sirloin of beef—was removed from the dish.

"When you steal your own cream, my dear," was a saying of his to ladies, "don't take just a spoonful on a bit of bread, but clear the whole pan with a great ladle and no bread."

One story about a breakdown when driving has been told: another incident of the same description shall be given in his own words:—

Nov. 4, 1856. *My dear Sir*,—When I relate the history of our recent transit through Poughill by night, I think you will allow that I am not nervous beyond measure when I say that I am obliged through fear to deny myself the pleasure of joining your hospitable board on Thursday next. Before we had crossed Summerleaze one lamp went out; another languished. My clumsy servant John had broken both springs. A lantern, which we borrowed at Lake Cottage of a woman called Barrett, held aloft by our boy, just enabled us to creep along amid a thorough flood of cold rain, until we arrived at Stowe. There we succeeded in negotiating a loan of another piece of candle, and moved on, a rare and rending headache meanwhile throbbing under my hat. Half-way down Stowe hill, the drag-chain broke suddenly, and but for extreme good behaviour on the part of the horses—shall I add good driving on mine?—we must have gone over in a heap, to the great delight of the Dissenters in this district. We did at last arrive home, but it was in a very disconsolate condition. Still, good came of our journey; for Mrs. Hawker cannot deny that I drove in a masterly manner, and therefore is bound to travel anywhere with me by *day*. We mean, with your leave, to come down to you early one day soon, and depart so as to be at home before dark. Tell your son that on Saturday night last, at eight o'clock, tidings came in that carriage-lamps flared along our in-road. I found at the door "a deputation from the Parent Society," the Rev. L. H——. Three friends had previously suggested his visit here, and all three had been snubbed. But he put into my hand a note from Leopold Ackland, so there was no longer any resistance. He had travelled far—Australia, Egypt, the Crimea during the Anglican defeat. So his talk amused us. With kindest regards to all at Flexbury, I remain, yours, my dear sir, very faithfully,

R. S. HAWKER.

T. CARNSEW, Esq.

Mr. Hawker, as has been already intimated, was rather peculiar in his dress. At first, soon after his induction to Morwenstow, he wore his cassock; but in time abandoned this inconvenient garb, in which he found it impossible to scramble about his cliffs. He then adopted a claret-coloured coat, with long tails. He had the greatest aversion to anything black: the only black things he would wear were his boots. These claret-coloured coats would button over the breast, but were generally worn open, displaying beneath a knitted blue fisherman's jersey. At his side, just where the Lord's side was pierced, a little red cross was woven into the jersey. He wore fishing-boots reaching above his knee.

The claret-coloured cassock coats, when worn out, were given to his servant-maids, who wore them as morning-dresses when going about their dirty work. "See there! the parson is washing potatoes!" or, "See there! the parson is feeding the pigs!" would be exclaimed by villagers, as they saw his servant girls engaged on their work, in their master's coats.

At first he went about in a college cap; but this

speedily made way for a pink or plum-coloured beaver hat without a brim, the colour of which rapidly faded to a tint of pink, the blue having disappeared. When he put on coat, jersey or hat he wore it till it was worn out: he had no best suit.

Once he had to go to Hartland, to the funeral of a relative. On the way he had an accident—his carriage upset, and he was thrown out. When he arrived at Hartland, his relations condoled with him on his upset. "Do, Hawker, let me find you a new hat: in your fall you have knocked the brim off yours," said one.

"My dear ——," he answered, "priests of the Holy Eastern Church wear no brims to their hats; and I wear none, to testify the connection of the Cornish Church with the East, before ever Augustine set foot in Kent." And he attended the funeral in his brimless hat. He wore one of these peculiar coloured hats, bleached almost white, at the funeral of his first wife, in 1863, and could hardly be persuaded to allow the narrowest possible band of black crape to be pinned round it.

The pink hats were, however, abandoned, partly because they would not keep their colour; and a priest's wide-awake, claret-coloured like the coat, was adopted in its place.

"My coat," said he, when asked by a lady why he wore one of such a cut and colour, "my coat is that of an Armenian archimandrite." But this he said only from his love of hoaxing persons who asked him impertinent questions.

When Mr. Hawker went up to London to be

married the second time, he lost his hat, which was carried away by the wind as he looked out of the window of the train, to become, perhaps, an inmate of a provincial museum as a curiosity. He arrived hatless in town after dark. He tied a large crimson silk handkerchief over his head, and thus attired paced up and down the street for two hours before his lodging, in great excitement at the thought of the change in his prospects which would dawn with the morrow. I must leave to the imagination of the reader the perplexity of the policeman at the corner over the extraordinary figure in claret-coloured clerical coat, wading-boots up to his hips, blue knitted jersey, and red handkerchief bound round his head. His gloves were crimson. He wore these in church as well as elsewhere.

In the dark chancel, lighted only dimly through the stained east window, hidden behind a close-grated screen, the vicar was invisible when performing the service, till, having shouted "Thomas," in a voice of thunder, two blood-red hands were thrust through the screen, with offertory bags, in which alms were to be collected by the churchwarden who answered the familiar call. Or, the first appearance of the vicar took place after the Nicene Creed, when a crimson hand was seen gliding up the banister of the pulpit, to be followed by his body, painfully worming its way through an aperture in the screen, measuring sixteen inches only; "the camel getting at length through the eye of the needle," as Mr. Hawker called the proceeding.

In church he wore a little black cap over his white

hair, rendered necessary by the cold and damp of the decaying old church.

At his side he carried a bunch of seals and medals. One of his seals bore the fish surrounded by a serpent biting its tail, and the legend ιχθυς. Another bore the pentacle, with the name of Jehovah in Hebrew characters in the centre. This was Solomon's seal. " With this seal," he said, " I can command the devils."

His command of the devil was not always successful. He built a barn on the most exposed and elevated point of the glebe; and when a neighbour expostulated with him, and assured him that the wind would speedily wreck it, " No," he answered: " I have placed the sign of the cross on it, and so the devil cannot touch it."

A few weeks after, a gale from the south-west tore the roof off.

" The devil," was his explanation, " was so enraged at seeing the sign of the cross on my barn, that he rent it and wrecked it."

A man whom he had saved from a wreck, in gratitude sent him afterwards, from the diggings in California, a nugget of gold he had found. This Mr. Hawker had struck into a medal or seal, and wore always at his side with the bunch.

Attached to the button-hole of his coat was invariably a pencil suspended by a piece of string.

He was a well-built man, tall, broad, with a face full of manly beauty, a nobly cut profile, dark, full eyes, and long, snowy hair. His expression was rapidly changing, like the sea as seen from his cliffs;

now flashing and rippling with smiles, and anon overcast and sad, sometimes stormy.

Mr. Hawker, some short time after his induction into Morwenstow, adopted an alb and cope which he wore throughout his ministrations at matins, litany and communion service. But he left off wearing the cope about ten or twelve years ago, and the reason he gave for doing so was his disapproval of the extravagances of the Ritualist party. Till the year before he died he had no personal knowledge of their proceedings, and related as facts the most ridiculous and preposterous fables concerning them which had been told him, and which he sincerely believed in.

The ceremonial he employed in his church was entirely of his own devising. When he baptised a child he raised it in his arms, carried it up the church in his waving purple cope, thundering forth, with his rich, powerful voice, the words: "We receive this child into the congregation of Christ's flock," etc. His administration of this sacrament was most solemn and impressive; and I know of parents who have gone to Morwenstow for the purpose of having their children baptised by him.

In celebrating marriage it was his wont to take the ring and toss it in the air before restoring it to the bridegroom. What was symbolised by this proceeding I have been unable to ascertain, unless it were to point out that marriage is always more or less of a toss-up.

After abandoning the cope for the reasons stated, his appearance in girdled alb was not a little peculiar. The alb, to any one not accustomed to see it, has much the look of a nightgown. Over his shoulders he wore a stole of which he was very fond. It was copied for him from one found at Durham, which had been placed in the shrine of St. Cuthbert, on the body. Mr. Hawker bore a special reverence for the memory of St. Cuthbert, who, living on his islet of Farne, the haunt of sea-mews, taming the wild birds, praying, meditating amidst the roar of the North Sea, he thought occupied a position not unlike his own. The week before he died, Mr. Hawker sent to Morwenstow for this stole, and was photographed in it.

"We are much taken with the old church," wrote a well-known public man a few years ago to a friend, "to say nothing of the vicar thereof, who reminds me immensely of Cardinal Wiseman. He is a sight to see, as well as a preacher to hear, as he stands in his quaint garb and quaint pulpit, and looks as if he belonged to the days of Morwenna Abbatissa herself."

He was usually followed to church by nine or ten cats, which entered the chancel with him and careered about it during service. Whilst saying prayers Mr. Hawker would pat his cats, or scratch them under their chins. Originally ten cats accompanied him to church; but one, having caught, killed and eaten a mouse on a Sunday, was excommunicated, and from that day was not allowed again within the sanctuary.

A friend tells me that on attending Morwenstow Church one Sunday morning, nothing amazed him more than to see a little dog sitting upon the altar step behind the celebrant, in the position which is usually attributed to a deacon or a server. He afterwards spoke to Mr. Hawker on the subject, and asked him why he did not turn the dog out of the chancel and church.

"Turn the dog out of the ark!" he exclaimed: "all animals, clean and unclean, should find there a refuge."

His chancel, as has been already said, was strewn with wormwood, sweet marjoram and wild thyme.

He had a garden which he called his church garden, below his house, in a spot sheltered by dwarfed trees. In this garden he grew such flowers as were suitable for church decoration, and were named in honour of the Virgin Mary or the saints, such as columbine, lilies, Barnaby's thistle, Timothy grass, the cowslip (St. Peter's flower), Lady's smock, etc.

Mr. Hawker's kindness to animals was a conspicuous feature in his character. The birds of Morwenstow became quite tame, and fluttered round him for food. "Ubi aves," he said, "ibi angeli." To the north side of the church, above the vicarage, is a small grove of trees, oaks and sycamores. There were nests in them of magpies: Mr. Hawker thought that they were those of jackdaws, but these birds do not build nests among branches. He was very anxious to get rooks to inhabit this grove; to obtain them he went to his chancel, and, kneeling before the altar, besought God to give him a rookery where he wanted. Having made his prayer, full of faith, he had a ladder put to the trees, and he carefully removed the nests to a chimney of his house which was rarely used.

"Jackdaws," said he, "I make you a promise: if you will give up these trees to rooks, you shall have the chimney of my blue room in *sæcula sæculorum*."

The jackdaws took him at his word, and filled the chimney with their piles of sticks which serve as nests. Somehow rooks were persuaded to settle among the tree-tops of his grove, and there the colony subsists to the present day.

Some years ago, when Dr. Phillpotts was Bishop of Exeter, a visit of the bishop to Morwenstow had been planned and decided upon. Mrs. Hawker insisted on having the blue room fitted up for his lordship. A fire would have to be lighted in the grate: the chimney would smoke unless cleared of nests.

Mr. Hawker stood by whilst Mrs. Hawker and the maid prepared the blue room. He would not have the jackdaws disturbed; he had given them his word of honour. Mrs. Hawker argued that necessity knows no law: the bishop must have a fire, and the jackdaws must make way for the bishop. She prevailed.

"I wrung my hands, I protested, entreated and foretold evil," was the vicar's account of the affair.

"Well, and did evil come of it?"

"Yes, the bishop never arrived, after all."

Mr. Hawker was warmly attached to the Bishop of Exeter, and was accustomed to send him some braces of woodcocks every October.

Not far from the church and vicarage was the Well of St. John, a spring of exquisitely clear water, which he always employed for his font.

Sir J. Buller, afterwards Lord Churston, claimed the well, and an expensive lawsuit was the result.

The vicar carried his right to the well, and Sir J. Buller had to pay expenses. Mr. Hawker would tell his guests that he was about to produce them a bottle of the costliest liquor in the county of Cornwall, and then give them water from the Well of St. John. The right to this water had cost several thousands of pounds.

A letter dated 7th Feb., 1852, to a young friend going up to the university, refers to his cats and dogs, and to his annual gift of woodcocks to the bishop, and may therefore be quoted at the conclusion of this chapter.

> Our roof bends over us unchanged. Berg (his dog) is still in our confidence, and well deserves it. The nine soft, furry friends of ours are well, and Kit rules them with a steady claw. Peggy is well and warm. . . . I never knew game so scarce since I came to Morwenstow; except some woodcocks, which I sent to the bishop as usual in October and November, we have had literally none.
>
> And now for one of those waste things, a word of advice. You are in what is called by snobs a fast college. I earnestly advise you to eschew fast men. I am now suffering from the effects of silly and idle outlay in Oxford. I do hope that nothing will induce you to accept that base credit which those cormorants, the Oxford tradesmen, always try to force on freshmen, in order to harass and rob them afterwards. No fast undergraduate in all my remembrance ever settled down into a respectable man. Ask God for strong angels, and He will fulfil your prayer. Never forget Him, and He will never neglect you.

CHAPTER V

The Inhabitants of Morwenstow in 1834—Cruel Coppinger—Whips the Parson of Kilkhampton—Gives Tom Tape a Ride—Tristam Pentire—Parminter and his Dog Satan—The Gauger's Pocket—Wrecking—The Wrecker and the Ravens—The Loss of the *Margaret Quail*—The Wreck of the *Ben Coolan*—"A Croon on Hennacliff"—Letters concerning Wrecks—The Donkeys and the Copper Ore—The Ship *Morwenna*—Flotsam and Jetsam—Wrecks on 14th Nov., 1875—Bodies in Poundstock Church—The Loss of the *Caledonia*—The Wreck of the *Phœnix* and of the *Alonzo*.

WHEN the Rev. R. S. Hawker came to Morwenstow in 1834, he found that he had much to contend with, not only in the external condition of church and vicarage, but also in that which is of greater importance.

A writer in the *John Bull* says: "He found a manse in ruins, and partly used as a barn; a parish peopled with wreckers, smugglers and Dissenting Bryanites; and a venerable church, deserted and ill-cared for, amidst a heap of weeds and nettles. Desolate as was the situation of the grey old sanctuary and tower, standing out upon the rugged incline that shelves down a descent of 300 feet to the beach, it was not more barren of external comfort than was the internal state of those who had been confided to his pastoral care.

"The farmers of the parish were simple-hearted and respectable; but the denizens of the hamlet, after receiving the wages of the harvest time, eked out a precarious existence in the winter, and watched eagerly and expectantly for the shipwrecks that were certain to happen, and upon the plunder of which they surely calculated for the scant provision of their families. The wrecked goods supplied them with the necessaries of life, and the rended planks of the dismembered vessel contributed to the warmth of the hovel hearthstone.

"When Mr. Hawker came to Morwenstow, 'the cruel and covetous natives of the strand, the wreckers of the seas and rocks for flotsam and jetsam,' held as an axiom and an injunction to be strictly obeyed:—

> Save a stranger from the sea,
> And he'll turn your enemy!

"The Morwenstow wreckers allowed a fainting brother to perish in the sea before their eyes without extending a hand of safety—nay, more, for the egotistical canons of a shipwreck, superstitiously obeyed, permitted and absolved the crime of murder by 'shoving the drowning man into the sea,' to be swallowed by the waves. Cain! Cain! where is thy brother? And the wrecker of Morwenstow answered and pleaded in excuse, as in the case of undiluted brandy after meals, 'It is Cornish custom'. The illicit spirit of Cornish custom was supplied by the smuggler, and the gold of the wreck paid him for the cursed abomination of drink."

One of Mr. Hawker's parishioners, Peter Barrow,* had been, for full forty years, a wrecker, but of a much more harmless description: he had been a watcher of the coast for such objects as the waves might turn up to reward his patience. Another was Tristam Pentire,* a hero of contraband adventure, and agent for sale of smuggled cargoes in bygone times. With a merry twinkle of the eye, and in a sharp and ringing tone, he loved to tell such tales of wild adventure, and of " derring-do," as would make the foot of the exciseman falter, and his cheek turn pale.

During the latter years of last century there lived in Wellcombe, one of Mr. Hawker's parishes, a man whose name is still remembered with terror—Cruel Coppinger. There are people still alive who remember his wife.

Local recollections of the man have moulded themselves into the rhyme:—

> Will you hear of Cruel Coppinger?
> He came from a foreign land:
> He was brought to us by the salt water,
> He was carried away by the wind!

His arrival on the north coast of Cornwall was signalised by a terrific hurricane. The storm came up Channel from the south-west. A strange vessel of foreign rig went on the reefs of Harty Race, and was broken to pieces by the waves. The only man who came ashore was the skipper. A crowd was gathered on the sand, on horseback and on foot, women as well as men, drawn together by the tidings of a probable wreck. Into their midst rushed the dripping stranger, and bounded suddenly upon the crupper of a young damsel who had ridden to the beach to see the sight. He grasped her bridle, and, shouting in some foreign tongue, urged the double-laden animal into full speed, and the horse naturally took his homeward way. The damsel was Miss Dinah Hamlyn. The stranger descended at her father's door, and lifted her off her saddle. He then announced himself as a Dane, named Coppinger. He took his place at the family board, and there remained till he had secured the affections and hand of Dinah. The father died, and Coppinger at once succeeded to the management and control of the house, which thenceforth became a den and refuge of every lawless character along the coast. All kinds of wild uproar and reckless revelry appalled the neighbourhood day and night. It was discovered that an organised band of smugglers, wreckers and poachers made this house their rendezvous, and that "Cruel Coppinger" was their captain. In those days, and in that far-away region, the peaceable inhabitants were unprotected. There was not a single resident gentleman of property and weight in the entire district. No revenue officer durst exercise vigilance west of the Tamar; and, to put an end to all such surveillance at once, the head of a gauger was chopped off by one of Coppinger's gang, on the gunwale of a boat.

Strange vessels began to appear at regular intervals on the coast, and signals were flashed from the headlands to lead them into the safest creek or cove. Amongst these vessels, one, a full-rigged schooner, soon became ominously conspicuous. She was for long the chief terror of the Cornish Channel. Her name was *The Black Prince.* Once, with Coppinger on board, she led a revenue-cutter into an intricate channel near the Bull Rock, where, from knowledge of the bearings, *The Black Prince* escaped scathless, while the king's vessel perished with all on board. In those times, if any landsman became obnoxious to Coppinger's men, he was seized, and carried on board *The Black Prince* and obliged to save his life by enrolling himself in the crew. In 1835 an old man, of the age of ninety-seven, related to Mr. Hawker that he had been so abducted, and after two years' service had been ransomed by his friends with a large sum. "And all," said the old man very simply, "because I happened to see one man kill another, and they thought I would mention it."

Amid such practices, ill-gotten gold began to flow and ebb in the hands of Coppinger. At one time he had enough money to purchase a freehold farm bordering on the sea. When the day of transfer came he and one of his followers appeared before the lawyer, and paid the money in dollars, ducats, doubloons and pistols. The man of law demurred, but Coppinger with an oath bade him take this or none. The document bearing Coppinger's name is still extant. His signature is traced in stern, bold characters, and under his autograph is the word "Thuro" (thorough) also in his own handwriting.

Long impunity increased Coppinger's daring. There were certain bridle-roads along the fields over which he exercised exclusive control. He issued orders that no man was to pass over them by night, and accordingly from that hour nóne ever did. They were called "Coppinger's Tracks." They all converged at a headland which had the name of Steeple

Brink. Here the cliff sheered off, and stood 300 feet of perpendicular height, a precipice of smooth rock towards the beach, with an overhanging face 100 feet down from the brow. Under this was a cave, only reached by a cable ladder lowered from above, and made fast below on a projecting crag. It received the name of "Coppinger's Cave." Here sheep were tethered to the rock, and fed on stolen hay and corn till slaughtered; kegs of brandy and hollands were piled around; chests of tea; and iron-bound sea-chests contained the chattels and revenues of the Coppinger royalty of the sea.

The terror linked with Coppinger's name throughout the coast was so extreme that the people themselves, wild and lawless as they were, submitted to his sway as though he had been lord of the soil and they his vassals. Such a household as Coppinger's was, of course, far from happy or calm. Although when his father-in-law died he had insensibly acquired possession of the stock and farm, there remained in the hands of the widow a considerable amount of money as her dower. This he obtained from the helpless woman by instalments, and by this cruel means. He fastened his wife to the pillar of her oak bedstead, and called her mother into the room. He then assured her he would flog Dinah with a cat-o'-nine-tails till her mother had transferred to him the amount of her reserved property that he demanded. This act of brutal cruelty he repeated till he had utterly exhausted the widow's store.

The Kilkhampton parson hated rook-pie. Coppinger knew it.

He invited him to dine with him one day. A large rook-pie was served at one end of the table, and roast rooks at the other; and the parson, who was very hungry, was forced to eat of them. When he departed he invited Coppinger to dine with him on the following Thursday. The smuggler arrived, and was regaled on pie, whether rabbit or hare he could not decide. When he came home he found a cat's skin and head stuffed into his coat-pocket, and thereby discovered what he had been eating.

Coppinger was furious. He had a favourite mare, so indomitable that none but he could venture on her back, and so fleet and strong that he owed his escape from more than one menacing peril to her speed and endurance.

Shortly after the dinner off cat-pie, the rector of Kilkhampton was walking homeward along a lane when he heard behind him the clattering of horse-hoofs; and Cruel Coppinger bore down on him, seated on his mare, whirling his double-thonged whip round his head. He lashed the back of the unfortunate parson, pursued him, struck and struck again till he had striped him like a zebra, and then galloped off with the parting scoff: "There, parson, I have paid my tithe in full; never mind the receipt."

On the selfsame animal Coppinger is related to have performed another freak. He had passed a festive evening at a farmhouse, and was about to take his departure, when he spied in the corner of the hearth a little old tailor who went from house to house in exercise of his calling. His name was uncle Tom Tape.

"Ha! Uncle Tom," cried Coppinger, "we both travel the same road, and I don't mind giving you a hoist behind me on the mare."

The old man cowered in the settle. He would not encumber the gentleman; was unaccustomed to ride such a spirited horse. But Coppinger was not to be put off. The trembling old man was mounted on the crupper of the capering mare. Off she bounded; and Uncle Tom, with his arms cast with the grip of terror round his bulky companion, held on like grim death. Unbuckling his belt, Coppinger passed it round Uncle Tom's thin body, and buckled it on his own front. When he had firmly secured his victim, he loosened his reins, and urged the mare into a furious gallop. Onwards they rushed, till they fled past the tailor's own door, where his startled wife, who was on the watch, afterwards declared "she caught sight of her husband clinging to a rainbow".

At last the mare relaxed her pace; and then Coppinger, looking over his shoulder said: "I have been under long promise to the Devil that I would bring him a tailor to make and mend for him; and I mean to keep my word to-night."

The agony of terror produced by this announcement caused such struggles that the belt gave way, and the tailor fell among the gorse at the roadside. There he was found next morning in a semi-delirious state, muttering: "No, no; I never will. Let him mend his breeches with his own drag-chain. I will never thread a needle for Coppinger or his friend."

One boy was the only fruit of poor Dinah's marriage with the Stranger. He was deaf and dumb, and mischievous and ungovernable from his youth. His cruelty to animals, birds and to other children was intense. Any living thing that he could torture yielded him delight. With savage gestures and jabbering moans he haunted the rocks along the shore, and seemed like some uncouth creature cast up by the sea. When he was only six years old, he was found one day on the brink of a cliff, bounding with joy, and pointing downwards to the beach with convulsions of delight. There, mangled by the fall, and dead, they found the body of a neighbour's child of his own age; and it was believed that little Coppinger had wilfully cast him over. It was a saying in the district that, as a judgment on his father's cruelty, his child had been born without a human soul.

But the end arrived. Money became scarce, and more than one armed king's cutter was seen day and night hovering off the land. So he "who came with the water went with the wind." His disappearance, like his arrival, was commemorated by a storm.

A wrecker who had gone to watch the shore saw, as the sun went down, a full-rigged vessel standing off and on. Coppinger came to the beach, put off in a boat to the vessel and jumped on board. She spread canvas, stood off shore, and, with Coppinger in her, was seen no more. That night was one of storm. Whether the vessel rode it out or was lost none knew.[1]

[1] *Footprints of Former Men*. I have followed Mr. Hawker's tale closely, except in one point, where I have told the story as related to me in the neighbourhood differently from the way in which he has told it. Coppinger was really an Irishman, with a wife at Trewhiddle, Cornwall, by whom he had a daughter, who married a son of Lord Clinton. He gave as her portion £40,000. Trewhiddle is near St. Austell.

Tristam Pentire* has already been mentioned. He was the last of the smugglers, and became Mr. Hawker's servant-of-all-work. The vicar had many good stories to relate of his man.

"There have been divers parsons in this parish since I have been here," said Tristam, "some strict, and some not; and there was one that had very mean notions about running goods, and said it was wrong to do so. But even he never took no part with the gauger—never. And besides," said old Trim, "wasn't the exciseman always ready to put *us* to death if he could?"

One day he asked Mr. Hawker: "Can you tell me the reason, sir, that no grass will ever grow on the grave of a man that's hanged unjustly?"

"No, indeed, Tristam: I never heard of the fact before."

"That grave on the right hand of the path as you go down to the porch has not one blade of grass on it, and never will. That's Will Pooly's grave, that was hanged unjustly."

"Indeed! How came that about?"

"Why, you see, they got poor Will down to Bodmin, all among strangers; and there was bribery and false swearing; and so they agreed together, and hanged poor Will. But his friends begged the body, and brought the corpse home here to his own parish; and they turfed the grave, and they sowed the grass twenty times over; but 'twas all of no use, nothing would grow—he was hanged unjustly."

"Well, but, Tristam, what was he accused of? What had Will Pooly done?"

"Done, your honour? Done? Oh! nothing at all, except killed an exciseman."

Among the "king's men" whose achievements haunted the old man's memory with a sense of mingled terror and dislike, a certain Parminter and his dog occupied a principal place.

"Sir," said old Tristam one day to the vicar, "that villain Parminter and his dog murdered with their shetting-irons no less than seven of our people at divers times, and they peacefully at work at their calling all the while."

Parminter was a bold officer, whom no threats could deter, and no money bribe. He always went armed to the teeth, and was followed by a large fierce dog, which he called Satan. This animal he had trained to carry in his mouth a carbine or a loaded club, which, at a signal from his master, Satan brought to the rescue.

"Ay, they was audacious rascals—that Parminter and his dog; but he went rather too far one day, as I reckon," said old Tristam, as he leaned on his spade talking to the vicar.

"Did he, Trim? in what way?"

"Why, your honour, the case was this. Our people had a landing down at Melhuach, in Johnnie Mathey's hole; and Parminter and his dog found it out. So they got into the cave at ebb tide, and laid in wait; and when the first boat-load came ashore, just as the keel took the ground, down storms Parminter, shouting for Satan to follow. But the dog knew better, and held back, they said, for the first time in all his life: so in leaps Parminter smack into the boat, alone, with his cutlass drawn, but "—with a kind of inward ecstasy—" he didn't do much harm to the boat's crew."

" Why not ? "

" Because, your honour, they chopped off his head on the gunwale."

Near Tonacombe Cross is a stone called the Witanstone. To that Tristam one day guided his master, the vicar.

" And now, your honour," he said, " let me show you the wonderfullest thing in all the place, and that is the Gauger's Pocket." He then showed him, at the back of the Witan-rock, a dry secret hole, about an arm's-length deep, closed by a moss-grown stone. " There, your honour," said he, with a joyous twinkle in his eye, " there have I dropped a little bag of gold, many and many a time, when our people wanted to have the shore quiet, and to keep the exciseman out of the way of trouble; and then he would go, if he were a reasonable officer; and the byword used to be, when 'twas all right, one of us would meet him, and say: ' Sir, your pocket is unbuttoned"; and he would smile, and answer: ' Ay, ay! but never mind, my man, my money's safe enough.' And thereby we knew that he was a just man, and satisfied, and that the boats would take the roller in peace; and that was the very way it came to pass that this crack in the stone was called evermore the Gauger's Pocket."

In former times, when a ship was being driven on the rocks on Sunday, whilst divine service was going on, news was sent to the parson, who announced the fact from the pulpit, or reading-desk, whereupon ensued a rapid clearance of the church. The story is told of a parson at Poughill, near Morwenstow, who, on hearing the news, proceeded down the nave in his surplice as far as the font; and the people, supposing there was to be a christening, did not stir. But when he was near the door he shouted: "My Christian brethren, there's a ship wrecked in the cove: let us all start fair!" and, flinging off his surplice, led the way to the scene of spoliation.

"I do not see why it is," said a Cornish clerk one day, "why there be prayers in the Buke o' Common Prayer for rain and for fine weather, and thanksgivings for them and for peace, and there's no prayer for wrecks, nor thanksgiving for a really gude one when it is come."

Mr. Hawker relates a good story in his *Footprints*, which was told him by an old man in his parish named Tony Cleverdon.

"There was once a noted old wrecker, named Kinsman: he lived in my father's time; and when no wreck was onward he would get his wages by raising stone in a quarry by the seashore. Well, he was to work one day over yonder, half-way down the Tower-cliff, when all at once he saw two old ravens flying round and round very near his head. They dropped down into the quarry two pieces of wreck-candle just at the old man's feet." (Very often wreckers pick up Neapolitan wax candles from vessels in the Mediterranean trade that have been lost in the Channel.) "So when Kinsman saw the candles, he thought in his mind, 'There is surely wreck coming in upon the beach'; so he packed his tools together, and left them just where he stood, and went his way wrecking. He could find no jetsam, however, though he searched far and wide. Next day he went back to quarry to his work. And he used to say it was as true as a proverb—there the tools were all buried deep out of sight, for the crag had given way; and if he had tarried an hour longer he must have been crushed to death. So you see, sir, what knowledge those ravens must have had; how well they knew the old man, and how dearly fond he was of wreck; how crafty they were to hit upon the only plan that would ever have slocked him away."

Wrecks are terribly frequent on this coast. Not a winter passes without several. There are men living who can remember eighty.

If wrecking is no longer practised, the wrecking spirit can hardly be said to be extinct, as the following facts will testify:—

In 1845 a ship came ashore in Melhuach Bay, between Boscastle and Bude. The surge burst against the cliffs, and it was impossible to launch a lifeboat; but a rocket was fired over the vessel, and so successfully that the hawser was secured to the ship. Every life would, in all probability, have been saved, had not some wretches cut through the rope, more greedy for prey than careful to save life. Of all the crew the only person saved was the captain. He confirmed the opinion of the coast-guard, that, but for the cutting through of the hawser, every one on board would have been rescued.

In 1864 a large ship was seen in distress off the

coast. The Rev. A. Thynne, rector of Kilkhampton, at once drove to Morwenstow. The vessel was riding at anchor a mile off shore, west of Hartland Race. He found Mr. Hawker in the greatest excitement, pacing his room, and shouting for some things he wanted to put in his greatcoat-pockets, and irritably impatient because his carriage was not round. With him was the Rev. W. Valentine, rector of Whixley in Yorkshire, then resident at Chapel, in the parish of Morwenstow.

"What are you going to do?" asked the rector of Kilkhampton: "I intend to drive at once to Bude for the lifeboat."

"No good!" thundered the vicar, "no good comes out of the West. You must go East. I shall go to Clovelly, and then, if that fails, to Appledore. I shall not stop till I have got a lifeboat to take those poor fellows off the wreck."

"Then," said the rector of Kilkhampton, "I shall go to Bude, and see to the lifeboat there being brought out."

"Do as you like; but mark my words, no good comes of turning to the West. Why," said he, "in the primitive Church they turned to the West to renounce the Devil."

His carriage came to the door, and he drove off with Mr. Valentine, as fast as his horses could spin him along the hilly, wretched roads.

Before he reached Clovelly, a boat had put off with the mate from the ship, which was the *Margaret Quail*, laden with salt. The captain would not leave the vessel; for, till deserted by him, no salvage could be claimed. The mate was picked up on the way, and the three reached Clovelly.

Down the street proceeded the following procession—the street of Clovelly being a flight of steps:—

First, the vicar of Morwenstow in a claret-coloured coat, with long tails flying in the gale, blue knitted jersey, and pilot-boots, his long silver locks fluttering about his head. He was appealing to the fishermen and sailors of Clovelly to put out in their lifeboat, to rescue the crew of the *Margaret Quail*. The men stood sulky, lounging about with folded arms, or hands in their pockets, and sou'-westers slouched over their brows. The women were screaming at the tops of their voices, that they would not have their husbands and sons and sweethearts enticed away to risk their lives to save wrecked men. Above the clamour of their shrill tongues, and the sough of the wind, rose the roar of the vicar's voice: he was convulsed with indignation, and poured forth the most sacred appeals to their compassion for drowning sailors.

Second in the procession moved the Rev. W. Valentine, with purse full of gold in his hand, offering any amount of money to the Clovelly men, if they would only go forth in the lifeboat to the wreck.

Third came the mate of the *Margaret Quail*, restrained by no consideration of cloth, swearing and damning right and left, in a towering rage at the cowardice of the Clovelly men.

Fourth came John, the servant of Mr. Hawker, with bottles of whisky under his arm, another inducement to the men to relent, and be merciful to their imperilled brethren.

The first appeal was to their love of heaven, and to their humanity; the second was to their pockets, their love of gold; the third to their terrors, their fear of Satan, to whom they were consigned; and the fourth to their stomachs, their love of grog.

But all appeals were in vain. Then Mr. Hawker returned to his carriage and drove away, farther east, to Appledore, where he secured the lifeboat. It was mounted on a waggon. Ten horses were harnessed to it; and, as fast as possible, it was conveyed to the scene of distress.

But, in the meanwhile, the captain of the *Margaret Quail*, despairing of help, and thinking that his vessel would break up under him, came off in his boat, with the rest of the crew, trusting rather to a rotten boat, patched with canvas which they had tarred over, than to the tender mercies of the covetous Clovellites, in whose veins ran the too recent blood of wreckers. The only living being left on board was a poor dog.

No sooner was the captain seen to leave the ship, than the Clovelly men lost their repugnance to go to sea. They manned boats at once, gained the *Margaret Quail*, and claimed £3000 for salvage.

There was an action in court, as the owners refused to pay such a sum; and it was lost by the Clovelly men, who, however, got an award of £1200. The case turned somewhat on the presence of the dog on the wreck; and it was argued that the vessel was not deserted, because a dog had been left on board, to keep guard for its masters. The owner of the cargo failed; and the amount actually paid to the salvors was £600 to two steam-tugs (£300 each), and £300 to the Clovelly skiff and sixteen men. The ship and cargo, minus masts, rigging, cables and anchors, were valued at £5000.

Mr. Hawker went round the country indignantly denouncing the boatmen of Clovelly, and with justice. It roused all the righteous wrath in his breast. And, as may well be believed, no love was borne him by the inhabitants of that little fishing village. They would probably have made a wreck of him, had he ventured among them.

Another incident, at Bude, called forth a second burst of indignation, but this time not so justly.

A fine vessel, the *Ben Coolan*, laden with Government stores for India, ran ashore on the sand, outside Bude Haven. The lifeboat was got out; but the sea was terrible, and there was no practised crew to man her. Crowds were on the pier, hooting the boatmen, and calling them cowards, because they would not put to sea, and save those on the vessel; but an old Oxford eight man, who was present, assures me that the crew were not up to facing such a sea: they were gardeners, land-labourers, canal-men, not one among them who, when he rowed, did not look over his shoulder to see where he was going. The crew shirked putting out in the tremendous sea that was bowling in; and the vessel broke up under the eyes of those who stood on the pier and cliffs. The first rocket that was fired fell short. The second went beyond the bows. The third went over the ship. The mate was seen to run forward to catch the rope, when a wave burst against the side, and spun him up in the foam, and he was seen no more. The ship turned broadside to the waves, which tore her to pieces with great rapidity. Only a few of the crew were saved. The captain was drowned.

Mr. Hawker wrote shortly afterwards :—

A CROON ON HENNACLIFF.

Thus said the rushing raven
  Unto his hungry mate:
" Ho, gossip! for Bude Haven!
  There be corpses six or eight.
Cawk, cawk! the crew and skipper
  Are wallowing in the sea,
So there's a savoury supper
  For my old dame and me!"

" Cawk! gaffer! thou art dreaming:
  The shore hath wreckers bold,
Would rend the yelling seamen
  From the clutching billows' hold!
Cawk, cawk! they'd bound for booty
  Into the dragon's den,
And shout, ' For death or duty! '
  If the prey were drowning men."

Loud laughed the listening surges
  At the guess our grandam gave:
You might call them Boanerges
  From the thunder of their wave!
And mockery followed after
  The sea-bird's jeering brood,
That filled the skies with laughter
  From Lundy Light to Bude.

" Cawk, cawk!" then said the raven:
  " I am fourscore years and ten,
Yet never in Bude Haven
  Did I croak for rescued men!

"They will save the captain's girdle,
   And shirt,[1] if shirt there be,
But leave their blood to curdle
   For my old dame and me."

So said the rushing raven
   Unto his hungry mate:
"Ho, gossip! for Bude Haven!
   There be corpses six or eight.
Cawk, cawk! the crew and skipper
   Are wallowing in the sea:
Oh, what a dainty supper
   For my old dame and me!"

A gentleman who was a witness of this wreck tells me: "We saw the carpenter swimming ashore. He was a magnificent man, largely built, with sinews and muscles of great strength. He swam boldly and desperately, but badly, as he kept his breast above the water, so that he must have been much beaten and bruised by the waves. We saw how his strength gradually gave way, and then he seemed to rally, and make another despairing effort. We succeeded in getting hold of him at last, and brought him ashore. Unfortunately there was no doctor by, or any one who was experienced in dealing with cases of drowning. We did as best we knew, following the old usage of throwing him across a barrel. *Now* I know that it was the worst treatment possible. Had a medical man been at hand, it is my conviction that the poor fellow would have been saved. His blood was not curdled when we got him ashore, and I saw it settle into his breast afterwards. It is an un-

---

[1] A fact: the shirt was secured.

pleasant thought, that a life was sacrificed for want of knowledge."

Those of the crew who were saved proved to be a sad set of fellows. They got so drunk, that they could not attend the burial of their comrades.

MORWENSTOW, Sept. 18, 1869. *My dear Mr. Martyn,*—I will not say, forgive me for my silence. You must do that; but how can I state my miseries? First of all, for a fortnight I have been a cripple from sciatica, only able to creep bent double from room to room.[1] On Sunday night a hurricane smote my house at midnight, burst in the whole of our bedroom window at a blow, and drove us out of bed to dress and go down. Two lights of the drawing-room window were also blown in, one broken to smash. No man or boy in the house. Well, we had a bed made up in the servants' room till the morning. At dawn tidings came that a large vessel was ashore in Vicarage Bay, just under the hut. I was put into the gig, and carried out. Found the crew in death-horrors. Rocket apparatus arrived, and fifteen men were dragged ashore alive. The other seven (blacks) were drowned among my rocks. Guess my state. The whole glebe alive with people. Seven corpses came ashore for burial one by one. Graves already dug, and shrouds prepared; but more yet. The cargo, coals, sixteen hundred tons, vessel nineteen hundred tons, largest ever seen here. Broken up to-night. My path down is now made for donkeys. What can be saved is to be brought up and sold, as well as the broken ship. Cannot you get help for one Sunday, and come over? It would be the act of an angel to come to my rescue. You have your house, and you could do much that I ought to do and cannot. Come, I entreat you. God bless you, and help me; for I am indeed in much anguish, and my poor Pauline worn out. Love to all.

Yours faithfully,

R. S. H.

[1] The handwriting of this letter is very shaky, and different from the usual bold writing of the vicar.

Morwenstow, Oct. 9, 1869. *My dear Mr. Martyn,*—I have devoted to you my first interval of freedom from pains and crushing worry. Let no man hereafter ever accuse me of shrinking from duty. I was assisted up to the churchyard by Cann to bury the last sailor, in such an anguish from sciatic pains, that I had faintness on me all the time; and on returning from the grave my leg gave way under me, and I fell. However, I have done it so far single-handed, and I am thankful. . . .

Yours faithfully,
R. S. Hawker.

Not long after a Spanish vessel came ashore a little lower down the coast. There were on her a number of Lascars. When the coast-guard officer went on board, the Lascars, supposing him to be a wrecker, drew their knives on him. He had the presence of mind to show them his buttons with the crown stamped on them, and so to satisfy them that he was a government officer. The crew were much bruised and injured. They were taken into Stowe and other farmhouses in the neighbourhood, and kindly nursed till well. The captain was a gallant little Spanish don.

The rector of Kilkhampton, who diligently visited the sailors, urged on the captain, when all were well, the advisability of the crew coming to church to return thanks for their rescue. He hesitated, saying he was a Roman Catholic: but the rector urged that all worshipped the same God, and had the same Saviour; and, after having revolved the matter in his own mind, he agreed.

Accordingly the whole crew with the captain came to Kilkhampton Church, a beautiful restored building, filled with old carved seats, rich modern stained glass, and where the service is choral, and rendered with great beauty and reverence.

The Spaniards and Lascars behaved with the utmost devotion and recollection. After service they adjourned to Penstowe, where they were hospitably entertained with a dinner. The captain and the mate dined with the family, the sailors in the hall. The captain took in the lady of the house. On the other side of him at table, sat one of the farmers who had received the shipwrecked mariners into his house. The Spaniard helped the lady to wine, half-filling her glass; but was nudged by the farmer, who bade him give her a brimmer. The little captain turned round, and looked him in the face with an astonished stare, which said plainly enough: "Do you, a Cornish clown, think to teach manners to a Spanish don?" The burly Cornish farmer withered at the glance.

In 1853 a vessel laden with copper ore was wrecked in the bay below Morwenstow Church. The ore was recovered, and carried up the cliff on the backs of donkeys; but it was a tedious process, and occupied two or three months. Mr. Hawker was touched with the sufferings of the poor brutes, zigzagging up a precipice, heavily laden with ore; and, during all the time, had water drawn for them, and a feed of corn apiece, to recruit their exhausted strength as they reached the top of the cliff. His compassion for the donkeys made a profound impression on the people, and is one of their favourite stories about him when they want to tell of the goodness of his kind heart.

During these two or three months, the agent for

the firm which owned the vessel lived in the vicarage and was entertained royally. When everything had been recovered, and he was about to depart, he thanked the vicar for his great kindness, and begged to know, on the part of the firm, if there was anything he could do, or give him, which would be acceptable as some recognition for his kindness.

"No," answered the vicar; "nothing. If paid by you, God will not repay me."

The agent again, and in more forcible terms, assured him that the firm would not be happy unless they could make him some acknowledgment for his services and hospitality, out of the common way.

"Then I will ask one thing," he said; "give the captain another ship."

The agent hesitated, and then said that what he asked was an impossibility. The firm had no other ships which were not then provided with captains. They could not, in justice, displace one of them, to instal in his room the captain of the wrecked ship.

"Never mind," said Mr. Hawker; "this is the only thing I have asked of you, and this is refused me."

A few days after, the agent came to him to inform him that the firm purposed laying the keel of a new vessel, and that the captain for whom he pleaded should be appointed to her.

The ship was built, and was baptised *Morwenna*. She now sails to and fro along this coast, and, whenever she passes Morwenstow, runs up a flag, as a mark of deference to the spot whence she derives her name.

The flotsam and jetsam of a wreck are the property of the Crown. The coast-guard are on the *qui-vive* after a storm, and there is no chance now for village wreckers. They may carry off small articles, which they can put in their pockets; but so many have been had up of late years before the magistrates, and fined, that the officers of government have it nearly all to themselves. When, however, a keg of brandy is washed ashore, the villagers go down to the beach with bottles, break in the head of the cask, and fill their bottles. Should a coastguard officer appear, the keg is kicked over, and they make off with their liquor. The bottles are sometimes kept in a cave, or hidden in the sand, and removed at night. The coast-guardsmen may suspect that the head of the cask was stove in purposely, but cannot prove it. When the shore is strewn with articles, an auction is held on the spot. The farmers are the principal buyers, and they get the goods very cheap. They have their donkeys at hand, to remove up the cliffs what they have purchased. The expense of transport prevents others at a distance from entering into competition with them.

After all has been sold, portions of the beach are let by auction for a week or fortnight; and those who take the beach are entitled to claim, as their own, whatever is thrown up by the sea during their tenure. A wreck does not come ashore at once, but by instalments; nor always at one place, but all along the coast.

Should there not be sufficient articles found by the coast-guard to make it worth their while to call in an auctioneer, they hold an auction of their own; but, not being licensed, they cannot run the price of the articles *up*, they therefore run them *down*. For instance, a piece of wood comes ashore, worth, may be, half a crown. The coast-guard offers it for ten shillings; and, if no one will give that for it, it is offered for nine, then eight, and so on, after the manner of a cheap-jack.

I had got as far as this in my memoir on Saturday night, 13th Nov., 1875. On the following morning I went to Morwenstow, to take duty in the church. The wind was blowing a hurricane from the south-west. I had to hold on to the grave-stones, to drag myself through the churchyard in the teeth of the storm, to the church porch.

There were few present that morning. No woman could have faced the wind. The roar of the ocean, the howling of the blast, the clatter of the glass in the windows, united, formed such a volume of sound that I had to shout my loudest to be heard when reading the service.

When morning prayer was over, I went into the porch. A few men were there, holding their hats on their heads, and preparing for a battle with the wind.

"Not many at church this morning," I said. "No, your honour," was the answer; "the wind would blow the women away; and the men are most of 'em on the cliffs, looking out if there be wrecks."

Two vessels were caught sight of between the scuds of rain, now on the top of a billow, then lost in the trough of the waves.

They had been driven within the fatal line between Hartland Head and Padstowe Point.

" Is there no chance for them ? "

" None at all."

That evening we sang in church the hymn for those at sea, in " Ancient and Modern." Whilst it was being sung, one vessel foundered; but the crew, six Frenchmen, came ashore in a boat. An hour or two earlier the other went down, with all hands on board.

On Monday and Tuesday bits of the wreck came up in the coves, with *Wilhelmina* on them, but no bodies.

After a storm the corpses are fearfully mangled on the sharp rocks, and are cut to pieces by the slate as by knives, and bits of flesh come ashore. These are locally called " gobbets "; and Mr. Hawker, after a wreck, used to send a man with a basket along the beaches of the coves in his parish, collecting these " gobbets," which he interred in his churchyard, on top of the cliffs.

In 1845, after a wreck, nine corpses were taken into Poundstock Church. The incumbent was wont to have daily service. The nine corpses lay along in the aisle that morning. It was the twenty-second day of the month, and he read the Psalm cvii. :—

They that go down to the sea in ships, and occupy their business in great waters; these men see the works of the Lord, and His wonders in the deep. For at His word the stormy wind ariseth, which lifteth up the waves thereof. They are carried up to the heaven, and down again to the deep; their soul melteth away because of the trouble. They reel to and fro, and stagger like a drunken man, and are at their wits' end. So when they cry unto the Lord in their trouble, He delivereth them out of their distress. For He maketh the storm to cease, so that the waves thereof are still. Then are they glad, because they are at rest; and so He bringeth them unto the haven where they would be.

This psalm coming in its proper order seemed strangely appropriate, read with those dead mariners for a congregation.

The narrative of the wreck of the *Caledonia* in 1843 must not be told by any other than Mr. Hawker himself. The following is extracted from his "Remembrances of a Cornish Vicar,"[1] slightly shortened.

At daybreak of an autumn day I was aroused by a knock at my bedroom door: it was followed by the agitated voice of a boy, a member of my household: "Oh, sir, there are dead men on Vicarage Rocks!"

In a moment I was up, and in my cassock and slippers rushed out. There stood my lad, weeping bitterly, and holding out to me in his trembling hands a tortoise alive. I found afterwards that he had grasped it on the beach, and brought it in his hand as a strange and marvellous arrival from the waves, but in utter ignorance of what it might be. I ran across my glebe, a quarter of a mile, to the cliffs, and down a frightful descent of three hundred feet to the beach. It was indeed a scene to be looked on only once in a human life. On a ridge of rock, just left bare by the falling tide, stood a man, my own servant: he had come out to see my flock of ewes, and had found the awful wreck. There he stood, with two dead sailors at his feet, whom he had just drawn out of the water, stiff and stark. The bay was tossing and seething with a tangled mass of rigging and broken fragments of a ship; the billows rolled up yellow with corn, for the cargo of the vessel had been

[1] *Footprints of Former Men in Far Cornwall*, pp. 182-221.

foreign wheat; and ever and anon there came up out of the water, as though stretched out with life, a human hand and arm. It was the corpse of another sailor drifting out to sea. "Is there no one alive?" was my first question to my man. "I think there is, sir," he said, "for just now I thought I heard a cry." I made haste in the direction he pointed out; and on turning a rock, just where a brook of fresh water fell to the sea, there lay the body of a man in a seaman's garb. He had reached the water faint with thirst, but was too much exhausted to swallow or drink. He opened his eyes at our voices; and, as he saw me leaning over him in my cassock, he sobbed with a piteous cry: "Oh, mon père, mon père!" Gradually he revived; and when he had fully come to himself with the help of cordials and food, we gathered from him the mournful tale of his vessel and her wreck. He was a Jersey man by birth, and had been shipped at Malta, on the homeward voyage of the vessel from the port of Odessa with corn.

Mr. Hawker wrote this account for a periodical, without giving the name of the place, or signing the article. This explains a few trifling deviations from fact. He goes on to relate how he took Le Daine into his house. This was not strictly true. Le Daine was found by another gentleman, and taken by him into his father's house in Morwenstow parish, where he was carefully and kindly nursed till his recovery. Mr. Hawker continues his narrative thus:—

I returned to the scene of death and danger, where my man awaited me. He had found, in addition to the two corpses, another dead body, jammed under a rock. By this time a crowd of people had arrived from the land, and at my request they began to search anxiously for the dead. It was indeed a terrible scene. The vessel, a brig of five hundred tons, had struck, as we afterwards found, at three o'clock that morning; and, by the time the wreck was discovered, she had been shattered into broken pieces by the fury of the sea. The rocks and water bristled with fragments of mast and spar and rent timbers; the cordage lay about in tangled masses. The rollers tumbled in volumes of corn, the wheaten cargo; and amidst it all the bodies of the helpless dead—that a few brief hours before had walked the deck, the stalwart masters of their ship—turned their disfigured faces towards the sky, pleading for sepulture. We made a temporary bier of the broken planks, and laid thereon the corpses, decently arranged. As the vicar, I led the way, and my people followed with ready zeal as bearers; and in sad procession we carried our dead up the steep cliff, by a difficult path, to await, in a room at my vicarage which I allotted them, the inquest. The ship and her cargo were, as to any tangible value, utterly lost.

The people of the shore, after having done their best to search for survivors and to discover the lost bodies, gathered up fragments of the wreck for fuel and shouldered them away; not perhaps a lawful spoil, but a venal transgression when compared with the remembered cruelties of Cornish wreckers. Then ensued my interview with the rescued man. His name was Le Daine. I found him refreshed, collected and grateful. He told me his tale of the sea. The captain and all the crew but himself were from Arbroath in Scotland. To that harbour also the vessel belonged. She had been away on a two-years' voyage, employed in the Mediterranean trade. She had loaded last at Odessa. She touched at Malta; and there Le Daine, who had been sick in the hospital, but recovered, had joined her. There also the captain had engaged a Portuguese cook; and to this man, as one link in a chain of causes, the loss of the vessel might be ascribed. He had been wounded in a street quarrel the night before the vessel sailed from Malta and lay disabled and useless in his cabin throughout the homeward voyage. At Falmouth, whither they were bound for orders, the cook died. The captain and all the crew, except the cabin-boy, went ashore to attend the funeral. During their absence the boy, handling in his curiosity the barometer, had broken the tube and the whole of the quicksilver had run out. Had this instrument, the pulse of the storm, been preserved, the crew would have received warning of the sudden and unexpected hurricane and might have stood out to sea; whereas they were caught in the chops of the Channel, and thus, by this small incident, the vessel and the mariners found their fate on the rocks of a remote headland in my lonely parish. I caused Le Daine to relate in detail the closing events.

"We received orders," he said, "at Falmouth to make for Gloucester to discharge. The captain and mate and another of the crew were to be married on their return to their native town. They wrote, therefore, to Arbroath from Falmouth, to announce their safe arrival from their two-years' voyage, and their hope in about a week to arrive at Arbroath for welcome there."

But in a day or two after this joyful letter there arrived in Arbroath a leaf torn out of my pocket-book and addressed "To the Owners of the Vessel the *Caledonia* of Arbroath," with the brief and thrilling tidings, written by myself in pencil, among the fragments of their wrecked vessel, that the whole crew, except one man, were lost "upon my rocks." My note spread a general dismay in Arbroath, for the crew, from the clannish relationship among the Scotch, were connected with a large number of the inhabitants. But to return to the touching details of Le Daine.

"We rounded the Land's End," he said, "that night all well, and came up Channel with a fair wind. The captain turned in. It was my watch. All at once, about nine at night, it began to blow in one moment as if the storm burst out by signal; the wind went mad; our canvas burst in bits. We reeved fresh sails: they went also. At last we were under bare poles. The captain had turned out when the storm began. He sent me forward to look out for Lundy Light. I saw your cliff." [This was a bluff and broken headland just by the southern boundary of my own glebe.] "I sang out, 'Land!' I had hardly done so when she struck with a blow and stuck fast. Then the captain sang out, 'All hands to the maintop!' and we all went up. The captain folded his arms and stood by silent."

Here I asked him, anxious to know how they expressed themselves at such a time, "But what was said afterwards, Le Daine?"

"Not one word, sir; only once, when the long boat went over, I said to the skipper: 'Sir, the boat is gone.' But he made no answer."

How accurate was Byron's painting!—

"Then shrieked the timid, and stood still the brave."

"At last there came on a dreadful wave, mast-top high, and away went the mast by the board, and we with it, into the sea. I gave myself up. I was the only man on the ship that could not swim; so, where I fell into the water, there I lay. I felt the waves beat me and send me on. At last there was a rock under my hand. I clung on. Just then I saw Alick Kant, one of our crew, swimming past. I saw him lay his hand on a rock, and I sang out, 'Hold on, Alick!' But a wave rolled and swept him away, and I never saw his face more. I was beaten onward and onward among the rocks and the tide, and at last I felt the ground with my feet. I scrambled on. I saw the cliff, steep and dark, above my head. I climbed up until I reached a kind of platform with grass; and there I fell down flat upon my face, and either I fainted away, or I fell asleep. There I lay a long time, and when I awoke it was just the break of day. There was a little yellow flower under my head; and, when I saw that, I knew I was on dry land." This was a plant of the bird's-foot clover, called in old times, Our Lady's Finger. He went on: "I could see no house or sign of people, and the country looked to me like some wild and desert island. At last I felt very thirsty, and I tried to get down towards a valley where I thought I should find water. But before I could reach it I fell and grew faint again; and there, thank God, sir, you found me."

Such was Le Daine's sad and simple story; and no one could listen unmoved to the poor solitary survivor of his shipmates and crew. The coroner arrived, held his 'quest, and the usual verdict of "Wrecked and cast ashore" empowered me to inter the dead sailors, found and future, from the same vessel, with the service in the Prayer Book for the Burial of the Dead. This decency of sepulture is the result of a somewhat recent statute, passed in the reign of George III. Before that time it was the common usage of the coast to dig, just above high-water mark, a pit on the shore, and therein to cast, without inquest or religious rite, the carcasses of shipwrecked men. My first funeral of those lost mariners was a touching and striking scene. The three bodies first found were buried at the same time. Behind the coffins, as they were solemnly borne along the aisle, walked the solitary mourner, Le Daine, weeping bitterly and aloud. Other eyes were moist; for who could hear unsoftened the greeting of the Church to these strangers from the sea, and the "touch that makes the whole earth kin," in the hope we breathed, that we too might one day "rest as these our brethren did"? It was well-nigh too much for those who served that day. Nor was the interest subdued when, on the Sunday after the wreck, at the appointed place in the service, just before the General Thanksgiving, Le Daine rose up from his place, approached the altar, and uttered in an audible but broken voice, his thanksgiving for his singular and safe deliverance from the perils of the sea.

The text of the sermon that day demands its history. Some time before, a vessel, *The Hero*, of Liverpool, was seen in distress, in the offing of a neighbouring harbour, during a storm. The crew, mistaking a signal from the beach, betook themselves to their boat. It foundered; and the whole ship's company, twelve in number, were drowned in sight of the shore. But the stout ship held together, and drifted on to the land, so unshattered by the sea, that the coast-guard, who went immediately on board, found the fire burning in the cabin. When the vessel came to be examined, they found in one of the berths a Bible, and between its leaves a sheet of paper, whereon some recent hand had transcribed verses, the twenty-first, twenty-second and twenty-third of the thirty-third chapter of Isaiah. The same hand had also marked the passage with a line of ink along the margin. The name of the owner of the book was also found inscribed on the fly-leaf. He was a youth of eighteen years of age, the son of a widow; and a statement under his name recorded that the Bible was "a reward for his good conduct in a Sunday school." This text, so identified and enforced by a hand that soon after grew cold, appeared strangely and strikingly adapted to the funeral of shipwrecked men; and it was therefore chosen as the theme for our solemn day. The very hearts of the people seemed hushed to hear it; and every eye was turned towards Le Daine, who bowed his head upon his hands and wept. These are the words: "But there the glorious Lord will be unto us a place of broad rivers and streams; wherein shall go no galley with oars, neither shall gallant ships pass thereby. For the Lord is our Judge, the Lord is our Lawgiver, the Lord is our King; He will save us. Thy tacklings are loosed; they could not well strengthen their mast, they could not spread the sail: then is the prey of a great spoil divided; the lame take the prey." Shall I be forgiven for the vaunt, if I declare that there was not literally a single face that day unmoistened and unmoved? Few, indeed, could have borne without deep emotion to see and hear Le Daine. He remained at Morwenstow six weeks; and during the whole of this time we sought diligently, and at last we found the whole crew, nine in number. They were discovered, some under rocks, jammed in by the force of the water, so that it took sometimes several ebb-tides, and the strength of many hands to extricate the corpses. The captain I came upon myself, lying placidly upon his back, with his arms folded in the very gesture which Le Daine had described as he stood amid the crew on the main-top. The hand of the spoiler was about to assail him, when I suddenly appeared, so that I rescued him untouched. Each hand grasped a small pouch or bag. One contained his pistols, the other held two little log-reckoners of brass; so that his last thoughts were full of duty to his owners and his ship, and his last efforts for rescue and defence. He had been manifestly lifted by a billow, and hurled against a rock, and so slain; for the victims of our cruel sea are seldom drowned, but beaten to death by violence and the wrath of the billows. We gathered together one poor fellow in five parts: his limbs had been wrenched off and his body rent. During our search for his remains, a man came up to me with something in his hand, inquiring: "Can you tell me, sir, what is this? Is it a part of a man?" It was the mangled seaman's heart; and we restored it reverently to its place, where it had once beat high with life and courage, with thrilling hope and sickening fear. Two or three of the dead were not discovered for four or five weeks after the wreck; and these had become so loathsome from decay, that it was at peril of health and life to perform the last duties we owe to our brother-men. But hearts and hands were found for the work; and at last, the good ship's company, captain, mate and crew, were laid at rest, side by side, beneath our churchyard trees. Groups of grateful letters from Arbroath are to this day among the most cherished memorials of my escritoire. Some, written by the friends of the dead, are marvellous proofs of the good feeling and educated ability of the Scotch people. One from a father breaks off in irrepressible pathos, with a burst of "Oh my son, my son!" We placed at the foot of the captain's grave the figure-head of his vessel. It is a carved image, life-size of his native Caledonia, in the garb of her country, with sword and shield.[1]

At the end of about six weeks Le Daine left my house on his homeward way, a sadder and a richer man. Gifts had been proffered from many a hand, so that he was able to return to Jersey with happy and joyful mien, well clothed and with thirty pounds in his purse. His recollections of our scenery were not such as were in former times associated with the Cornish shore: for three years afterward he returned to the place of his disaster accompanied by his uncle, sister and affianced wife, and he had brought them, that, in his own joyous words, "they might see the spot of his great deliverance"; and there, one summer day, they stood, a group of happy faces, gazing with wonder and gratitude on our rugged cliffs, that were then clad in that gorgeous vesture of purple and gold which the heather and gorse wind and weave along the heights; and the soft blue wave lapping the sand in gentle cadence, as though the sea had never wreaked an impulse of ferocity, or rent a helpless prey. Nor was the thankfulness of the sailor a barren feeling. Whensoever after-

---

[1] A copy of verses to Mr. Hawker, thanking him for his conduct, was written, printed and circulated in Arbroath. They are by one David Arnott, and dated 13th Oct., 1842. They are of no merit. They end thus:—

> Such deeds as thine are registered in heaven,
> And there alone can due reward be given.

ward the vicar sought to purchase for his dairy a Jersey cow, the family and friends of Le Daine rejoiced to ransack the island until they had found the sleekest, loveliest, best, of that beautiful breed ; and it is to the gratitude of that poor seaman and stranger from a distant abode, that the herd of the glebe has long been famous in the land ; and hence, as Homer would have sung, hence came

    Bleehtah, and Lilith, Neelah, Evan, Neelah, and Katy.

Strange to say, Le Daine has been twice shipwrecked since his first peril, with similar loss of property, but escape of life ; and he is now the master of a vessel in the trade of the Levant. In the following year a new and another wreck was announced in the gloom of night. A schooner under bare poles had been watched for many hours from the cliffs, with the steersman fastened at the wheel. All at once she tacked, and made for the shore, and just as she had reached a creek between two reefs of rock, she foundered and went down. At break of day only her vane was visible to mark her billowy grave. Not a vestige could be seen of her crew. But in the course of the day her boat was drifted ashore, and we found from the name on the stern that the vessel was the *Phœnix* of St. Ives. A letter from myself by immediate post brought up next day from that place a sailor who introduced himself as the brother of the young man who had sailed as mate in the wrecked ship. He was a rough, plain-spoken man, of simple religious cast, without guile or pretence ; one of the good old seafaring sort ; the men who " go down to the sea in ships, and occupy their business in great waters" ; these, as the Psalmist chants, " see the wonders of the Lord, and His glories in the deep." At my side he paced the shore day after day, in weary quest of the dead. " If I could but get my poor brother's bones," he cried out yearningly, again and again, "if I could but lay him in the earth, how it would comfort dear mother at home !" We searched every cranny in the rocks, and we watched every surging wave, until hope was exchanged for despair. A reward, of meagre import, it is true, offered by the Seaman's Burial Act, to which I have referred, and within my own domain doubled always by myself, brought us many a comrade in this sickening scrutiny; but for long it was in vain. At last, one day while we were scattered over a broken stretch of jumbled rocks that lay in huddled masses along the base of the cliffs, a loud and sudden shout called me where the seaman of St. Ives stood. He was gazing down into the broken sea— it was on a spot near low-water mark—and there, just visible from underneath a mighty fragment of rock, was seen the ankle of a man, and a foot still wearing a shoe! "It is my brother!" wailed the sailor bitterly; "it is our dear Jim; I can swear to that shoe!" We gathered around: the tide ebbed a very little after this discovery, and only just enough to leave dry the surface of the rock under which the body lay. Soon the sea began again to flow, and very quickly we were driven by the rising surges from the spot. The anguish of the mourner for his dead was thrilling to behold and terrible to hear. "Oh my brother! my brother!" was his sob again and again, "what a burial-place for our own dear boy!" I tried to soothe him, but in vain: the only theme to which he could be brought to listen was the chance—and I confess it seemed to my own secret mind a hopeless thought—that it might be possible at the next ebb tide, by skill and strength combined, to move, if ever so little, the monstrous rock, and so recover the corpse. It was low water at evening tide, and there was a bright November moon. We gathered in numbers; for among my parishioners there were kind and gentle-hearted men, such as had "pity, tenderness and tears"; and all were moved by the tale of the sailor hurled and buried beneath a rock by the strong and cruel sea. The scene of our first nightly assemblage was a weird and striking sight. Far, far above, loomed the tall and gloomy headlands of the coast; around us foamed and raged the boiling waves; the moon cast her massive lowering shadows on rock and sea;

> And the long moonbeam on the cold, wet sand
> Lay, like a jasper column, half-upreared.

Stout and stalwart forms surrounded me, wielding their iron bars, pickaxes and ropes. Their efforts were strenuous but unavailing. The tide soon returned in its strength, and drove us, baffled from the spot, before we had been able to grasp or shake the ponderous mass. It was calculated by competent judges that its weight was full fifteen tons: neither could there be a more graphic image of the resistless strength of the wrathful sea, than the aspect of this and similar blocks of rifted stone, that were raised and rolled **perpetually by the power** of the billows, and hurled, as in some pastime of the giants, along the shuddering shore! Deep and bitter was the **grief of** the **sailor at our failure** and retreat. His piteous wail **over the dead** recalled the agony **of** those who are recorded in Holy Writ—they who grieved for their lost ones, and would not be comforted, because they were not! That night an inspiration visited me in my wakeful bed. At a neighbouring harbour dwelt a relative of mine, who was an engineer, in charge of the machinery on a breakwater and canal. To him, at morning light, I sent an appeal for succour; and he immediately responded with aid and advice. Two strong windlasses, worked by iron chains, and three or four skilful men, were sent up by him next day with instructions for their work. Again at evening ebb we were all on the spot. One of our new **assistants**, a very Tubal Cain in aspect and stature, and of the same craft with that smith before **the** flood, **plunged** upon the rock **as the water reluctantly revealed its upper side,** and drilled a **couple of holes in the surface with rapid** energy, to receive, each of them, that which he called a Lewis-wedge and a ring. To these the chains of the windlasses were fastened on. They then looped a rope around the ankle of the corpse, and gave it, as the post of honour, **to me** to hold. It was on the evening of Sunday[1] that all this was done; and I have deemed it a venial breach of discipline **to** omit the nightly service of the **church**, in order to suit the tide. Forty strong parishioners, all absentees from evening prayer, manned the double windlass power; I intoned the pull; **and by a strong and** blended effort, the **rocky mass was** slowly, silently **and** gently upheaved; **a slight haul at the rope,** and up to our startled view and **to the sudden** lights, came forth the altered, ghastly, flattened semblance of a

---

[1] A man present on this occasion tells me that the recovery of the body took place on a Monday, and not on a Sunday. Mr. Hawker had daily prayer in his church.—S. B.-G.

man! "My brother! my brother!" shrieked a well-known voice at my side, and tears of gratitude and suffering gushed in mingled torrent over his rugged cheek. A coffin had been made ready, under the hope of final success; and therein we reverently laid the disfigured carcass of one who, a little while before, had been the young and joyous inmate of a fond and happy home. We had to clamber up a steep and difficult pathway along the cliff with the body, which was carried by the bearers in a kind of funeral train. The vicar of course led the way.[1] When we were about half-way up, a singular and striking event occurred, which moved us all exceedingly. Unobserved, for all were intent in their solemn task, a vessel had neared the shore: she lay to, and, as it seemed, had watched us with nightglasses from the deck, or had discerned us from the torches and lanterns in our hands. For all at once there sounded along the air three deep and thrilling cheers! And we could see that the crew on board had manned their yards. It was manifest that their loyal and hearty voices and gestures were intended to greet our fulfilment of duty to a brother mariner's remains. The burial-place of the dead sailors in this churchyard is a fair and fitting scene for their quiet rest. Full in view, and audible in sound, for ever rolls the sea. Is it not to them a soothing requiem that

> Old Ocean, with its everlasting voice,
> As in perpetual jubilee, proclaims
> The praises of the Almighty?

Trees stand, like warders, beside their graves; and the Norman shingled church, "the mother of us all," dwells in silence by, to watch over her safe and slumbering dead. And it recalls the imagery of the Holy Book wherein we read of the gathered reliques of the ancient slain: "And Rizpah the daughter of Aiah took sackcloth, and spread it for her upon the rock from the beginning of harvest until water dropped upon them out of heaven, and suffered neither the birds of the air to rest on them by day, nor the beasts of the field by night".

A year had passed away when the return of the equinox

[1] With cross going before him, in his surplice, reciting psalms.

admonished us again to listen for storms and wrecks. There are men in this district whose usage it is at every outbreak of a gale of wind to watch the cliffs from rise to set of sun. Of these my quaint old parishioner, Peter Barrow, was one. On a wild winter day I found myself seated on a rock with Peter standing by, at a point that overhung the sea. We were both gazing with anxious dismay at a ship which was beating to and fro in the Channel, and had now drifted much too near to the shore: she had come into sight some hours before, struggling with Harty Race, the local name of a narrow boisterous run of sea between Lundy and the land; and she was now within three or four miles of our rocks. "Ah, sir!" said Peter, "the coast-men say—

> From Padstowe Point to Lundy Light,
> Is a watery grave by day or night.

And I think the poor fellows off there will find it so." All at once, as we still watched the vessel labouring in the sea, a boat was launched over her side, and several men plunged into it one by one. With strained and anxious eyes we searched the billows for the course of the boat. Sometimes we caught a glimpse as it rode upon some surging wave; then it disappeared a while. At last we could see it no more. Meanwhile the vessel had held down Channel, tacked and steered as if still beneath the guidance of some of her crew, although it must have been in sheer desperation that they still hugged the shore. What was to be done? If she struck, the men still on board must perish without help, for nightfall drew on. If the boat reappeared, Peter could make a signal where to land. In hot haste then I made for the vicarage, ordered my horse, and returned towards the cliffs. The ship rode on, and I accompanied her way along the shore. She reached the offing of Bude Haven, and there grounded on the sand. No boatman could be induced to put off, and thick darkness soon after fell. I returned worn, heartsick, and weary on my homeward way; there strange tidings greeted me: the boat which we had watched so long had been rolled ashore by the billows, empty. Peter Barrow had hauled her above high-water mark, and had found a name, the *Alonzo* of Stockton-on-Tees, on her stern. That night I wrote as usual to the owner, with news of the wreck, and the next day we were able to guess at the misfortunes of the stranded ship: a boat had visited the vessel, and found her freighted with iron from Gloucester for a Queen's yard round the Land's End. Her papers in the cabin showed that her crew of nine men had been reported all sound and well three days before. The owners' agent arrived; and he stated that her captain was a brave and trusty officer, and that he must have been compelled by his men to join them when they deserted the ship. They must all have been swamped and lost not long after the launch of the boat, and while we watched for them in vain amid the waves. Then ensued what has long been with me the saddest and most painful duty of the shore: we sought and waited for the dead. Now, there is a folk-lore of the beach, that no corpse will float or be found until the ninth day after death. The truth is, that about that time the body proceeds to decompose; and as a natural result it ascends to the surface of the current, is brought into the shallows of the tide, and is there found. The owners' representative was my guest for ten days; and with the help of the ship's papers and his own personal knowledge we were able to identify the dead. First of all, the body of the captain came in: he was a fine, stalwart, and resolute-looking man. His countenance, however, had a grim and angry aspect, just such an expression as would verify the truth of our suspicion that he had been driven by others to forsake his deck. Then arrived the mate and three other men of the crew. None were placid of feature or calm and pleasant in look, as those usually are who are accidentally drowned, or who die in their beds.

But one day my strange old man, Peter Barrow, came to me in triumphant haste with the loud greeting, "Sir! we have got a noble corpse down on your beach. We have just laid him down above high-water mark, and he is as comely a body as a man shall see!" I made haste to the spot; and there lay, with the light of a calm and wintry day falling on his manly form, a fine and stately example of a man: he was six feet two inches in height, of firm and accurate proportion throughout; and he must have been, indeed, in life a shape of noble symmetry and grace. On his broad smooth chest was tattooed a rood, that is to say, our blessed Saviour on His cross, with on the one hand His mother, and on the other St. John the Evangelist: underneath were the initial letters of a name, P. B. His arms also were marked with tracery in the same blue lines. On his right arm was engraved P. B. again, and E. M., the letters linked with a wreath; and on his left arm was an anchor, as I imagined the symbol of hope, and the small blue forget-me-not flower. The greater number of my dead sailors—and I have myself said the burial-service over forty-two such men rescued from the sea—were so decorated with some distinctive emblem and name; and it is their object and intent, when they assume these signs, to secure identity for their bodies if their lives are lost at sea. We carried the strangely decorated man to his comrades of the deck; and gradually in the course of one month we discovered and carefully buried the total crew of nine strong men. These gathered strangers, the united assemblage from many a distant and diverse abode, now calmly slept among our rural and homely graves, the stout seamen of the ship *Alonzo* of Stockton-on-Tees. The boat which had foundered with them we brought also to the churchyard; and there, just by their place of rest, we placed her beside them, keel upward to the sky, in token that her work, too, was over, and her voyage done. There her timbers slowly moulder still; and by-and-by her dust will mingle in the scenery of death with the ashes of those living hearts and hands that manned her, in their last unavailing launch, and fruitless struggle for the mastery of life.[1] But the history of the *Alonzo* is not yet closed. Three years afterwards a letter arrived from the Danish consul at a neighbouring seaport town, addressed to myself as the vicar of the parish; and the hope of the writer was that he might be able to ascertain through myself, for two anxious and grieving parents in Denmark, tidings of their lost son. His name, he said, was Philip Bengstein; and it was in the correspondence that this strange and

---

[1] The boat is rotted nearly away, the bows alone remain tolerably entire.—S. B.-G.

touching history transpired. The father, who immediately afterward wrote to my address, told me in tearful words that his son, bearing that name, had gone away from his native home because his parents had resisted a marriage which he was desirous to contract. They found that he had gone to sea before the mast, a position much below his station in life; and they had traced him from ship to ship, until at last they found him on the papers of the *Alonzo* of Stockton-on-Tees. Then their inquiry as to the fate of that vessel had led them to the knowledge, through the owners, that the vicar of a parish on the seaboard of North Cornwall could in all likelihood convey to them some tidings of their long lost son. I related in reply the history of the death, discovery and burial of the unfortunate young man. I was enabled to verify and to understand the initial letters of his own name, and of her who was not to become his bride, although she still clung to his memory in loving loneliness in that foreign land. Ample evidence, therefore, verified his corpse; and I was proudly enabled to certify to his parents the reverent burial of their child. A letter is treasured among my papers filled to overflowing with the strong and earnest gratitude of a stranger and a Dane for the kindness we had rendered to one who loved "not wisely" perchance, "but too well," to that son who had been lost, and was found too late; one, too, whose "course of true love" had brought him from distant Denmark to a green hillock among the dead, beneath a lonely tower among the trees, by the Cornish sea. What a picture was that which we saw painted upon the bosom and limbs of a dead man, of fond and faithful love, of severed and broken hearts, of disappointed hope, of a vacant chair and a hushed voice in a far away Danish home!

CHAPTER VI

Wellcombe—Mr. Hawker Postman to Wellcombe—The Miss Kitties—Advertisement of Roger Giles—Superstitions—The Evil Eye—The Spiritual Ether—The Vicar's Pigs Bewitched—Horse killed by a Witch—He finds a lost Hen—A Lecture against Witchcraft—Its Failure—An Encounter with the Pixies—Curious Picture of a Pixie Revel—The Fairy-Ring—Antony Cleverdon and the Mermaids.

ABOUT three miles from Morwenstow as the crow flies, and five or six by road, on the coast, is a little church and hamlet called Wellcombe. The church probably occupies the site of a cell of St. Nectan, and is dedicated to him. It is old and was interesting.[1] The parish forms a horseshoe with the heels toward the sea, which is here reached by a rapidly descending glen ending in a cove. It is a small parish, with some 230 inhabitants, people of a race different from those in the adjoining parishes, with black eyes and hair, and dark-skinned. "Dark-grained as a Wellcombe woman," is a saying in the neighbourhood when a brunette is being described. The people are singularly ignorant and superstitious: they are a religious people, and attend church with great regularity and devotion.

[1] Alas! here the wrecker has been at work. There were carved bench-ends with curious heads, technically called poppy-heads, but unlike any I have seen elsewhere, unique, I believe. These heads have been cut off, thrown away and the bench ends stuck against the screen. The seats are now of deal.

The chief landowner and lord of the manor is Lord Clinton, and the vicarage is in his gift. It is worth only seventy pounds, and there is neither glebe nor parsonage house; consequently Wellcombe formerly went with Hartland or Morwenstow.

When Mr. Hawker became vicar of Morwenstow, Wellcombe was held by the vicar of Hartland; but on his death, in 1851, Lord Clinton gave it to Mr. Hawker.

Mr. Hawker accordingly took three services every Sunday. He had his morning prayer at Morwenstow, at eleven, and then drove over to Wellcombe, where he had afternoon service at two P.M., and then returned to Morwenstow for evening prayer at five P.M.

He never ate between services. Directly morning prayer was over, he got into his gig; a basket of pipes, all loaded, was handed in, and he drove off to Wellcombe, smoking all the way; and, after having taken duty, he smoked all the way back. Once a month he celebrated the holy communion at Wellcome; and then, through the kindness of the rector of Kilkhampton, the morning service at Morwenstow was not allowed to fall through.

Mr. Hawker for long acted as postman to Wellcombe. The inhabitants of that remote village did not often get letters; when missives arrived for them, they were left at Morwenstow vicarage, and on the following Sunday a distribution of the post took place in the porch after divine service.

But the parishioners of Wellcombe were no "scholards"; and the vicar was generally required to read their letters to them, and sometimes to write the answers.

On one occasion he was reading a letter to an old woman of Wellcombe, whose son was in Brazil. Part of the letter ran as follows: "I cannot tell you, dear mother, how the muskitties [mosquitoes] torment me. They never leave me alone, but pursue me everywhere."

"To think of that!" interrupted the old woman. "My Ezekiel must be a handsome lad! But I'm interrupting. Do you go on, please, parson."

"Indeed, dear mother," continued the vicar, reading, "I shut my door and window of an evening, to keep them out of my room."

"Dear life!" exclaimed the old woman, "what will the world come to next!"

"And yet," continued the vicar, "they do not leave me alone. I believe they come down the chimney to get at me."

"Well, well, now, parson!" exclaimed the mother, holding up her hands; "to think how forward of them!"

"Of whom?"

"Why, the Miss Kitties, sure. When I were young, maidens would have blushed to do such a thing. And come down the chimbley too!" After a pause, mother's pride overmastering sense of what befitted her sex: "But Ezekiel must be rare handsome, for the maidens to be after him so. And, I reckon, the Miss Kitties is quality-folk too."

Mr. Hawker thus describes the Wellcombe people: "They have amongst them no farrier for their cattle, no medical man for themselves, no beer-house, no shop; a man who travels for a distant town (Stratton) supplies them with sugar by the ounce, or tea in smaller quantities still. Not a newspaper is taken in throughout the hamlet, although they are occasionally astonished and delighted by the arrival, from some almost forgotten friend in Canada, of an ancient copy of *The Toronto Gazette*. This publication they pore over to weariness; and on Sunday they will worry the clergyman with questions about transatlantic places and names, of which he is obliged to confess himself utterly ignorant. An ancient dame once exhibited her prayer-book, very nearly worn out, printed in the reign of George II., and very much thumbed at the page from which she assiduously prayed for the welfare of Prince Frederick."

The people of Wellcombe were very ignorant. Indeed, a good deal of ignorance lingered late in the West of England. The schoolmaster had not thrown a great blaze of light on the Cornish mind in the first half of the present century.

I give a specimen of English composition by a schoolmaster of the old style in Devonshire; and it may be guessed that the Cornish fared not better for teachers than their Wessex neighbours.

This is an advertisement, said to have been written over a little shop:—

Roger Giles, Surgin, Parish clark and Skulemaster, Groser, and Hundertaker, Respectably informs ladys and gentlemen that he drors teef without wateing a minit, applies laches every hour, blisters on the lowest tarms, and vizicks for a penny a peace. He sells Godfather's Kordales, kuts korns, bunyons, dokters hosses, clips donkies, wance a munth, and undertakes to luke arter every bodies nayls by the ear. Joes-harps, penny wissels, brass kanel-sticks, fryinpans, and other moozikal hinstrumints hat grately reydooced figers. Young ladys and genelmen larnes their grammur and langeudge, in the purtiest manner, also grate care taken off their morrels and spellin. Also zarm-zinging, tayching the base vial, and all other zorts of vancy-work, squadrils, pokers, weazils, and all country dances tort at home and abroad at perfekshun. Perfumery and znuff, in all its branches. As times is cruel bad, I begs to tell ey that i his just beginned to sell all sorts of stashonary ware, cox, hens, vouls, pigs, and all other kinds of poultry. Blakin-brishes, herrins, coles, skrubbin-brishes, traykel, godly bukes and bibles, mise-traps, brick-dist, whisker-seed, morrel pokkerankerchers, and all zorts of swatemaits, including taters, sassages, and other gardin stuff, bakky, zigars, lamp oyle, tay-kittles, and other intoxzikatin likkers; a dale of fruit, hats, zongs, hare oyle, pattins, bukkits, grindin stones, and other aitables, korn and bunyon zalve and all hardware. I as laid in a large azzortment of trype, dogs' mate, lolipops, ginger-beer, matches, and other pikkles, such as hepsom salts, hoysters, Winzer sope, anzetrar.

P.S.—I tayches gografy, rithmetic, cowstiks, jimnastiks, and other chynees tricks.

I should have held this to be an invention inspired by Caleb Quotem, in George Colman's play "The Review," but that Mr. Burton of the Curiosity Shop, Falmouth, has shown me old signboards almost as absurd.

The people of Wellcombe were not only ignorant, but superstitious. Mr. Hawker shared at least some of their superstitions. Living as he did in a visionary dream-world of spirits, he was ready to admit, without questioning, the stories he heard of witchcraft and the power of the evil eye.

Whenever he came across any one with a peculiar eyeball, sometimes bright and clear, and at others covered with a filmy gauze, or a double pupil, ringed twice, or a larger eye on the left than on the right side, he would hold the thumb, fore and middle fingers in a peculiar manner, so as to ward off the evil effect of the eye.

He had been descanting one day on the blight which such an eye could cast, when his companion said: "Really, Mr. Hawker, you do not believe such rubbish as this in the nineteenth century."

He turned round and said gravely: "I do not pretend to be wiser than the Word of God. I find that the evil eye is reckoned along with 'blasphemy, pride and foolishness,' as things that defile a man."[1]

Mr. Hawker had a theory that there was an atmosphere which surrounded men, imperceptible to the senses, which was the vehicle of spirit, in which angels and devils moved, and which vibrated with spiritual influences affecting the soul. Every passion man felt set this ether trembling, and made itself felt throughout the spiritual world. A sensation of love or anger or jealousy felt by one man was like a stone thrown into a pool; and it sent a ripple throughout the spiritual universe which touched and communicated itself to every spiritual being. Some mortal men, having a highly refined soul, were as conscious of these pulsations as disembodied beings; but the majority are so numbed in their spiritual part as to make no response to these movements.

---

[1] Mark vii. 21; cf. also Prov. xxiii. 6, xxviii. 22; Matt. vi. 23; Luke xi. 34; Matt. xx. 15.

He pointed out that photography has brought to light and taken cognisance of a chemical element in the sun's rays of which none formerly knew anything, but the existence of which is now proved; so, in like manner, was there a spiritual element in the atmosphere of which science could not give account, as its action could only be registered by the soul of man, which answered to the calms and storms in it as the barometer to the atmosphere and the films of gold-leaf in the magnetometer to the commotions of the magnetic wave.

There was an old woman at Morwenstow who he fully believed was a witch. If any one combated his statement he would answer: "I have seen the five black spots placed diagonally under her tongue, which are evidences of what she is. They are like those in the feet of swine, made by the entrance into them of the demons at Gadara."

This old woman came every day to the vicarage for skimmed milk. One day there was none and she had to leave with an empty can. "As she went away," said the vicar, "I saw her go mumbling something beside the pig-sty. She looked over at the pigs and her eye and incantation worked. I ran out ten minutes after to look at my sow, which had farrowed lately; and there I saw the sow, which, like Medea, had taken a hatred to her own offspring, spurning them away from her milk; and there sat all the nine sucking-pigs on their tails, with their fore-paws in the air, begging in piteous fashion; but the evil eye of old Cherry had turned the mother's heart to stone, and she let them die one by one before her eyes."

Some years agone a violent thunderstorm passed over the parish and wrought great damage in its course. Trees were rooted up, cattle killed, and a rick or two set on fire.

"It so befel that I visited, the day after, one of the chief agricultural inhabitants of the village; and I found the farmer and his men standing by a ditch wherein lay, heels upward, a fine young horse, quite dead. 'Here, sir,' he shouted, as I came on, 'only please to look: is not this a sight to see?' I looked at the poor animal and uttered my sympathy and regret at the loss. 'One of the fearful results,' I said, 'of the storm yesterday.' 'There, Jem,' said he to one of his men triumphantly, 'didn't I say the parson would find it out? Yes, sir,' he said, 'it is as you say: it is all that wretched old Cherry Parnell's doing, with her vengeance and her noise.' I stared with astonishment at this unlooked-for interpretation which he had put into my mouth, and waited for him to explain. 'You see, sir,' he went on to say, 'the case was this: Old Cherry came up to my place, tottering along, and mumbling that she wanted a fagot of wood. I said to her: "Cherry, I gave you one only two days agone, and another two days before that; and I must say that I didn't make up my woodrick altogether for you." So she turned away, looking very grany, and muttering something. Well, sir, last night as I was in bed, I and my wife, all to once there bursted a thunderbolt and shaked the very room and house. Up we started, and my wife says: "Oh, father, old Cherry's up! I wish I had gone after her with that there faggot." I confess

I thought in my mind, I wish she had; but it was too late then, and I would try to hope for the best. But now, sir, you see with your own eyes what that revengeful old woman has been and done. And I do think, sir,' he went on to say, changing his tone to a kind of indignant growl, 'I do think, that when I call to mind how I've paid tithe and rates faithfully all these years and kept my place in church before your reverence every Sunday and always voted in the vestries that what hath and be ought to be—I do think that such ones as old Cherry Parnell never ought to be allowed to meddle with such things as thunder and lightning.' "

A farmer came to Mr. Hawker once with the complaint: " Parson, I've lost my brown speckled hen; I reckon old Cherry have been and conjured her away. I wish you'd be so gude as to draw a circle, and find out where my brown speckled hen have been spirited away to."

The vicar had his cross-handled walking-stick in his hand, a sort of Oriental pastoral staff; and he forthwith drew a circle in the dust and sketched a pentacle within it—Solomon's seal, in fact—whilst he thought the matter over.

"I believe, Thomas," said he, "the brown speckled hen has never got out of your lane; the hedges are walled and high."

In the afternoon back came the farmer. "Parson, you've done for old Cherry with your circle. I found the brown speckled hen in our lane."

Not twenty miles from Morwenstow, a few years ago, occurred the following circumstances, which I know are true, and which I give here as an illustration of the superstition which prevails in Devon and Cornwall.

A boy of the parish of Bratton Clovelly, proving intelligent in the national school, was sent by the rector to Exeter to the training college, in time passed his examination and obtained his certificate. He then returned for a holiday to his native village and volunteered to deliver in the schoolroom a lecture on "Popular Superstitions."

The lecture was announced, the rector took the chair, the room was crowded, and a very fair discourse was delivered against the prevailing belief in witchcraft. The lecturer was heard patiently to the close, and then up rose one of the principal farmers in the place, Brown by name.

"Mr. Lecturer," said he, "and all good people here assembled: You've had your say against witchcraft, and you says that there ain't nothing of the sort. Now, I'll tell'y a thing or two—facts; and a pinch of facts is worth a bushel of reasons. There was, t'other day, my cow Primrose, the Guernsey, and as gude a cow for milk as ever was. Well, on that day, when my missus put the milk on the fire to scald 'un, it wouldn't hot. She put on a plenty of wood, and turves, and brimmel-bushes, but 'twouldn't hot noways. And sez she to me, as I comes in, 'I'll tell'y what tez, Richard, Primrose has been overlooked by old Betty Spry. Now, you go off as fast as you can to the White Witch up to Exeter.' Well, I did so; and when I came to the White Witch, as lives nigh All Hallows on the Walls, I was shown into a room; and there was a farmer stamping about, in just such a predicament as me. Sez I, 'Are you come to see the White Witch?'—'Ah, that I be!' sez he; 'my old cow has fallen ill, and won't give no milk.'—'Why,' sez I, 'my cow's milk won't hot, and the missus has put a lot of fire underneath.'—'Do you suspect anybody?' sez he.—'I do,' sez I; 'there's old Betty Spry has an evil eye, and her's the one as has done it.' Just then the door opens, and the maiden looks in, and sez to me, 'Mr. Brown, the White Witch will speak with you.' And then I am shown into the next room. Well, directly I come in, sez he to me, 'I know what you've come for before you speak a word: your cow's milk won't scald. I'll tell'y why: she's been overlooked by an old woman named Betty Spry.' He said so to me, as sure as eggs is eggs, and I never had told him not one word. Then sez he to me, 'You go home, and get sticks out four different parishes, and set them under the milk, and her'll boil.' Well, I paid 'un a crown, and then I came here; and I fetched sticks from Lew Trenchard, and from Stowford, and from German's Week, and from Broadwood Widger; and no sooner were they lighted under the pan than the milk boiled."

Then up rose Farmer Tickle, very red in the face, and said: "Mr. Lecturer: You've said that there be no such things as spirits and ghosts. I'll tell'y something. I was coming over Broadbury one night, and somehow or other I lost my way. I was afraid of falling into the bog—you know all about that bog, don't'y, by the old Roman castle? There was a gentleman—a sort of traveller, in my recollection—

was driving over Broadbury in a light tax-cart, and suddenly he went into the bog, and his horse and cart were swallowed up, and he had much ado to save himself. Well, he didn't want to lose his tax-cart and harness, for the tax-cart contained bales of cloth and the harness was new; so he went to the blacksmith at the cross, and got him to come there with his man and grappling-irons. They let the irons down into the bog, and presently they got hold of something and began to draw it up. It was a horse; and they threw it on the side and said, 'There, sir, now you have your horse.'—'No,' answered he, looking hard at it, 'this is a hunter, with saddle and stirrups. Let down the irons again.' So they felt about once more, and presently they pulled up another horse and laid him on the side. 'There, sir, is this yours?' sez the blacksmith; 'he's in gig-harness all right.'—'No,' sez the traveller; 'my horse was a dapple, and this is a grey. Down with the irons again.' This time they cries out, 'Yo, heave-oh! we've got hold of the tax-cart!' But when they pulled 'un up it was a phaeton. So they let their grappling-irons down again, and presently up came another horse, and this was in harness; but sez the traveller, 'He's not mine, for mine was a mare. Try again, my fine fellows.' Next as came up had no harness at all on; and the next had blinkers with Squire G——'s crest on them. Well, they worked all day, and they got up a dozen horses and three carriages, but they never found the traveller's tax-cart and the dapple mare.

"But, Lor' bless me! I've been wandering again

on Broadbury, and now I must return to the point. Knowing what I did about the bog, I was a bit frighted of falling into her. Presently I came to a bit of old quarry and rock, and I thought there might be some one about, so I shouted at the top of my voice, 'Farmer Tickle has lost his way.' Well, just then a voice from among the stones answered me, and said, 'Who? who?'—'Farmer Tickle of X——, I say.' Then the voice answered again, asking: 'Who? who? who?'—'Are ye hard of hearing?' I shouted. 'I say tez Farmer Tickle, as live in the old rummling farm of Southcot in X—— parish.' As imperent as possible again the voice asked: 'Who? who? who?' 'Tez Farmer Tickle, I tell'y!' I shouted; 'and if you axes again I'll come along of you with my stick.'—'Who? who? who?' I ran to the rocks and beat about with my stick; and then a great white thing rushed out——"

"It was an owl," said the lecturer scornfully.

"An owl!" echoed Farmer Tickle. "I put it to the meeting. A man as says this was an owl, and not a pixie, would say anything!" and he sat down amidst great applause.

Then up rose Farmer Brown once more.

"Gentlemen, and labouring men, and also women," he began, "I'll give you another pinch of facts. Before I was married I was going along by Culmpit one day, when I met old Betty Spry, and she sez to me, 'Cross my hand with silver, my pretty boy, and I'll tell you who your true love will be.' So I thinks I'd like to know that, and I gives her a sixpence. Then sez she, 'Mark the first maiden that you meet as you go along the lane that leads to Eastway House: she's the one that will make you a wife.' Well, I was going along that way, and the first maiden I met was Patience Kite. I thought she was comely and fresh-looking; so, after going a few steps on, I turns my head over my shoulder and looks back at her; and what in the world should she be doing at exactly the same minute but looking back at me! Then I went after her and said, 'Patience, will you be Mrs. Brown?' and she said, 'I don't mind, I'm noways partickler.' And now she is my wife. Look at her yonder, as red as a turkey-cock; there she sits, and so you may know my story is true. But how did Betty Spry know this before ever I had spoken the words? That beats me!"

Then, once more, up stood Farmer Tickle.

"Mr. Lecturer, Mr. Chairman, I puts it to you. First and last we must come to Holy Scripter. Now, I ask you, Mr. Chairman, being our parson, and you, Mr. Lecturer, being a scholard, and all you as have got Bibles, whether Holy Scripter does not say, 'Thou shalt not suffer a witch to live,'—whether Holy Scripter does not say that the works of the flesh are idolatry, witchcraft, hatred, variance, emulations, and such like? Now, if witchcraft be all moonshine, then I reckon so be hatred, variance, and emulations too. Now, I put it to the meeting, which is true? Which does it vote for, the Holy Bible and witchcraft, or Mr. Lecturer and his new-fangled nonsense? Those in favour of Scripter and witches hold up their hands."

Need I say that witchcraft carried the day.

One of Mr. Hawker's parishioners had an encounter with pixies. Pixies, it must be explained, are elves, who dance on the sward and make fairy-rings; others work in mines; others, again, haunt old houses.

This man had been to Stratton market. On his way home, as he was passing between dense hedges, suddenly he saw a light, and heard music and singing. He stood still, and looked and listened. Passing through the hedge, he saw the little people in a ring dancing; and there sat on a toadstool an elf with a lantern in his hand, made of a campanula, out of which streamed a greenish-blue light. As the pixies danced, they sang.

"Sir,"—this is the man's own account,—"I looked and listened a while, and then I got quietly hold of a great big stone, and heaved it up, and I dreshed in amongst them all; and then I up on my horse, and galloped away as hard as I could, and never drew rein till I came home to Morwenstow. But, when the stone fell among them all, out went the light. You don't believe me? But it be true, true as gospel; for next day I went back to the spot, and there lay the stone, just where I had dreshed it."

I have got a curious oil-painting in Lew Trenchard House, dating from the reign of William and Mary as I judge by the costume. It represents a pixie revel. In the background is an elfin city, illumined by the moon. Before the gates is a ring of tiny beings, dancing merrily around what is probably a corpse-candle: it is a candle-stump, standing on the ground, and the flame diffuses a pallid white light.

In the foreground is water, on which floats a pumpkin, with a quarter cut out of it, so as to turn it into a boat with a hood. In this the pixie king and his consort are enthroned, while round the sides of the boat sit the court, dressed in the costume of the period of William of Orange. On the hood sits a little elf, with a red toadstool, as an umbrella, over the heads of the king and queen. In the bow sits Jack-o'-lantern, with a cresset in his hands, dressed in a red jacket. Beside him is an elf playing on a Jew's-harp, which is as large as himself; and another mischievous red-coated sprite is touching the vibrating tongue of the harp with a large extinguisher, so as to stop the music.

The water all round the royal barge is full of little old women and red-jacketed hobgoblins in egg-shells and crab-shells; whilst some of the pixies, who have been making a ladder of an iron boat-chain, have missed their footing, and are splashing about in the water. In another part of the picture the sprites appear to be illumining the window of a crumbling tower.

Mr. Hawker had a curious superstition about fairy-rings. There was one on the cliff. Some years ago he was visited by Lady ———, who drove over from Bude. As he walked with her on the sward, they came to the ring in the grass, and she was about to step into it, when he arrested her abruptly, and said: " Beware how you set foot within a fairy-ring : it will bring ill-luck."

"Oh, nonsense, Mr. Hawker! the circle is made by toadstools. See, here is one : I will pick it."

"If you do, there will be shortly a death in your house."

She neglected the warning, and picked one of the fairy champignons.

Within a week a little daughter died.

Another similar coincidence confirmed him in his belief. The curate of Bridgerule and his wife came to see him, and much the same scene took place. The curate, in spite of his warning, kicked over a toadstool in the ring, and handed it to his wife.

Ten days after, Mr. Hawker got a heart-broken letter from the wife, an Irish lady, in which she said: "Oh, why did we neglect your prophecy! why did we give no heed to your word! When we returned to Bridgerule, our little Mary sickened; and now we have just laid her in her grave."

He was staying with a friend. Suddenly the table gave a crack. Mr. Hawker started, and, laying his hand on the table, said: "Mark my words, there has been a death in my family."

By next post came news of the death of one of the Miss I'ans.

At Wellcombe was an old man, Antony Cleverdon, from whom Mr. Hawker learned many charms, some of which he has given in his *Footprints of Former Men*. This old man, commonly called Uncle Tony, was a source of great amusement to the vicar, who delighted to visit and converse with him.

"Sir," said Uncle Tony to him one day, "there is one thing I want to ask you, if I may be so free, and it is this: Why should a merrymaid (the local name for mermaid), that will ride upon the waters in such terrible storms, never lose her looking-glass and comb?"

"Well, I suppose," answered the vicar, "that, if there are such creatures, Tony, they must wear their looking-glasses and combs fastened on somehow—like fins to a fish."

"See!" said Tony, chuckling with delight, "what a thing it is to know the Scriptures like your reverence: I never should have found it out. But there's another point, sir, I should like to know, if you please: I've been bothered about it in my mind hundreds of times. Here be I, that have gone up and down Wellcombe cliffs and streams fifty years come next Candlemas, and I've gone and watched the water by moonlight and sunlight, days and nights, on purpose, in rough weather and smooth (even Sundays too, saving your presence)—and my sight as good as most men's—and yet I never could come to see a merrymaid in all my life! How's that, sir?"

"Are you sure, Tony," the vicar rejoined, "that there are such things in existence at all?"

"Oh, sir, my old father seen her twice! He was out once by night for wreck (my father watched the coast like many of the old people formerly), and it came to pass that he was down by the Duck Pool on the sand at low-water tide, and all at once he heard music in the sea. Well, he croped on behind a rock, like a coast-guard man watching a boat, and got very near the noise. He couldn't make out the words, but the sound was exactly like Bill Martin's voice that singed second counter in church: at last he got very near, and there was the merrymaid very plain to be seen, swimming about on the waves like a woman bathing, and singing away. But my father said it was very sad and solemn to hear—more like the tune of a funeral hymn than a Christmas carol, by far—but it was so sweet that it was as much as he could do to hold back from plunging into the tide after her. And he an old man of sixty-seven, with a wife and a houseful of children at home! The second time was down here by Wellcombe Pits. He had been looking out for spars: there was a ship breaking up in the Channel, and he saw some one move just at half-tide mark. So he went on very softly, step and step, till he got nigh the place; and there was the merrymaid sitting on a rock—the bootifullest merrymaid that eye could behold—and she was twisting about her long hair, and dressing it just like one of our girls getting ready for her sweetheart on a Sunday. The old man made sure he should greep hold of her round the waist, before ever she found him out; and he had got so near that a couple of paces more, and he would have caught her, as sure as tithe or tax, when, lo and behold, she looked back and glimpsed him! So in one moment she dived head foremost off the rock, and then tumbled herself topsy-turvy about in the water, and cast a look at my poor father, and grinned like a seal!"

CHAPTER VII

Condition of the Church last Century—Parson Radford—The Death of a Pluralist—Opposition Mr. Hawker met with—The Bryanites—Hunting the Devil—Bill Martin's Prayer-meeting—Mr. Pengelly and the Candle-end—Cheated by a Tramp—Mr. Hawker and the Dissenters—Mr. B——'s Pew—A Special Providence over the Church—His Prayer when threatened with the Loss of St. John's Well—Objections to Hysterical Religion—Mr. Vincent's Hat—Regard felt for him by old Pupils—"He did not appreciate me"—Modryb Marya—A Parable—A Carol—Love of Children—Angels—A Sermon, "Here am I".

THE condition of the Church in the diocese of Exeter at the time when John Wesley appeared was piteous in the extreme. Non-residence was the rule: the services of the sanctuary were performed in the most slovenly manner, the sacraments were administered rarely and without due reverence in too many places, and pastoral visitation was neglected. The same state of things continued, only slightly improved, to the time when Mr. Hawker began his ministrations at Morwenstow.

There was a story told of a fox-hunting parson, Mr. Radford, in the north of Devon, when I was a boy. He was fond of having convivial evenings in his parsonage, which often ended uproariously.

Bishop Phillpotts sent for him, and said: "Mr. Radford, I hear, but I can hardly believe it, that men fight in your house."

"Lor', my dear," answered Parson Radford, in

broad Devonshire, "doant'y believe it. When they begin fighting, I take and turn them out into the churchyard."

The Bishop of Exeter came one day to visit him without notice. Parson Radford, in scarlet, was just about to mount his horse and gallop off to the meet, when he heard that the bishop was in the village. He had barely time to send away his hunter, run upstairs, and jump, red coat and boots, into bed, when the bishop's carriage drew up at the door.

"Tell his lordship I'm ill, will ye?" was his injunction to his housekeeper, as he flew to bed.

"Is Mr. Radford in?" asked Dr. Phillpotts.

"He's ill in bed," said the housekeeper.

"Dear me! I am so sorry! Pray ask if I may come up and sit with him," said the bishop.

The housekeeper ran upstairs in sore dismay, and entered Parson Radford's room. The parson stealthily put his head out of the bedclothes, but was reassured when he saw his room was invaded by his housekeeper, and not by the bishop.

"Please, your honour, his lordship wants to come upstairs, and sit with you a little."

"With me, good heavens!" gasped Parson Radford. "No. Go down and tell his lordship I'm took cruel bad with *scarlet fever:* it is an aggravated case, and very catching."

In the neighbourhood of Morwenstow, a little before Mr. Hawker's time, was a certain Parson Winterton.* He was rector of Eastcote, rector of Eigncombe, rector of Marwood, rector of Westcote, and vicar of Barton. Mr. Hawker used to tell the following story:—

When Parson Winterton lay on his death-bed, he was visited and prepared for dying by a neighbouring clergyman.

"What account can you render for the talents committed to your charge? What use have you made of them?" asked the visitor.

"Use of my talents?" repeated the dying man. And then, thrusting his hands out from under the bedclothes, he said: "I came into this diocese with nothing—yes, with nothing—and now," and he began to check off the names on the fingers of the left hand with the forefinger of the right hand, "I am rector of Eigncombe, worth £80; rector of Marwood, worth £450; rector of Westcote, worth £560; vicar of Barton, worth £300; and rector of Eastcote, worth a £1000. If that is not making use of one's talents, I do not know what is. I think I can die in peace."

Morwenstow, as has been already said, had been without a resident vicar for a century before Mr. Hawker came there. When he arrived, it was with his great heart overflowing with love, and burning to do good to the souls and bodies of his people. He was about the parish all day on his pony, visiting every one of his flock, taking vehement interest in all their concerns, and doing everything he could think of to win their hearts.

But two centuries of neglect by the Church was not to be remedied in a generation. Mr. Hawker was surprised that he could not do it in a twelvemonth. He was met with coldness and hostility by most of the farmers, who were, with one or two exceptions,

Wesleyans or Bible Christians. The autocrat of the neighbourhood was an agent for the principal landowner of the district, and he held the people under his thumb. With him the vicar speedily quarrelled: their characters were as opposed as the poles, and it was impossible that they could work together. Mr. Hawker thought—rightly or wrongly, who shall decide?—that this man thwarted him at every turn, and urged on the farmers to oppose and upset all his schemes for benefiting the parish, spiritually and temporally. Mutual antipathy caused recriminations, and the hostility became open. The agent thought he had dealt the vicar a severe blow when he persuaded Sir J. Buller to claim St. John's Well. Mr. Hawker found himself baffled by the coldness of the Dissenters, and the hostility of the agent, which he had probably brought upon himself; and it struck a chill to his heart, and saddened it.

The vicar was, however, not blameless in the matter. He expected all opposition to melt away before his will; and if a parishioner, or any one else with whom he had dealings, did not prove malleable, and submit to be turned in his hands like a piece of wax, he had no patience with him. He could not argue, but he could make assertions with the force and vehemence which tell with some people as arguments.

The warmth with which Mr. Hawker took up the cause of the labourers, his denunciation of the truck-system, and the forcible way in which he protested against the lowness of the wage paid the men, conduced, no doubt, to set the farmers against him. But he was the idol of the workmen. Their admiration and respect for him knew no bounds. "If all gentlemen were like our vicar," was the common saying, "the world would have no wrongs in it."

When Mr. Hawker's noble face was clouded with trouble, as he talked over the way in which he had been thwarted at every turn by the agent and the farmers, if a word were said about the poor, the clouds cleared from his brow, his face brightened at once: "'The poor have ye always with you,' said our Lord, and the word is true—is true."

In a letter written in 1864 to a former curate of Wellcombe, now an incumbent in Essex, he says:—

> The only parish of which I can report favourably is my own cure of Wellcombe. Morwenstow is, as it always was, Wesleyan to the backbone; but at Wellcombe the church attendance is remarkable. The same people are faithful and constant as worshippers, and the communicants from two hundred and four souls are fourteen. When any neighbouring clergyman has officiated for me, he is struck with the number and conduct of the congregation. The rector of Kilkhampton often declares Wellcombe to be the wonder of the district. This is to me a great compensation for the unkindly Church feeling of Morwenstow.

The opposition of the Wesleyans and Bryanites caused much bitterness, and he could not speak with justice and charity of John Wesley. He knew nothing of the greatness, holiness and zeal of that zealous man: he did not consider how dead the Church was when he appeared and preached to the people. When he was reproached for his harsh speeches about Wesley, his ready answer was: "I judge of him by the deeds of his followers."

One of his sayings was: "John Wesley came into Cornwall and persuaded the people to change their vices." Once, when the real greatness of Wesley was being pressed upon him, he said sharply: "Tell me about Wesley when you can give me his present address."

If this vehement prejudice seems unjust and unchristian, it must be remembered that Mr. Hawker had met with great provocation. But it was not this provocation which angered him against Methodists and Bryanites, for he was a man of large though capricious charity: that which cut him to the quick was the sense that Cornish Methodism was demoralising the people. Wesleyanism was not so much to blame as Bryanism.

The Cornish Bryanites profess entire freedom from obligation to keep the law, and the complete emancipation from irksome moral restraint of those who are children of God, made so by free grace and a saving faith. One of their preachers was a man of unblushingly profligate life: the details of his career will not bear relation. Mr. Hawker used to mention some scandalous acts of his to his co-religionists, but always received the cool reply: "Ah! maybe; but after all he is a *sweet Christian.*"

A favourite performance in a Bryanite meeting, according to popular report, is to "hunt the Devil out." The preacher having worked the people up into a great state of excitement, they are provided with sticks, and the lights are extinguished. A general *mêlée* ensues. Every one who hits thinks he is dealing the Devil his death-blow; and every one who receives a blow believes it is a butt from the Devil's horns.

Mr. Hawker had a capital story of one of these meetings.

The preacher had excited the people to a wild condition by assuring them he saw the Devil in person—there! there! there!

"Where, where is he?" screamed some of the people.

"Shall I hit 'un down with my umbrella?" asked a farmer.

"He'll burn a great hole in it if ye do," said his wife; "and I reck'n he won't find you another."

Sticks were flourished, and all rushed yelling from their pews.

"Where is he? Let us catch a glimpse of the end of his tail, and we'll pin him."

The shouting and the uproar became great.

"I see 'un, I see 'un!" shouted the preacher; and, pointing to the door, he yelled, "He is there!"

At that very moment the door of the Bryanite meeting-house was thrown open and there stood R——, the dreaded steward of Lord ——, with his grey mare. He had been riding by, and astonished at the noise, had dismounted and opened the door to learn what had occasioned it.

I give the account of a private Bible Christian meeting from the narrative of an old Cornish woman of Kilkhampton.

"Some thirty or more years agone, Long Bill Martin was converted and became a very serious character in Kilkhampton; and a great change that was for Bill. Prayer-meetings were now his delight, especially if young women were present—then he did warm up, I tell'y. He could preach, he could, just a word or two at a time; and then, when he couldn't find words, he'd roar. He was a mighty comfortin' preacher, too, especially to the maidens. Many was the prayer-meeting which he kept alive; and if things was going flat—for gospel ministers du go flat sometimes, tell'y, just like ginger-beer bottles if the cork's out tu often. And, let me tell'y, talkin' of that, there comed a Harchdeacon here one day: I seed 'un, and he had strings tied about his hat, just as they du corks of lemonade, to keep the spirit in him down; he was nat'rally very uppish, I reck'n. But to go back to Bill. When he couldn't speak, why, then he'd howl, like no sucking dove: 'Ugh! the devil! drive the devil!' Yu could hear him hunting the devil of nights a hundred yards or more off from the cottage where he was leading prayer. One day he settled to have a meeting down near the end of the village and sent in next door to borrow a form (not a form of prayer, yu know, for he didn't hold to that), and invited the neighbours to join. 'You'd better come. We'm goin' to have a smart meetin' t'night, can tell'y.'

"So us went in, and they set to to pray: fust won and then another was called upon to pray. 'Sister, you pray.' 'Brother Rhicher (Richard), you pray.' So to last Rhicher Davey he beginned: 'My old woman,' sez he, 'she's hoffal bad in her temper, and han't got no saving grace in her, not so much as ye might put on the tail of a flea,' sez he; 'but we hopps for better things, and I prays for improvement,' he went on; 'and if improvement don't come to her, why, improvement might come to me, by her bein' taken where the wicked cease from troubling, and so leave weary me at rest.' Then I began to laugh; but Long Bill he ketched me up and roared, 'Pray like blazes, Nanny Gilbert, do'y!' So I kep my eye fixed to her, and luked at her hard and steadfast, I did, for I knew what the latter hupshot would be with her; and her beginned, 'We worms of hearth!' and there her ended. So we waited a bit; and then Bill Martin says, 'Squeedge it hout, Nanny, squeedge it hout!' But it were all no good. Never another word could she utter, though I saw she was as red as a beet-root with tryin' to pray. She groaned, but no words. Then out comed old Bill—Long Bill us called 'un, but Bill Martin was his rightful name—'Let us pray, my friends,' he sez. 'Honly believe,' he sez. 'Drive the devil,' he roars. 'There he is! There he is!' he sez. 'Do'y not see un! Do'y not smell un?'—'It's the cabbidge,' sez Nanny Gilbert; 'there's some, and turnips tu, and a bit of bacon, biling in the pot over the turves.' For her was a little put out at not being able to pray. It was her cottage in which the prayer-meeting was being held, yu know. Well, Long Bill didn't stomach the cabbidge, so he roars louder than afore, 'FAITH! my friends; have *faith!* and then yu can see and smell the devil.'—'If it's the cabbidge yu mean,' sez Nanny, 'I can smell 'un by my nat'ral faculties.'—'There's the devil!' shouts Bill Martin, growing excited. 'Ugh! drive the hold devil! Faith! my friends, have faith, hell-shaking faith, conquering faith, devil-driving faith, a damned lot of faith!' And then he roars, 'There he is! I can zee 'un afluttering hover your heads, ye sinners, just like my hands afluttering over the cann'l!'

"So I titched her as was next me, and I sez: 'Where is 'un? I doan't see 'un, d'yu?'—'Yer han't got faith,' sez she. 'But I can feel 'un just as if he was acrigglin' and acrawlin' in my head where the partin' is.'

"Well, just then—and I am sure I can't tell yu whether it happened afore Bill Martin speaked, or after—but he roars out, 'I see 'un! he's flown up the chimley!' And just then—as I sed, I cannot say whether it was afore he speaked or after—down came a pailful of soot right into the midst of old Nanny's pot of cabbage and turnips.

"Well, I tell'y, when old Nanny Gilbert seed that, her was as mad as Parson Hawker during a wreck. She ups off her chair and runs first to the pot and looks what's done there; and then she flies to Bill Martin—Long Bill, yu know—and ketches him by the ear and drags him forward to the pot and sez, flaming like a bit of fuzz, 'Yer let the devil loose out of your own breast and sent 'um flittering up my chimley, the wiper! and he's smutted all my supper, as was biling for me and my old man and the childer. And I'll tell'y what, if yu don't bring your devil down by his tail, that I may rub his nose in it, I'll dip yours, I will.'

"Well, yu may believe me, Bill tremmled as a blank-mange—that's a sort of jelly stuff I seed one day in a gentleman's house to Bude, when the servant was carrying it in to dinner; it shooked all hover like. For I tell'y, a woman as has had her biling of cabbage and turnips spoiled, especial if there be a taste of bacon in it, ain't to be preached peaceable.

"After that I can't tell'y 'xactly what took place. We wimin set up screaming and scuffled about like bats in the light. But I seed Nanny giving Long Bill a sort of a chuck with one hand where his coat-tails would have grown, only he didn't wear a coat, only a jacket. P'raps, though, yu know, he'd nibbled 'em off like the monkey as Parson Davies keeped in the stable for his childer. That monkey had the beautifullest tail—after a peacock—when first he came to Kilkhampton; but he bit it off in little portions. And then, poor thing, at last he got himself into a sort of tangle or slip-knot in twisting himself about to bite right off the last fag-end of stump. And when Ezekiel—that's the groom—comed in of the morning with his bread and milk, the poor beast stretched his head out with a jerk to get his meat and forgot he had knotted himself up with his own body, and so got strangled in himself. Well, but I was telling yu about Bill Martin and not Parson Davies's monkey. So after that meetin' his nose was a queer sort of mixture of scald-red and black. He was never very partial to water, was Bill: and so the scald and smut stuck there, maybe one year, maybe two. But all this happened so long ago that I couldn't take my Bible oath that it wasn't more— say three, then: odd numbers is lucky."

Mr. Hawker had a story of a Wellcombe woman whom he visited after the loss of her husband.

"Ah! thank the Lord," said she, "my old man is safe in Beelzebub's bosom."

"Abraham's bosom, my good woman," said the vicar.

"Ah! I dare say. I am not acquainted with the quality, and so don't rightly know their names."

While on the subject of the Devil, I cannot omit a story told of a certain close-fisted Cornish man, whom we will call Mr. Pengelly, as he is still alive. The story lost nothing in the vicar's mouth.

Mr. Pengelly was very ill and like to die. So one night the Devil came to the side of his bed, and said to him: "Mr. Pengelly, I will trouble yu, if you please."

"Yu will trouble me with what, your honour?" says Mr. Pengelly, sitting up in bed.

"Why, just to step along of me, sir," says the Devil.

"Oh! but I don't please at all," replies Mr. Pengelly, lying down again and tucking his pillow under his cheek.

"Well, sir, but time's up, yu know," was the remark the Devil made thereupon; "and whether it pleases yu or no, yu must come along of me to once, sir. It isn't much of a distance to speak of from Morwenstow," says he by way of apology.

"If I must go, sir," says Mr. Pengelly, wiping his nose with his blue pocket-handkerchief covered with white spots, and R. P. marked in the corner in red cotton, "why, then, I suppose yu ain't in a great hurry. Yu'll give me ten minutes?"

"What do'y want ten minutes for, Mr. Pengelly?" asks the Devil.

"Why, sir," says Mr. Pengelly, putting his blue pocket-handkerchief over his face, "I'm ashamed to name it, but I shu'd like to say my prayers. Leastwise, they couldn't du no harm," exclaimed he, pulling the handkerchief off and looking out.

"They wouldn't du yer no gude, Mr. Pengelly," says the Devil.

"I shu'd be more comfable in my mind, sir, if I said 'em," says he.

"Now, I'll tell yu what, Mr. Pengelly," says the Devil after a pause, "I'd like to deal handsome by yu. Yu've done me many a gude turn in your day. I'll let you live as long as yonder cann'l-end burns."

"Thank'y kindly, sir," says Mr. Pengelly. And presently he says, for the Devil did not make signs of departing: "Would yu be so civil as just tu step into t'other room, sir? I'd take it civil. I can't pray comfably with yu here, sir."

"I'll oblige yu in that too," said the Devil; and he went out to look after Mrs. Pengelly.

No sooner was his back turned, than Mr. Pengelly jumped out of bed, extinguished the candle-end, clapped it in the candle-box, and put the candle-box under his bed. Presently the Devil came in, and said: "Now, Mr. Pengelly, yu're all in the dark: I see the cann'l's burnt out, so yu must come with me."

"I'm not so much in the dark as yu, sir," says the sick man, "for the cann'l's not burnt out, and isn't like to. He's safe in the cann'l-box. And I'll send for yu, sir, when I want yu."

Mr. Pengelly is still alive; but let not the visitor to his farm ask him what he keeps in his candle-box, or, old man of seventy-eight though he is, he will jump out of his chair, and lay his stick across the shoulders of his interrogator. "They du say," said my informant, "that Mrs. Pengelly hev tried a score of times to get hold of the cann'l-end, and burn it out; but the master is tu sharp for his missus, and keeps it as tight from her as he does from the Devil."

Mr. Pengelly has the credit of having been only once in his life cheated, and that was by a tramp, in this wise:—

One day a man in tatters, and with his shoes in fragments, came to his door, and asked for work.

"I like work," says the man, "I love it. Try me."

"If that's the case," says Mr. Pengelly, "yu may dig my garden for me, and I will give yu one shilling and twopence a day." Wages were then eighteen pence, or one and eightpence.

"Done," said the man.

So he was given a spade, and he worked capitally. Mr. Pengelly watched him from his windows, from behind a wall, and the man never left off work except to spit on his hands; that was his only relaxation, and he did not do that over-often.

Mr. Pengelly was mighty pleased with his workman; he sent him to sleep in the barn, and paid him his day's wage that he might buy himself a bit of bread.

Next morning Mr. Pengelly was up with the lark. But the workman was up before Mr. Pengelly or the lark either, and was digging diligently in the garden.

Mr. Pengelly was more and more pleased with his man. He went to him during the morning; then the fellow stuck his spade into the ground, and said:

"I'll tell yu what it is, sir, I like work! I love it! but I cannot dig without butes or shoes. Yu may look: I've no soles to my feet, and the spade nigh cuts through them."

"Yu must get a pair of shoes," said Mr. Pengelly.

"That's just it," says the man; "but no bootmaker will trust me; and I cannot pay down, for I haven't the money, sir."

"What would a pair of shoes cost, now?" asks his employer, looking at the man's feet wholly devoid of leather soles.

"Fefteen shilling, maybe," says he.

"Fefteen shilling!" exclaims Mr. Pengelly; "yu'll never get that to pay him."

"Then I must go to some other farmer who'll advance me the money," says the man.

"Now don't'y be in no hurry," says Mr. Pengelly, in a fright lest he should lose a man worth half a crown a day by his work. "Suppose I were to let'y have five shilling. Then yu might go to Stratton, and pay that, and in five days you would have worked it out, keeping twopence a day for your meat; and that will do nicely if yu're not dainty. Then I would let'y have another five shilling, till yu'd paid up."

"Done," says the man.

So Mr. Pengelly pulled the five shillings out, in two half-crown pieces, and gave them to the man.

Directly he had the money in his hand, the fellow drove the spade into the ground, and, making for the gate, took off his hat and said: "I wish yu a gude morning, Mr. Pengelly, and many thanks for the crown. Now I'm off to Taunton like a long dog."

And like a long dog (greyhound) he went off, and Mr. Pengelly never saw him or his two half-crowns again. So the man who cheated the Devil was cheated by a tramp: that shows how clever tramps are.

But to return to the vicar of Morwenstow, and the Dissenters in his parish. Although very bitter in speech against Dissent, he was ready to do any kindness that lay in his power to a Dissenter. He took pains to instruct in Latin and Greek a young Methodist preparing for the Wesleyan ministry, and read with him diligently out of free good-nature. His pupil is now, I believe, a somewhat distinguished preacher in his connection. He was always ready to ask favours of their landlords for Dissenting farmers, and went out of his way to do them exceptional kindnesses.

Some one rallied him with this:—

"Why, Hawker, you are always getting comfortable berths for schismatics."

"So one ought," was his ready reply. "I try my best to make them snug in this world, they will be so uncommonly miserable in the next."

He delighted in seeing persons of the most opposed religious or political views meet at his table. A Roman Catholic, an Independent minister, a Nothingarian and a High Anglican, were once lunching with him.

"What an extraordinary thing, that you should have such discordant elements unite harmoniously at your table!" said a friend.

"Clean and unclean beasts feeding together in the ark," was his reply.

"But how odd that you should get them to meet!"

"Well, I thought it best: they never will meet in the next world."

One day he visited the widow of a parishioner who was dead. As he entered, he met the Methodist preacher coming out of the room where the corpse lay.

"When is poor Thomas to be buried?" asked the vicar.

"We are going to take him out of the parish," answered the widow; "we thought you would not bury him, as he was a Dissenter."

"Who told you that I would not?"

The widow lady looked at the Nonconformist minister.

"Did you say so?" he asked of the preacher abruptly.

"Well, sir, we thought, as you were so mighty particular, you would object to bury a Dissenter."

"On the contrary," said the vicar, "do you not know that I should be but too happy to bury you all?"

He was highly incensed at Mr. Cowper Temple's abortive proposal for admitting Dissenters to the pulpits of the Church. "What!" said he in wrath, "suffer a Dissenting minister to invade our sacred precincts, to draw near to our pulpits and altars! It is contrary to Scripture; for Scripture says: 'If a beast do but touch the mountain, let him be stoned or thrust through with a dart.'"

As an instance of despotic conduct towards a parishioner, it would be difficult to match the following incident: A wealthy yeoman of Morwenstow, Mr. B——, was the owner of a tall pew, which stood like a huge sentry-box, in the nave of the church. Most of the other pew-owners had consented to the removal of the doors, curtains and panelling which they had erected upon or in place of their old family seats to hide themselves from the vulgar gaze; but no persuasion of the vicar had any effect upon the stubborn Mr. B——. The pew had been constructed and furnished with a view to comfort; and, like the famous Derbyshire farmer, Mr. B—— could " vould his arms, shut his eyes, dra' out his legs and think upon nothin' " therein, unnoticed by any one but the parson. Moreover, Mr. B—— had, it was said, a faculty-right to the hideous enclosure. He was therefore invulnerable to all the coaxing, reasoning, threatening and preaching which could be brought to bear upon him. Weeks after all the other pews had been swept away, he intrenched himself in his ecclesiastical fortress, and looked defiance at the outside world. At last the vicar resolved to storm the enemy, and gave him due notice, that, on a certain day and hour, it was his intention to demolish the pew. Mr. B—— was present at the appointed time to defend his property, but was so taken aback at the sight of the vicar entering the church armed with a large axe, that he stood dumfounded with amazement, whilst, without uttering a word, the vicar strode up to the pew, and with a few lusty blows literally smashed it to pieces, and then flung the fragments outside the church door. To the credit of Mr. B——, he still continued to attend church; but he took on one occasion an unseasonable opportunity of rebuking the vicar for his violence. It was on the parish feast day, or "revel" as the inhabitants of the parish called it; and, as was his wont, the vicar was expatiating in the pulpit on the antiquity of the church, and how the shrine of St. Morwenna had been preserved unchanged whilst dynasties had perished and empires had been overthrown. Whereupon Mr. B—— exclaimed in a voice of thunder, "No such thing: you knacked down my pew!" The vicar, however, was still more than a match for him. Without the least embarrassment, he turned from St. Morwenna to the parable of the rich man and Lazarus, and, in describing the life and character of Dives, drew such a vivid portrait of Mr. B——, that the poor man rushed out of church when the preacher began to consign him to his place of torment.

The impression was strong upon him, that he and the Church were under special Divine protection, and he would insist that no misfortune ever befel his cows or sheep. When, however, after some years he was unlucky, he looked on every stroke of misfortune as an assault of Satan himself, allowed to try him as he had tried Job.

This belief that he had, of a special Providence watching over him, must explain the somewhat painful feature of his looking out for the ruin of those who wrought evil against the Church. He bore them no malice; but he looked upon such wrongs done as done to God, and as sure to be avenged by Him. He had always a text at hand to support his view. "I have no personal enemies," he would say, "but

Uzziah cannot put his hand to the ark without the Lord making a breach upon him."

His conviction that the Church was God's kingdom was never shaken. "No weapon formed against thee shall prosper," he said; "that was a promise made by God to the Church, and God does not forget His promises. Why, I have *seen* His promise kept again and again. I know that God is no liar."

"But look at the hostility to the Church in Mr. M——, what efforts he has made in Parliament, and throughout the country, agitating men's minds, and all for the purpose of overthrowing the Church. He prospers."

"My friend," said the vicar, pausing, and laying his hand solemnly on his companion's arm, "God does not always pay wages on Saturday night."

When an attempt was made in 1843 to wrest the Well of St. John from him, he went thrice a day, every day during that Lent, whilst the case was being tried, till 27th March, and offered up before the altar the following prayer :—

Almighty and most merciful God! the Protector of all that trust in Thee! We most humbly beseech Thee that Thou wouldest be pleased to stretch forth Thy right hand to rescue and defend the possessions of this Thy sanctuary from the envy and violence of wicked and covetous men. Let not an adversary despoil Thine inheritance, neither suffer Thou the evil man to approach the waters that flow softly for Thy blessed baptism, from the well of Thy servant St. John.

And, O Almighty Lord, even as Thou didst avenge the cause of Naboth the Jezreelite, upon angry Ahab and Jezebel his wife; and as Thou didst strengthen the hands of Thy blessed apostle St. Peter, insomuch that Ananias and Sapphira could not escape just judgment when they sought to keep back a part of the possession from Thy Church ; even so now, O Lord God, shield and succour the heritage of Thy holy shrine! Show some token upon us for good, that they who see it may say, " This hath God done ". Be Thou our hope and fortress, O Lord, our castle and deliverer, as in the days of old, such as our fathers have told us. Show forth Thy strength unto this generation, and Thy power unto them that are yet for to come. So shall we daily perform our vows, through Jesus Christ our Lord. Amen.

The attempt to deprive him of the Well of St. John signally failed.

> They dreamed not in old Hebron, when the sound
>   Went through the city, that the promised son
>   Was born to Zachary, and his name was John,—
> They little thought that here, in this far ground
>   Beside the Severn Sea, that Hebrew child
>   Would be a cherished memory of the wild !—
> Here, where the pulses of the ocean bound
>   Whole centuries away, while one meek cell,
>   Built by the fathers o'er a lonely well,
> Still breathes the Baptist's sweet remembrance round.
>   A spring of silent waters with his name,
>   That from the angel's voice in music came,
> Here in the wilderness so faithful found,
> It freshens to this day the Levite's grassy mound.

MORWENSTOW, Sept. 20, 1850. *My dear Mrs. M*——,— . . . I have but a sullen prospect of winter tide. I had longed to go on with another window. But my fate, which in matters of *l. s. d.* is always mournful, paralyses my will. A west window in my tower is offered me by Warrington for the cost of carriage and putting together. But—but—but. Fifteen years I have been vicar of this altar ; and all that while no lay person, landlord, tenant, parishioner or steward, has ever proffered me even one kind word, much less aid or coin. Nay, I have found them all bristling with dislike. All the great men have been hostile to me in word or deed. Yet I thank my Master and His angels, I have accomplished in and around my church a thousand times more than the great befriended clergy of this deanery. Not one thing has failed. When I lack aid to fulfil, I go to the altar and ask it. Is it conceded? So fearfully that I shudder with thanksgiving. A person threatened me with injury on a fixed day. I besought rescue. On that very day that person died. A false and treacherous clergyman came to a parish close by. I shook with dread. I asked help. It came. He entered my house five days afterwards to announce some malady unaccountable to him. He went. It grew. He resigned his cure last week.

And these are two only out of forty miracles.

Yours faithfully,
R. S. HAWKER.

It is painful to record this side of the vicar's character; but without it this would be but an imperfect sketch. He was, it must be borne in mind, an anachronism. He did not belong to this century or this country. His mind and character pertained to the Middle Ages and to the East.

He is not to be measured by any standard used for men of our times.

MORWENSTOW, July 24, 1857. *My dear Mrs. M———,*—All my pets are dead, and I cannot endure my lonely lawn. I want some ewe lamb, "to be unto me a daughter." T——— is a parish famous for sheep: are there any true Church farmers among the sheep-masters, to whom, with Dr. C———'s introduction, I could write, in order to obtain the animals I seek? I want to find a man, or men, who would deal honestly and sincerely by me, and in whom I could trust. Will you ask your father if he would have the kindness to instruct me hereon? I want soft-eyed, well-bred sheep, the animal which was moulded in the mind of God the Trinity, to typify the Lamb of Calvary.

Yours always,
R. S. HAWKER.

He had the greatest objection to hysterical religion.

"Conversion," he said, "is a spasm of the ganglions." "Free justification," was another of his sayings, "is a bankrupt's certificate, whitewashing him, and licensing him to swindle and thieve again."

"There was a young Wesleyan woman at Shop" (this is one of his stories) "who was ill; and her aunt, a trusty old Churchwoman, was nursing her. The sick woman's breast was somewhat agitated, and rumblings therein were audible. 'Aunt,' said she, 'do you hear and see? There is the clear witness of the Spirit speaking within!'—'Lor', my dear,' answered the old woman, 'it's not that: you can get the better of it with three drops of peppermint on a bit of loaf-sugar.'"

On the occasion of a noisy revival in the parish, he wrote the following verses, to describe what he believed to be the true signs of spiritual conversion —very different from the screeching and hysterics of the revival which had taken place among his own people, the sad moral effect of which on the young women he learned by experience.

> When the voice of God is thrilling,
>   Breathe not a sound;
> When the tearful eye is filling,
>   Breathe not a sound;
> When the memory is pleading,
> And the better mind succeeding,
> When the stricken heart is bleeding,
>   Breathe not a sound.
>
> When the broad road is forsaken,
>   Breathe not a sound;
> And the narrow path is taken,
>   Breathe not a sound;

> When the angels are descending,
> And the days of sin are ending,
> When heaven and earth are blending,
> Breathe not a sound.

A Dissenter at Bude considered this sentiment so unsuited to evangelical religion, and so suitable for the dumb dogs of the Established Church, that he had it printed on a card, and distributed it among his co-religionists, in scorn, with a note of derision of his own appended.

Mr. Hawker was walking one day on the cliffs near Morwenstow, with the Rev. W. Vincent,* when a gust of wind took off Mr. Vincent's hat, and carried it over the cliff.

Within a week or two a Methodist preacher at Truro was discoursing on prayer, and in his sermon he said: "I would not have you, dear brethren, confine your supplications to spiritual blessings, but ask also for temporal favours. I will illustrate my meaning by narrating an incident, a fact, that happened to myself ten days ago. I was on the shore of a cove near a little, insignificant place in North Cornwall, named Morwenstow, and about to proceed to Bude. Shall I add, my Christian friends, that I had on my head at the time a shocking bad hat, and that I somewhat blushed to think of entering that harbour, town and watering-place, so ill-adorned as to my head? Then I lifted up my prayer to the Almighty, that He would pluck me out of the great strait in which I found myself, and clothe me suitably as to my head; for He painteth the petals of the polyanthus, and colours the calyx of the coreopsis. At that solemn moment I raised my eyes to heaven; and I saw, in the spacious firmament on high, the blue, ethereal sky, a black spot. It approached, it largened, it widened, it fell at my feet. It was a brand-new hat, by a distinguished London maker. I cast my battered beaver to the waves, and walked into Bude as fast as I could, with the new hat on my head."

The incident got into *The Methodist Reporter*, or some such Wesleyan publication, under the heading of "Remarkable Answer to Prayer." "And," said the vicar, "the rascal made off with Vincent's new hat from Bennett's; there was no reaching him, for we were on the cliff, and could not descend the precipice. He was deaf enough, I promise you, to our shouts."

That Mr. Hawker was appreciated by some, the following note received by me will show:—

Nov. 16, 1875. In the spring of this year, and consequently before there could have been any idea of "De mortuis," etc., I happened to find myself in company with two Morwenstow people, returning to their old home. One of them was a prosperous-looking clerk or shopman from Manchester, the other a nice, modest-looking servant girl. On recognising each other, which they did not do at once, their talk naturally turned to old days. The Sunday School, Morwenstow and its vicar were discussed; and it was very remarkable to see how lively was their remembrance of him, how much affection and reverence they entertained for him, how keen was their appreciation of the great qualities of his head and heart, and how much delight they testified in being able to see his honoured face and white head, and hear the well-remembered tones of his voice once more. It may seem but a trivial incident; but to those who know how constant is the complaint, and, indeed, how well founded, that our children, when they leave school, leave us altogether, such attestation to his work and influence is not without its value. I remain, etc., W. C——.

"Talking of *appreciation*," as Mr. Hawker said once, "the Scripture-reader, Mr. Bumpus,* at ——, came to me the other day, and said: 'Please, sir, I have been visiting and advising Farmer Matthews, but he did not quite appreciate me. In fact, he kicked me downstairs.'"

Mr. Hawker could not endure to hear the apostles or evangelists spoken of by name without their proper prefix or title of "Saint." If he heard any one talk of Mark, or John, or Paul, he would say: "Look here. There was a professor at Oxford in my time who lectured on divinity. One day a pert student began to speak about 'Paul's opinion.' 'Paul's opinion, sir!' said the professor. 'Paul is not here to speak for himself; but if Paul were, and heard you talk thus disrespectfully of him, it is my belief that Paul would take you by the scruff of your neck and chuck you out of the window. As I have Paul in honour, if I hear you speak of him disrespectfully again, I will kick you from the room.'"

"Never boast," was a favourite saying of the vicar's. "The moment you boast, the Devil obtains power over you. You notice if it be not so. You say, 'I now never catch cold,' and within a week you have a sore throat. 'I am always lucky in my money ventures'; and the next fails. So long as you do not boast, the Devil cannot touch you; but, the moment you have boasted, virtue has gone from you, and he obtains power. Nebuchadnezzar was prosperous till he said, 'Is not this great Babylon, that I have built for the house of the kingdom by the might of my power, and for the honour of my majesty?' It was while the word was in the king's mouth that the voice fell from heaven which took it from him."

MORWENSTOW, Jan. 2, 1850. *My dear Mrs. M——,*—I know not when I have been more shocked than by the sudden announcement of the death of good Bishop Coleridge. For good he verily and really was. What a word that is, "suddenly"! The Lord opened the eyes of the young man, and, behold, there were horses and chariots of fire round about Elisha. May God grant us Sir T. More's prayer, "that we may all meet and be merry in heaven"! . . . I am to do something again for the new series of *Tracts for the Christian Seasons.* Did you detect my "Magian Star" and "Nain, the lovely city"?

I hope to hear from you what is going on in the out-world. Here within the ark we hear only the voices of animals and birds, and the sound of many waters. "The Lord shut him in." Give my real love to P——, and say I will write her soon a letter, with a psalm about "her dear Aunt Mary."

Yours faithfully,
R. S. HAWKER.

The psalm came in due time with this introduction:—

MODRYB MARYA: AUNT MARY.
A CHRISTMAS CHANT.

[In old and simple-hearted Cornwall, the household names "uncle" and "aunt" were uttered and used as they are to this day in many countries of the East, not only as phrases of kindred, but as words of kindly greeting and tender respect. It was in the spirit, therefore, of this touching and graphic usage, that they were wont, on the Tamar side, to call the Mother of God, in their loyal language, Modryb Marya, or Aunt Mary.]

Now, of all the trees by the king's highway,
    Which do you love the best?
Oh! the one that is green upon Christmas Day,
    The bush with the bleeding breast!

Now, the holly, with her drops of blood, for me;
For that is our dear Aunt Mary's tree!

Its leaves are sweet with our Saviour's name,
   'Tis a plant that loves the poor:
Summer and winter it shines the same,
   Beside the cottage door.
Oh! the holly, with her drops of blood, for me;
For that is our kind Aunt Mary's tree!

'Tis a bush that the birds will never leave,
   They sing in it all day long;
But, sweetest of all, upon Christmas Eve,
   Is to hear the robin's song.
'Tis the merriest sound upon earth and sea,
For it comes from our own Aunt Mary's tree!

So, of all that grow by the king's highway,
   I love that tree the best:
'Tis a bower for the birds upon Christmas Day,
   The bush of the bleeding breast.
Oh! the holly, with her drops of blood, for me;
For that is our sweet Aunt Mary's tree!

The following was sent to the same young girl, P—— M——:—

Morwenstow, February, 1853. *Dear P——,*—I have copied a little parable-story for you. Tell me if you can understand it. May God bless you, my dear child, whom I love for your father's sake!   Yours faithfully,
                                    R. S. Hawker.

Natum ante omnia sæcula.

The first star gleamed over Nazareth, when thus the Lady said unto her Son: "Jesu, wilt thou not arise and go with me into the field that we may hear the sweet chime of the birds as they chant their evening psalm?"—"Yea, Mary, mother," answered the awful Boy, "yea, for I love their music well.

I have loved it long. I listened, in My gladness, to the first-born voices of the winged fowl, when they brake forth into melody among the trees of the Garden, or ever there was a man to rejoice in their song. Twain, moreover, after their kind, the eagle and the dove, did My Father and I create, to be the token-birds of our Spirit, when He should go forth from us to thrill the world of time."

His theory was that the eagle symbolised the Holy Ghost in His operation under the old covenant, and the dove His work in the Church. The double-headed eagle, so often found in mediæval churches—and there is one carved on a boss at Morwenstow—he thought represented the twofold effusion of the Spirit in two dispensations.

The following "Carol of the Kings" was written during the Epiphany of 1859, and published with the signature "Nectan" in a Plymouth paper:—

A CAROL OF THE KINGS.

[It is chronicled in an old Armenian myth [1] that the wise men of the East were none other than the three sons of Noe, and that they were raised from the dead to represent, and to do homage for, all mankind in the cave at Bethlehem! Other legends are also told: one, that these patriarch-princes of the Flood did not ever die, but were rapt away into Enoch's Paradise, and were thence recalled to begin the solemn gesture of world-wide worship to the King-born Child! Another saying holds, that, when their days were full, these arkite fathers fell asleep, and were laid at rest in a cavern at Ararat until Messias was born, and that then an angel aroused them from the slumber of ages to bow down and to hail, as the heralds of many nations, the awful Child. Be this as it may—whether the mystic magi were Shem, Cham, and Japhet, in their first or second existence, under their own names or those of other men, or whether they were three long-descended and royal sages from the loins or the land of Baalam, one thing has been delivered to me for very record. The supernatural shape of clustering orbs which was embodied suddenly from surrounding light, and framed to be the beacon of

---

[1] How a thing can be "chronicled in a myth" is not easy to understand. Myths not infrequently get recorded, not chronicled.—S. B.-G.

that westward-way, was and is the Southern Cross! It was not a solitary signal-fire, but a miraculous constellation, a pentacle of stars, whereof two shone for the transom and three for the stock; and which went above and before the travellers, day and night, radiantly, until it came and stood over where the young Child lay! And then? What then? Must those faithful orbs dissolve and die? Shall the gleaming trophy fall? Nay—not so. When it had fulfilled the piety of its first-born office, it arose, and, amid the vassalage of every stellar and material law, it moved onward and onward, obedient to the impulse of God the Trinity, journeying evermore towards the south, until that starry image arrived in the predestined sphere of future and perpetual abode: to bend, as to this day it bends, above the peaceful sea, in everlasting memorial of the Child Jesus: the Southern Cross!]

> Three ancient men in Bethlehem's cave
>   With awful wonder stand:
> A voice had called them from their grave
>   In some far Eastern land.
>
> They lived, they trod the former earth,
>   When the old waters swelled:
> The ark, that womb of second birth,
>   Their house and lineage held.
>
> Pale Japhet bows the knee with gold,
>   Bright Shem sweet incense brings,
> And Cham the myrrh his fingers hold:
>   Lo! the three Orient kings!
>
> Types of the total earth, they hailed
>   The signal's starry frame:
> Shuddering with second life, they quailed
>   At the Child Jesu's name.
>
> Then slow the patriarchs turned and trod,
>   And this their parting sigh,—
> "Our eyes have seen the living God,
>   And now—once more to die."

We began this chapter with stories illustrating the harsh side of Mr. Hawker's character. We have slided insensibly into those which show him forth in his gentler nature. There was in him the eagle and the dove : it is pleasanter to think of the dove-like characteristics of this grand old man.

And naturally, when we speak of him in his softer moods, not when he is doing battle for God and the Church, and—it must be admitted—for his own whims, but when he is at peace and full of smiles, we come to think of him in his relations with children.

When his school was first opened he attended it daily ; but in after-years, as age and infirmities crept on, his visits were only once a week.

He loved children, and they loved him. It was his delight to take them by the hand and walk with them about the parish, telling them stories of St. Morwenna, St. Nectan, King Arthur, Sir Bevil Grenville, smugglers, wreckers, pixies and hobgoblins, in one unflagging stream. So great was the affection borne him by the children of his parish, that when they were ill, and had to take physic, and the mothers could not induce them to swallow the nauseous draught, the vicar was sent for, and the little ones, without further struggle, swallowed the medicine administered by his hand.

A child said to him one day : " Please, Mr. Hawker, did you ever see an angel ? "

" Margaret," he answered solemnly, and took one of the child's hands in his left palm, " there came to this door one day a poor man. He was in rags. Whence he came I know not. He appeared quite suddenly at the door. We gave him bread. There was something wonderful, mysterious, unearthly, in his face. And I watched him as he went away. Look, Margaret! do you see that hill all gold and crimson with gorse and heather? He went that way. I saw him go up through the gold and crimson, up, still upwards, to where the blue sky is, and there I lost sight of him all at once. I saw him no more; but I thought of the words, 'Be not forgetful to entertain strangers: for thereby some have entertained angels unawares.'"

A good idea of his notions about angels, and their guardianship of his church, may be gathered from a remarkable sermon he preached a few years ago, on St. John the Baptist's day, in his own church. It was heard by an old man, a builder in Kilkhampton; and it made so deep an impression on his mind, that he was able to repeat to me the outline of its contents, and to give me whole passages.

His text was 1 Sam. iii. 4, "*Here am I!*"

More than a thousand years ago St. Morwenna came from Wales, from Brecknockshire, where was her father's palace: she loved the things of God more than the things of men.

And then the wild Atlantic rolled against these cliffs as now, and the gorse flamed over them as now, and the little brook dived through fern, and foamed over the rocks to join the sea, as now. And there were men and women where you dwell, as now; and there were little children on their knees, as now. But then there was no knowledge of God in the hearts of men, as there is now. There was no church, as now; no Word of God preached, as now; no font where the water was sanctified by the brooding Spirit, as now; no altar where the bread of life was broken, as now. All lay in darkness and the shadow of death.

And God looked upon the earth, and saw the blue sea lashing our rocks, and the gorse flaming on our hills, and the brook murmuring into the sea, and men and women and children lying in the shadow of death; and it grieved Him. Then He called: "Who will come and plant a church in that wild glen, and bring the light of life into this lone spot?" and Morwenna answered with brave heart and childlike simplicity, "Here am I!"

And Morwenna came. She built herself a cell at Chapel-piece, where now no heather or furze or thorn will grow, for her feet have consecrated it for evermore; and she got a gift of land; and she built a church, and dedicated it to God the Trinity, and St. John the Baptiser, who preached in a wilderness such as this. And she gave the land for ever to God and His Church; and wheresoever the Gospel shall be preached, there shall also this, that this woman hath done, be told for a memorial of her.

Now a holy bishop came; and he accepted, in the name of God, this gift off her hands, and he consecrated for ever this church to God.

Now look you! This house is God's. These pillars are God's. These windows are God's. That door is God's. Every stone and beam is God's. The grass in the churchyard, the fern rooted in the tower, all are God's.

And when the holy bishop dedicated all to God, and consecrated the ground to the very centre of the earth, then he set a priest here to minister in God's name, to bless, baptise, and break the holy bread, and fill the holy cup, in God's name.

And God looked out over the earth, and He saw the building and the land Morwenna had given to Him; and He said: "Who will pasture My flock in this desert? Who will pour on them the sanctifying water? Who will distribute to them the bread of heaven?" And the priest standing here made answer, "Here am I!"

And God said: "Who will stand by My priest, and watch and ward My building and My land? Who will defend him against evil men? Who will guard My house from the spoiler? My land from those who would add field to field, till they can say, 'We are alone in the earth'?" And an angel answered, "Here am I!"

And the angel came down to keep guard here, with flaming sword that turneth every way, to champion the priest of God, and to watch the sanctuary of God.

More than one thousand years have rolled away since Morwenna gave this church to God; and since then never has there been a day in which, when God looked forth upon the earth, there has not been a priest standing at this altar, to say in answer to His call, "Here am I!"

A thousand years, and more, have swept away; and in all these ages there never has been a moment in which an angel, leaning on his flashing sword, has not stood here as sentinel, to answer to God's call, when foes assail, and traitors give the Judas kiss, and feeble hearts fail, "Here am I!"

And now, my brethren, I stand here.

Does God ask: "Who is there to baptise the children, and bring them to Me? Who is there to instruct the young in the paths of righteousness? Who is there to bless the young hands that clasp for life's journey? Who is there to speak the word of pardon over the penitent sinner who turns with broken and contrite heart to Me? Who is there to give the bread of heaven to the wayfarers on life's desert? Who is there to stand by the sick man's bed, and hold the cross before his closing eyes? Who is there to lay him with words of hope in his long home?" Why, my brethren, I look up in the face of God, and I answer boldly, confidently, yet humbly and suppliantly, "Here am I!"

I, with all my infirmities of temper and mind and body; I, broken by old age, but with a spirit ever willing; I, troubled on every side, without with fightings, within with fears; I—I—strengthened, however, by the grace of God, and commissioned by His apostolic ministry.

And am I alone? Not so. There are chariots and horses of fire about me. There are angels round us on every side.

You do not see them. You ask me, "Do you?"

And I answer, Yes, I do.

Am I weak? An angel stays me up. Do my hands falter? An angel sustains them. Am I weary to death with disappointment? My head rests on an angel's bosom, and an angel's arms encircle me.

Who will raise his hand to tear down the house of God? Who will venture to rob God of His inheritance? An angel is at hand. He beareth not the sword in vain: he saith to the assailer, "Here am I!"

And believe me: the world may roll its course through centuries more; the ocean may fret our rocks, and he has fretted them through ages past; but as long as one stone stands upon another of Morwenna's church, so long will there be a priest to answer God's call, and say, "Here am I!" and so long will there be an angel to stay him up in his agony and weakness, saying, "Here am I!" and to meet the spoiler, with his sword and challenge, "Here am I!"[1]

[1] This sermon is given approximately only. Mr. Hawker always preached extempore. It is a restoration; and a restoration from notes can never equal the original.

CHAPTER VIII

The Vicar of Morwenstow as a Poet—His Epigrams—"The Carol of the Pruss"—"Down with the Church"—"The Quest of the Sangreal"—Editions of his Poems—Ballads—"The Song of the Western Men"—"The Cornish Mother's Lament"—"A Thought"—Churchyards.

WHEN the vicar of Morwenstow liked, he could fire off a pungent epigram. Many of these productions exist; but, as most of them apply to persons or events with whom or with which the general reader has no acquaintance, it is not necessary to quote them. Some also are too keenly sharpened to bear publication.

The Hon. Newton Fellowes[1] canvassed for North Devon, at the time when the surplice controversy was at its height, and went before the electors as the champion of Protestantism, and "no washing of the parson's shirt."

On the hustings he declared with great vehemence that he "would never, never, never allow himself to be priest-ridden." Mr. Hawker heard him, and, tearing a leaf from his pocket-book, wrote on it:—

> Thou ridden ne'er shalt be, by prophet or by priest:
> Balaam is dead, and none but he would choose thee for his beast!

And he slipped the paper into the hand of the excited but not eloquent speaker.

[1] Afterwards Lord Portsmouth.

He had a singular facility for writing off an epigram on the spur of the moment. In the midst of conversation he would pause, his hand go to the pencil that dangled from his button-hole, and on a scrap of paper, the fly-leaf of a book, or a margin of newspaper, a happy, brilliant epigram was written on some topic started in the course of conversation, and composed almost without his pausing in his talk.

Many of his sayings were epigrammatical. On an extremely self-conceited man leaving the room one day, after he had caused some amusement by his self-assertion, Mr. Hawker said: "Conceit is the compensation afforded by benignant Nature for mental deficiency."

His "Carol of the Pruss," 1st Jan., 1871, is bitter:—

> Hurrah for the boom of the thundering gun!
>   Hurrah for the words they say!
> "Here's a merry Christmas for every one,
>   And a happy New Year's Day."
> Thus saith the king to the echoing ball:
> "With the blessing of God we will slay them all!"
>
> "Up!" saith the king, "load, fire and slay!"
>   'Tis a kindly signal given:
> However happy on earth be they,
>   They'll be happier in heaven.
> Tell them, as soon as their souls are free
> They'll sing like birds on a Christmas-tree.
>
> Down with them all! If they rise again,
>   They will munch our beef and bread:
> War there must be with the living men;
>   There'll be peace when all are dead!
> This earth shall be our wide, wide home:
> Our foes shall have the world to come.

Starve, starve them all, till through the skin
    You may count each **hungry bone**!
Tap, tap their veins, till the blood runs **thin**,
    And their sinful flesh is gone!
While life is strong in the German sky,
What **matters** it who besides may die?

No sigh so sweet as the cannon's breath,
    No music like to the gun!
There's a merry Christmas to war and death,
    And a happy New Year to none.
Thus saith the king to the echoing ball:
"With the blessing of God we will slay them all!"

Sir R. Vyvyan and Sir C. Lemon were standing for East Cornwall in the Conservative and Church interest. The opposition party was that of the Dissenters; and their cry was "Down with the Church!" Thereupon Mr. Hawker wrote the lines:—

    Shall the grey tower in ruin bow?
    Must the babe die with nameless brow?
    Or common hands in mockery fling
    The unblessed waters of the spring?
    No! while the Cornish voice can ring
    The Vyvyan cry, "Our Church and King!"

    Shall the grey tower in ruin stand
    When the heart thrills within the hand,
    And beauty's lip to youth hath given
    The vow on earth that links for heaven?
    Shall no glad peal from church-tower grey
    Cheer the young maiden's homeward way?
    No! while the Cornish voice can ring,
    And Vyvyan cry, "Our Church and King!"

    Shall the grey tower in ruins spread?
    And must the furrow hold the dead
    Without the toll of passing knell,
    Without the stolèd priest to tell

> Of Christ the first-fruits of the dead,
> To wake our brother from his bed ?[1]
> No! while the Cornish voice can ring,
> And Vyvyan cry, "Our Church and King!"

When the Irish Church was disestablished, the vicar was highly incensed, and at the election of 1873 voted for the Conservative candidate instead of holding fast in his allegiance to the Liberal. But when the Public Worship Bill was taken up by Mr. Disraeli, and carried through Parliament by the Conservative government, his faith in the Tory prime minister failed as wholly as it had in the leader of the Liberal party; and he wrote the following bitter epigram on the two prime ministers :—

> An English boy was born, a Jew, and then
> On the eighth day received the name of Ben.
> Another boy was born, baptised, but still
> In common parlance called the People's Will!
> Both lived impenitent, and so they died;
> And between both the Church was crucified.
> Which bore the brand, I pray thee, tell me true—
> The wavering Christian, or the doubtful Jew?

There is another epigram attributed to him, but whether rightly or not I am not in a position to state :—

> Doctor Hopwood,* the vicar of Calstock,* is dead;
> But, *De mortuis nil nisi bonum,* is said.
> Let this maxim be strictly regarded, and then
> Doctor Hopwood will never be heard of again!

The following pretty lines were addressed to a

---

[1] Four lines in the last verse I have supplied, as the copy sent me was defective.—*S.B.-G.*

child, the daughter of an attached friend, who was budding into beautiful womanhood. It was written in 1864.

> The eyes that melt, the eyes that burn,
> The lips that make a lover yearn,—
> These flashed on my bewildered sight
> Like meteors of the northern night.
>
> Then said I, in my wild amaze,
> "What stars be they that greet my gaze?"
> Where shall my shivering rudder turn?
> To eyes that melt, or eyes that burn?
>
> Ah! safer far the darkling sea
> Than where such perilous signals be;
> To rock and storm and whirlwind turn
> From eyes that melt, and eyes that burn.

A lady was very pressing that he should write something in her album—she thought his poems so charming, his ballads so delicious, his epigrams so delightful, etc. Mr. Hawker was impatient at this poor flattery, and, taking up her album, wrote in it:—

A best superfine coat	5	5 0
A pair of kerseymere small-clothes . .	2	14 0
A waiscoat with silk buttons . . .	1	10 0
	£9	9 0

Mr. Hawker was a poet of no mean order. His "Quest of the Sangreal," which is his most ambitious composition, is a poem of great power, and contains passages of rare beauty. It is unfortunate that he should have traversed the same ground as the Poet Laureate. The "Holy Grail" of the latter has eclipsed the "Quest" of the vicar of Morwenstow. But, if the two poems be regarded without previous knowledge of the name of their composers, I am not sure that some judges would not prefer the masterpiece of the Cornish poet to a piece in which Lord Tennyson scarcely rises to his true level. In his "Quest of the Sangreal" alone does the vicar of Morwenstow show his real power. His ballads are charming; but a ballad is never, and can never be, a poem of a high order; it is essentially a popular piece of verse, without any depth of thought; pleasing by its swing and spirit, but not otherwise a work of art or genius. Mr. Hawker was too fond of the ballad. His first successes had been won in that line, and he adhered to it till late. A few sonnets rise to the level of sonnets, also never a very exalted one. His "Legend of St. Cecily" and "St. Thekla," somewhat larger poems, are pleasing; but there is nothing in them which gives token of there lying in the breast of the Cornish vicar a deep vein of the purest poetical ore. That was revealed only by the publication of "The Quest of the Sangreal," which rose above the smaller fry of ballads and sonnets as an eagle above the songsters of the grove.

And yet this poem, belonging to the first order, as I am disposed to regard it, is disappointing—there is not enough of it. The poem is charged with ideas, crowded with conceptions full of beauty; but it is a torso, not a complete statue.

The subject of the poem is the Sangreal,[1] the true

---

[1] There is considerable doubt as to the origin of the name Sangraal, Sangrail or Sangreal. It has been variously derived from Sang-réal, True Blood, and from Sanc-Grazal, the provençal for Holy Cup. The latter is the most probable derivation.

blood of Christ, gathered by Joseph of Arimathea in a golden goblet from the side of the Saviour as He hung on the cross. This precious treasure he conveyed to Britain, and settled with it at Avalon, or Glastonbury. There it remained till

> Evil days came on,
> And evil men: the garbage of their sin
> Tainted this land, and all things holy fled.
> The Sangreal was not. On a summer eve
> The silence of the sky brake up in sound;
> The tree of Joseph glowed with ruddy light;
> A harmless fire curved like a molten vase
> Around the bush ——

and all was gone.

After the lapse of centuries King Arthur sends his knights in quest of the miraculous vessel. There is a long account given by Arthur of its history, then of the drawing of the lots by his knights to decide the directions in which they are to ride in quest of it, then of the knights departing, and a description of the blazon and mottoes on their shields; and then —after some 400 lines has led us to the beginning of the Quest, and we expect the adventures of Sir Percival, Sir Tristan, Sir Launcelot and Sir Galahad —it all ends in a vision unrolled before the eyes of King Arthur, of the fate of Britain, in about eighty lines.

We are disappointed; for Sir Thomas Malory's "Morte d'Arthur" supplies abundant material for a long and glorious poem on the achievements of the four knights.

The Poet Laureate's "Holy Grail" did not appear

till 1870, or we might suppose that the Cornish poet shrank from treading on the same ground. When we turn over Sir Thomas Malory's pages, it is with a feeling of bitter regret that we have not his story glorified by Mr. Hawker's poetry. The finding of the Grail by Sir Galahad, his coronation as King of Sarras, and his death, were subjects he could have rendered to perfection.

The name of the poem is a misnomer. There is no quest, only a starting on the quest.

But, in spite of this conspicuous fault, "The Quest of the Sangreal" is a great poem, containing passages of rare beauty. Of Joseph of Arimathea Mr. Hawker says,—

> He dwelt in Orient Syria, God's own land,
> The ladder-foot of heaven ; where shadowy shapes
> In white apparel glided up and down.
> His home was like a garner full of corn
> And wine and oil—a granary of God.
> Young men, that no one knew, went in and out
> With a far look in their eternal eyes.
> All things were strange and rare: the Sangreal
> As though it clung to some ethereal chain,
> Brought down high heaven to earth at Arimathèe.

The idea of the poet :—

> The conscious water saw its God, and blushed—

in reference to the miracle at Cana, occurs with a change in Mr. Hawker's verses, with reference to the Last Supper :—

> The selfsame cup, wherein the faithful wine
> Heard God, and was obedient unto blood.

After the loss of the Holy Grail :—

>The land is lonely now: Anathema.
>The link that bound it to the silent grasp
>Of thrilling worlds is gathered up and gone:
>The glory is departed, and the disk
>So full of radiance from the touch of God.
>This orb is darkened to the distant watch
>Of Saturn and his reapers when they pause,
>Amid their sheaves, to count the nightly stars.

The Eastward craving of Mr. Hawker, the point to which his heart and instincts turned, find expression in this poem repeatedly :—

>Eastward! the source and spring of life and light.
>Thence came, and thither went, the rush of worlds
>When the great cone of space was sown with stars.
>There rolled the gateway of the double dawn
>When the mere God shone down a breathing man.
>There, up from Bethany, the Syrian twelve
>Watched their dear Master darken into day.
>. . . . .
>Sir Galahad holds the Orient arrow's name,
>His chosen hand unbars the gate of day.
>There glows that Heart, filled with his mother's blood,
>That rules in every pulse the world of man,
>Link of the awful Three, with many a star.
>O blessed East! 'mid visions such as thine,
>'Twere well to grasp the Sangreal, and die.

In one passage Mr. Hawker seems to be speaking the feeling of loneliness that he ever felt in his own heart: he was, as he says in one of his letters, "the ever-alone."

>Ha! sirs, ye seek a noble crest to-day—
>To win and wear the starry Sangreal,
>The link that binds to God a lonely land.
>Would that my arm went with you like my heart!

But the true shepherd must not shun the fold;
For in this flock are crouching grievous wolves,
And chief among them all my own false kin.
Therefore I tarry by the cruel sea
To hear at eve the treacherous mermaid's song,
And watch the wallowing monsters of the wave,
'Mid all things fierce and wild and strange—*alone!*
Ay! all beside can win companionship:
The churl may clip his mate beneath the thatch,
While his brown urchins nestle at his knees;
The soldier gives and grasps a mutual palm,
Knit to his flesh in sinewy bonds of war;
The knight may seek at eve his castle-gate,
Mount the old stair, and lift the accustomed latch,
To find, for throbbing brow and weary limb,
That paradise of pillows, one true breast.
But he, the lofty ruler of the land,
Like yonder Tor, first greeted by the dawn,
And wooed the latest by the lingering day,
With happy homes and hearths beneath his breast,
Must soar and gleam in solitary snow:
The lonely one is ever more the king!

Here are some beautiful lines on Cornwall :—

Ah! native Cornwall! throned upon the hills,
Thy moorland pathways worn by angel feet,
Thy streams that march in music to the sea,
'Mid Ocean's merry noise, his billowy laugh!
Ah, me! a gloom falls heavy on my soul:
The birds that sang to me in youth are dead.
I think, in dreamy vigils of the night,
It may be God is angry with my land—
Too much athirst for fame, too fond of blood,
And all for earth, for shadows, and the dream,
To glean an echo from the winds of song!

Mr. Hawker's poems were republished over and over again, with a few, but only a few, additions.

The pieces written by him as a boy, *Tendrils, by Reuben*, were never reprinted, nor did they deserve it. He saw that clearly enough.

In 1832 he published his *Records of the Western Shore*; in 1836, the second series of the same. In these appeared his Cornish ballads.

They were republished in a volume entitled *Ecclesia*, in 1841; again, with some additions, under the title, *Reeds Shaken by the Wind*, in 1842; and the second cluster of the same in 1843.

They again appeared with "Genoveva," in a volume called *Echoes of Old Cornwall*, in 1845. "Genoveva" is a poem founded on the beautiful story of Geneviève de Brabant, and appeared first in *German Ballads, Songs*, etc., edited by Miss Smedley, and published by James Burns, no date.

His *Cornish Ballads*, and the *Quest of the Sangreal*, containing reprints of the same poems, came out in 1869. The *Quest of the Sangreal* was first published in 1864.

In 1870 he collected into a volume, entitled *Footprints of Former Men in Cornwall*, various papers on local traditions he had communicated to *Once a Week*, and other periodicals.

Of his ballads several have been given in this volume. Two more only are given here; one, "The Song of the Western Men," which deceived Sir Walter Scott and Lord Macaulay into the belief that it was a genuine ancient ballad.

Macaulay says, in speaking of the agitation which prevailed throughout the country during the trial of the seven bishops, of whom Trelawney, Bishop of

Bristol, was one, "The people of Cornwall, a fierce, bold and athletic race, among whom there was a stronger provincial feeling than in any other part of the realm, were greatly moved by the danger of Trelawney, whom they reverenced less as a ruler of the Church, than as the head of an honourable house, and the heir, through twenty descents, of ancestors who had been of great note before the Normans set foot on English ground. All over the country the peasants chanted a ballad, of which the burden is still remembered :—

And shall Trelawney die? and shall Trelawney die?
Then thirty thousand Cornish boys will know the reason why!

The miners from the caverns re-echoed the song with a variation :—

Then thirty thousand underground will know the reason why!

The refrain is ancient, but the poem itself was composed by Mr. Hawker. This is its earliest form: it afterwards underwent some revision.

THE SONG OF THE WESTERN MEN.

A good sword and a trusty hand,
  A merry heart and true,
King James's men shall understand
  What Cornish lads can do.
And have they fixed the where and when,
  And shall Trelawney die?
Then twenty thousand Cornish men
  Will know the reason why!
What! will they scorn Tre, Pol and Pen,
  And shall Trelawney die?
Then twenty thousand underground
  Will know the reason why!

Out spake the captain brave and bold,
    A merry wight was he:
"Though London's Tower were Michael's hold,
    We'll set Trelawney free.
We'll cross the Tamar hand to hand,
    The Exe shall be no stay;
We'll side by side, from strand to strand,
    And who shall bid us nay?
What! will they scorn Tre, Pol and Pen,
    And shall Trelawney die?
Then twenty thousand Cornish men
    Will know the reason why!

And when we come to London Wall,
    We'll shout with it in view,
"Come forth, come forth, ye cowards all!
    We're better men than you!
Trelawney, he's in keep and hold,
    Trelawney, he may die;
But here's twenty thousand Cornish bold
    Will know the reason why!"
What! will they scorn Tre, Pol and Pen,
    And shall Trelawney die?
Then twenty thousand underground
    Will know the reason why!

The other is a touching little ballad, the lament of a Cornish mother over her dead child; which well illustrates the sympathy which always welled up in the kind vicar's heart when he met with suffering or sorrow:—

    They say 'tis a sin to sorrow,
        That what God doth is best;
    But 'tis only a month to-morrow
        I buried it from my breast.

    I know it should be a pleasure
        Your child to God to send;

But mine was a precious treasure
   To me and to my poor friend.

I thought it would call me mother,
   The very first words it said:
Oh, I never can love another
   Like the blessed babe that's dead!

Well, God is its own dear Father;
   It was carried to church, and blessed;
And our Saviour's arms will gather
   Such children to their rest.

I will check this foolish sorrow,
   For what God doth is best;
But oh, 'tis a month to-morrow
   I buried it from my breast!

The following beautiful verses, of very high order of poetical merit, have not previously been published:—

A THOUGHT.

[30th Aug. 1866. Suggested by Gen. xviii. 1-3.]

A fair and stately scene of roof and walls
   Touched by the ruddy sunsets of the West,
Where, meek and molten, eve's soft radiance falls
   Like golden feathers in the ringdove's nest.

Yonder the bounding sea, that couch of God!
   A wavy wilderness of sand between;
Such pavement, in the Syrian deserts, trod
   Bright forms, in girded albs, of heavenly mien.

Such saw the patriarch in his noonday tent:
   Three severed shapes that glided in the sun,
Till, lo! they cling, and, interfused and blent,
   A lovely semblance gleams, the three in one!

> Be such the scenery of this peaceful ground,
>   This leafy tent amid the wilderness;
> Fair skies above, the breath of angels round,
>   And God the Trinity to beam and bless!

This poem was sent to an intimate friend with this letter:—

DEAR MRS. M——,—I record the foregoing thought for you, because it literally occurred to me as I looked from the windows of your house, across the sand towards the sea. Forgive the lines for the sake of their sincerity, etc. . . .

He wrote a poem of singular beauty on the auroral display of the night of 10th Nov. 1870, which was privately printed. In it he gave expression to the fancy, not original, but borrowed from Origen, or from North American Indian mythology, that the underworld of spirits is within this globe, and the door is at the North Pole, and the flashing of the lights is caused by the opening of the door to receive the dead. The following passage from his pen refers to the same idea:—

CHURCHYARDS.—The north side is included in the same consecration with the rest of the ground. All within the boundary, and the boundary itself, is alike hallowed in sacred and secular law. It is because of the doctrine of the Regions, which has descended unbrokenly in the Church, that an evil repute rests on the northern parts. The East, from whence the Son of Man came, and who will come again from the Orient to judgment, was, and is, his own especial realm. The dead lie with their feet and faces turned eastwardly, ready to stand up before the approaching Judge. The West was called the Galilee, the region of the people. The South, the home of the noonday, was the typical domain of heavenly things. But the North, the ill-omened North, was the peculiar haunt of evil spirits and the dark powers of the air. Satan's door stood in the north wall, opposite the font, and was duly opened at the exorcism in baptism for the egress of the fiend. When our Lord lay in the sepulchre, it was with feet towards the east, so that his right hand gave benediction to the South, and his left hand reproached and repelled the North. When the evil spirits were cast out by the voice of Messiah, they fled, ever more, northward. The god of the North was Baalzephon. They say that at the North Pole there stands the awful gate, which none may approach and live, and which leads to the central depths of penal life. R. S. H.

MORWENSTOW.

CHAPTER IX

Restoration of Morwenstow Church—The Shingle Roof—The First Ruridecanal Synod—The Weekly Offertory—Correspondence with Mr. Walter—On Alms—Harvest Thanksgiving—The School—Mr. Hawker belonged to no Party—His Eastern Proclivities—Theological Ideas—Baptism—Original Sin—His Preaching—Some Sermons.

THE church of Morwenstow was restored by Mr. Hawker in 1849; that is to say, he removed the pews that had been built about the old carved oak benches, pulled down the gallery, and put up a new pulpit, and made sundry other changes in the church.

The roof was covered with oak shingle in the most deplorable condition of decay. According to the description of a mason who went up the tower to survey it, "it looked, for all the world, like a wrecked ship thrown up on the shore."

Mr. Hawker was very anxious to have the roof reshingled, and this question was before the vestry during several years. The parish offered to give the church a roofing of the best Delabole slate, but the vicar stood out for shingle. The rate-payers protested against wasting their money on such a perishable material, but the vicar would not yield.

Vestry meeting after vestry meeting was called on this matter; one of the landowners remonstrated, but all in vain: Mr. Hawker remained unmoved; a shingle roof he would have, or none at all. A gentleman wrote to him, quoting a passage from Parker's *Glossary of Architecture* to show that anciently shingle roofs were put on only because more durable material was not available, and were removed when lead, slate or tiles were to be had. But Mr. Hawker remained unconvinced. "Our parson du stick to his maygaims," said the people shrugging their shoulders. He was very angry with the opposition to his shingle roof, and quarrelled with several of his parishioners about it.

He managed to collect money among his friends, and re-roofed the church, bit by bit, with oak shingle. But old shingle was made from heart of oak cut down in winter: the shingle he obtained was from oak cut in spring for barking, and therefore full of sap. The consequence was, that in a very few years it rotted, and let the water in as through a colander.

Enough money was thrown away on this roof to have put the whole church in thorough repair.

I pointed out to the vicar some years ago, when he was talking of repairing his church, that the stones in the arches and in the walls were of various sorts —some good building-stones, some rotten, some dark, some light—giving a patchwork appearance to the interior. I advised the removal of the poorer stones, and the insertion of better ones for the sake of uniformity. "No, never!" he answered. "The Church is built up of good and bad, of the feeble and the strong, the rich and the poor, the durable and the perishable. The material Church is a type of the Catholic Church, not the type of a sect."

In many ways Mr. Hawker was before his time, as in other ways he was centuries behind it.

He was the first to reinstitute ruridecanal synods which had fallen into disuse in Cornwall; and, when he was rural dean in 1844, he issued the following citation to all the clergy of the deanery of Trigg-Major:—

In obedience to the desire of many of the clergy, and with the full sanction of our Right Reverend Father in God, the lord bishop of this diocese, I propose, in these anxious days of the ecclesiate, to restore the ancient usuage of rural synods in the deanery of Trigg-Major. I accordingly convene you to appear, in your surplice, in my church of Morwenstow on the fifth day of March next ensuing, at eleven o'clock in the forenoon, then and there, after divine service, to deliberate with your brethren in chapter assembled. I remain, reverend sir, your faithful servant,

R. S. HAWKER,
The Rural Dean.

FEBRUARY, 1844.

Accordingly on 5th March, the clergy assembled in the vicarage, and walked in procession thence to the church in their surplices. The church was filled with the laity; the clergy were seated in the chancel. The altar was adorned with flowers and lighted candles. After service the laity withdrew, and the doors of the church were closed. The clergy then assembled in the nave, and the rural dean read them an elaborate and able statement of the case of rural chapters, after which they proceeded to business. His paper on Rural Synods was afterwards published by Edwards & Hughes, Ave Maria Lane, 1844.

It is remarkable that synods, which are now everywhere revived throughout the Church of England, meeting sometimes in vestries, sometimes in dining-rooms, were first restored, after the desuetude of three centuries, in the church of Morwenstow, and with so much gravity and dignity, over fifty years ago.

The importance of the weekly offertory is another thing now recognised. The Church seems to be preparing herself against possible disestablishment and disendowment, by reviving her organic life in synods, and by impressing on her people the necessity of giving towards the support of the services and the ministry. But the weekly offertory is quite a novelty in most places still. Almost the first incumbent in England to establish it was the vicar of Morwenstow, before 1843.

He entered into controversy on the subject of the offertory with Mr. Walter of *The Times*.

When the Poor Law Amendment Bill passed in 1834, and was amended in 1836 and 1838, it was thought by many that the need for an offertory in church was done away with, and that the giving of alms to the poor was an interference with the working of the Poor Law.

Mr. Hawker published a statement of what he did in this matter in *The English Churchman*, for 1844. Mr. Walter made this statement the basis of an attack on the system, and especially on Mr. Hawker, in a letter to *The Times*.

Mr. Hawker replied to this:—

SIR,—I regret to discover that you have permitted yourself to invade the tranquillity of my parish, and to endeavour to interrupt the harmony between myself and my parishioners, in a letter which I have just read in a recent number of *The Times*.

You have done so by a garbled copy of a statement which appeared in *The English Churchman*, of the reception and disposal of the offertory alms in the parish church of Morwenstow.

I say "garbled" because, while you have adduced just so much of the document as suited your purpose, you have suppressed such parts of it as might have tended to alleviate the hostility which many persons entertain to this part of the service of the Church.

With reference to our choice, as the recipients of Church money, of labourers whose " wages are seven shillings a week," and " who have a wife and four children to maintain thereon," you say, " Here is an excuse for the employer to give deficient wages ! "

In reply to this, I beg to inform you that the wages in this neighbourhood never fluctuate: they have continued at this fixed amount during the ten years of my incumbency. . . . Your argument, as applied to my parishioners, is this: Because they have scanty wages in that county, therefore they should have no alms; because these labourers of Morwenstow are restricted by the law from any relief from the rate, therefore they shall have no charity from the Church; because they have little, therefore they shall have no more. You insinuate that I, a Christian minister, think eight shillings a week sufficient for six persons during a winter's week, as though I were desirous to limit the resources of my poor parishioners to that sum. May God forgive you your miserable supposition ! I have all my life sincerely, and not to serve any party purpose, been an advocate of the cause of the poor. I, for many long years, have honestly, and not to promote political ends, denounced the unholy and cruel enactments of the New Poor Law. . . .

Let me now proceed to correct some transcendent misconceptions of yourself and others as to the nature and intent of the offertory in church. The ancient and modern division of all religious life was, and is, threefold—into devotion, self-denial and alms. No sacred practice, no Christian service, was or is complete without the union of these three. They were all alike and equally enjoined by the Saviour of man. The collection of alms was therefore incorporated in the Book of Common Prayer. But it was never held to be established among the services of the Church for the benefit of the poor alone: it was to enable the rich to enjoy the blessedness of almsgiving for their Redeemer's sake: it was to afford to every giver fixed and solemn opportunity to fulfil the remembrance, that whatsoever they did to the poor they did unto Him, and that the least of such their kindness would not be forgotten at the last day. "Let us wash," they said, "our Saviour's feet by alms". . . . But this practice of alms, whereunto the heavenly Head of the Church annexed a specific reward—this necessity, we are told, is become obsolete. A Christian duty become, by desuetude, obsolete! As well might a man infer that any other religious excellence ceased to be obligatory because it had been disused. The virtue of humility, for example, which has been so long in abeyance among certain of the laity, shall no longer, therefore, be a Christian grace! The blessing on the meek shall cease in 1844! . . . Voluntary kindness and alms have been rendered unnecessary by the compulsory payments enacted by the New Poor Law! As though the twenty-fifth chapter of St. Matthew had been repealed by Sir James Graham! As if one of the three conditions of our Christian covenant was to expire during the administration of Sir Robert Peel! . . .

And now, sir, I conclude with one or two parting admonitions to yourself. You are, I am told, an elderly man, fast approaching the end of all things, and, ere many years have passed, about to stand a separated soul among the awful mysteries of the spiritual world. I counsel you to beware, lest the remembrance of these attempts to diminish the pence of the poor, and to impede the charitable duties of the rich, should assuage your happiness in that abode where the strifes and the triumphs of controversy are unknown, "Because thou hast done this thing, and because thou hadst no pity". And lastly, I advise you not again to assail our rural parishes with such publications, to harass and unsettle the minds of our faithful people. We, the Cornish clergy, are a humble and undistinguished race; but we are apt, when unjustly assailed, to defend ourselves in straightforward language, and to utter plain admonitions, such as, on this occasion, I have thought it my duty to address to yourself; and I remain your obedient servant,

R. S. HAWKER.

Nov. 27, 1844.

Now there is scarcely a church in England in which a harvest thanksgiving service is not held. But probably the first to institute such a festival in the Anglican Church was the vicar of Morwenstow in 1843.

In that year he issued a notice to his parishioners to draw their attention to the duty of thanking God for the harvest, and of announcing that he would set apart a Sunday for such a purpose.

To the Parishioners of Morwenstow.

When the sacred Psalmist inquired what he should render unto the Lord for all the benefits that He had done unto him, he made answer to himself, and said: "I will receive the cup of salvation, and call upon the name of the Lord". Brethren, God has been very merciful to us this year also. He hath filled our garners with increase, and satisfied our poor with bread. He opened His hand, and filled all things living with plenteousness. Let us offer a sacrifice of thanksgiving among such as keep Holy Day. Let us gather together in the chancel of our church on the first Sunday of the next month, and there receive, in the bread of the new corn,[1] that blessed sacrament which was ordained to strengthen and refresh our souls. As it is written, "He rained down manna also upon them for to eat, and gave them food from heaven." And again, "In the hand of the Lord there is a cup, and the wine is red." Furthermore, let us remember, that, as a multitude of grains of wheat are mingled into one loaf, so we, being many, are intended to be joined together into one, in that holy sacrament of the Church of Jesus

---

[1] On 1st Oct., Lammas Day, the eucharistic bread was anciently made of the new corn of the recent harvest. This custom Mr. Hawker revived.

Christ. Brethren, on the first morning of October call to mind the word, that, wheresoever the body is, thither will the eagles be gathered together. "Let the people praise thee, O God, yea, let all the people praise thee! Then shall the earth bring forth her increase, and God, even our own God, shall give us His blessing. God shall bless us, and all the ends of the earth shall fear Him."

THE VICAR.

THE VICARAGE, MORWENSTOW, Sept. 13, 1843.

At much expense to himself he built and maintained a school in a central position in the parish. He called it St. Mark's School. It stands on a very exposed spot, and the site can hardly be considered as judiciously chosen. It is unnecessary here, it could hardly prove interesting, to quote numberless letters which I have before me, recounting his struggles to keep this school open, and obtain an efficient master for it. It was a great tax on his means, lightened, however, by the donations and subscriptions of landowners in the parish and personal friends towards the close of his life.

But in 1857 he wrote a letter to a friend, who has sent the letter to *The Rock*, from which I extract it.

It is said that Mr. Hawker is a very "eccentric" man. Now, I know not in what sense they may have intended the phrase, nor, in fact, what they wish to insinuate; so that I can hardly reply. If they mean to convey the ordinary force of the term, namely, a person out of the common, I am again at a loss. I wear a cassock, instead of a broadcloth coat, which is, I know, eccentric; but then, I have paid my parish school expenses for many years out of the difference between the usual clergyman's tailor's bill and my own cost in apparel; so that I do not, as they may have meant, feel ashamed or blush at such eccentricity. My mode of life, again, does differ from that of most of my clerical neighbours; for while they belong, some to one party in the Church and some to another, I have always lived aloof from them all, whether High or Low. And although there exist clerical clubs of both extremes in this deanery, and I have been invited to join by each, I never yet was present at a club meeting, dinner or a local synod. The time would fail me to recount the many modes and manners wherein I do differ from usual men. Be it enough that I am neither ashamed nor sorry for any domestic or parochial habit of life.

In 1845 he issued the following curious notice in reference to his daily prayer and his school :—

TAKE NOTICE.

The vicar will say Divine service henceforward every morning at ten and every evening at four. "Praised be the Lord daily, even the God that helpeth us, and poureth His benefits upon us" (Ps. lxviii. 19).

The vicar will attend at St. Mark's schoolroom every Friday at three o'clock, to catechise the scholars, and at the Sunday school at the usual hour. He will not from henceforth show the same kindness to those who keep back their children from school as he will to those who send them. "Thou shalt not seethe a kid in his mother's milk" (Exod. xxiii. 19).

Mr. Hawker was a High Churchman, but one of an original type, wholly distinct from the Tractarian of the first period, and the Ritualist of the second period, of the Catholic revival in the English Church. He never associated himself with any party. He did not read the controversial literature of his day, or interest himself in the persons of the ecclesiastical movement in the Anglican communion.

In November, 1861, he wrote :—

Dr. Bloxham was an ancient friend of mine (at Oxford). One of a large body of good and learned men, all now gone, and he only left. How I recollect their faces and words!

Newman, Pusey, Ward, Marriott—they used to be all in the common-room every evening, discussing, talking, reading. I remember the one to whom I did not take was Dr. Pusey. He never seemed simple in thought or speech; obscure and involved. He was the last in all that set—as I now look back and think—to have followers called by his name.

Mr. Hawker turned his eyes far more towards the Eastern Church than towards Rome. His mind was fired by Mr. Collins-Trelawney's *Peranzabuloe or the Lost Church Found*, the fourth edition of which appeared in 1839. It was an account of the ancient British chapel and cell of St. Piran, which had been swallowed up by the sands, but which was exhumed, and the bones of the saint, some ancient crosses, and early rude sculpture found. The author of the book drew a picture of the ancient British Church independent of Rome, having its own local peculiarities with regard to the observance of Easter, and the tonsure, etc., and argued that this church, which held aloof from St. Augustine, was of Oriental origin. He misunderstood the paschal question altogether, and his argument on that head falls to the ground when examined by the light which can be brought to bear on it from Irish sources. The ancient British, Scottish and Irish churches did not follow the Oriental rule with regard to the observance of Easter; but their calendar had got out of gear, and they objected to its revision.

However, the book convinced Mr. Hawker that he must look to the East for the ancestors of the Cornish Church, and not Rome-wards; and this view of the case lasted through his life, and coloured his opinions.

When Dr. J. Mason Neale's *History of the Holy Eastern Church* came out, he was intensely interested in it; and his Oriental fever reached its climax, and manifested itself in the adoption of a pink brimless hat, after the Eastern type. This Eastern craze also probably induced him, when he adopted a vestment, to put on a cope for the celebration of the holy communion; that vestment being used by the Armenian Church for the Divine Mysteries, whereas it is *never* so used in the Roman Church.

His theology assumed an Oriental tinge, and he expressed his views more as an Eastern than as a son of the West.

A few of his short notes of exposition on Holy Scripture have come into my hands, and I insert one or two of them as specimens of the poetical fancy which played round Gospel truths.

'Ο μεσίτης. A mediator is not one who prays. Christ's manhood is the intermediate thing which stands between the Trinity and man, to link and blend the natures human and Divine. It is the bridge between the place of exile and our native land. The presence of God the Son, standing with his wounds on the right hand of God the Father *is*, and constitutes, mediation.

His idea is that mediation is not intercession, but the serving as a channel of intercommunion between God and man. Thus there can be but one mediator, but every one may intercede for another. There can be no doubt that he was right.

His views with regard to baptism were peculiar. He seems to have retained a little of his grandfather's Calvinistic leaven in his soul, much as St.

Augustine's early Manichæism clung to him, and discoloured his later orthodoxy. The Catholic doctrine of the Fall is, that, by the first transgression of Adam, a discord entered into his constitution, so that thenceforth, soul and mind and body, instead of desiring what is good and salutary, are distracted by conflicting wishes, the flesh lusting against the spirit, and the mind approving that which is repugnant to the body. The object of the Incarnation is to restore harmony to the nature of man; and in baptism is infused into man a supernatural element of power for conciliating the three constituents of man. Fallen man is, according to Tridentine doctrine, a beautiful instrument whose strings are in discord; a chime

> Of sweet bells jangled, out of tune.

But he is provided with the Conciliator, with One whose note is so clear and true that he can raise the pitch of all his strings by that, and thus restore the lost music of the world.

Lutheran and Calvinistic teaching, however, are the reverse of this. According to the language of the "Formulary of Concord," man by the Fall has lost every element of good, even the smallest capacity and aptitude and power in spiritual things; he has lost the faculty of knowing God, and the will to do anything that is good; he can no more lead a good life than a stock or a stone; everything good in him is utterly obliterated. There is also a positive ingredient of sin infused into the veins of every man. Sin is, according to Luther, of the essence of man.

Original sin is not, as the Church teaches, the loss of supernatural grace co-ordinating man's faculties, and their consequent disorder; it is something born of the father and mother. The clay of which we are formed is damnable; the fœtus in the mother's womb is sin; man, with his whole nature and essence, is not only a sinner, but sin. Such are the expressions of Luther, indorsed by Carlstadt. Man, according to Catholic theology, still bears in him the image of God, but blurred. According to Melancthon, this image is wholly obliterated by an "intimate, most evil, most profound, inscrutable, ineffable corruption of our whole nature." Calvin clinches the matter by observing that from man's corrupted nature comes only what is damnable. "Man," says he, "has been so banished from the kingdom of God, that all in him that bears reference to the blessed life of the soul is extinct."[1] And if men have glimpses of better things, it is only that God may take from them every excuse when he damns them.[2]

Mr. Hawker by no means adopted the Catholic view of the Fall: the Protestant doctrine of the utter corruption and ruin of man's nature had been so deeply driven into his mind by his grandfather, that it never wholly worked itself out, and he never attained to the healthier view of human nature as a compound of good elements temporarily thrown in disarray.

This view of his appears in papers which are under my eye, as I write, and in his ballad for a cottage-wall, on Baptism.

[1] *Institutes*, lib. ii., c. 2, sect. 12. [2] *Ibid.*, sect. 18.

> Ah! woe is me! for I have no grace
>   Nor goodness as I ought:
> I never shall go to the happy place,
>   And 'tis all my parents' fault.

His teaching on the Eucharist he embodied in a ballad entitled "Ephphatha". An old blind man sits in a hall at Morwenstow, that of Tonacombe probably.

> He asks, and bread of wheat they bring;
> He thirsts for water from the spring
> Which flowed of old, and still flows on,
> With name and memory of St. John.

Bread and water are given him; and, through the stained windows, glorious rainbow tints fall over what is set before him. A page looking on him pities the old man, because—

> He eats, but sees not on that bread
> What glorious radiance there is shed;
> He drinks from out that chalice fair,
> Nor marks the sunlight glancing there.
>
> Watch! gentle Ronald, watch and pray!
> And hear once more an old man's lay:
> I cannot see the morning poured
> Ruddy and rich on this gay board;
> I may not trace the noonday light
> Wherewith my bread and bowl are bright;
> But thou, whose words are sooth, hast said
> That brightness falls on this fair bread;
> Thou sayest, and thy tones are true,
> This cup is tinged with heaven's own hue:
> I trust thy voice, I know from thee
> That which I cannot hear nor see.

The application of the parable is palpable. Mr. Hawker appended to the ballad the following note :—

I have sought in these verses to suggest a shadow of that beautiful instruction to Christian men, the actual and spiritual presence of our Lord in the second Sacrament of His Church; a primal and perpetual doctrine in the faith once delivered to the saints. How sadly the simplicity of this hath and has been distorted and disturbed by the gross and sensuous notion of a carnal presence, introduced by the Romish innovation of the eleventh century![1]

The following passage occurs in one of his sermons :—

If there be anything in all the earth to which our Lord did join a blessing, and that for evermore, it was the bread and the cup. Surely of this Sacrament, which the apostles served, it may be said, He that receiveth you receiveth Me. Now, nothing can be more certain than that our Lord and Master, before He suffered death, called into His presence the twelve men, the *equal* founders of His future Church. He stood alone with the twelve. There was nobody else there but those ministers and their Lord. Nothing is more manifest than that He took bread of corn, and showed the apostles in what manner and with what words to bless and to break it. Equally clear is it, that their Lord took into His hands, with remarkable gesture and deed, the cup, and taught the twelve also the blessing of the wine. Accordingly, after the Son of man went up, we read that the apostles took bread, and blessed, and gave it to the Church. Likewise also they took the cup.

And, although the Romish Dissenters keep it back to this day, the apostles gave the wine also to the people. St. Paul, who was not one of the twelve, but a bishop afterwards ordained, writes : "We have an altar". He speaks of the bread which he breaks, and the cup he was accustomed to bless. So we trace from those old apostolic days, down to our own, an

[1] Note in *Ecclesia*, 1841.

altar-table of wood in remembrance of the wooden cross, fine white bread, good and wholesome wine, a ministry descended **from the** apostles, to be in all ages and in every land the outward and visible signs of a great event—the eternal sacrifice of Jesus Christ our Lord.

Now, nothing can be more plain than that these things, so seen, and handled, and felt, and eaten, and drunk, were delivered to the Church to contain and to convey a deep blessing, an actual grace. They were ordained for this end by Christ Himself: He said of the bread, This is My body; *i.e.*, not a part of My flesh, but a portion of My spiritual presence, a share of that which is Divine.

Again, Jesus said about the cup, This is My blood; *i.e.*, not that which gushed upon the soldier's spear, but the life-blood **of** My heavenly heart, **that which shall be** shed on you from on high with the fruit of the vine—the produce of the everlasting veins of Him who is **on** the right hand of God.

So was it understood, **so** is it explained, by apostolic words. Thus said St. Paul, "The cup of blessing which we bless, is it not the communion—the common reception, that is—the communication to faithful lips of the blood of Christ?"

So we say in our Catechism, that the body and blood of Christ are verily and indeed taken and received. We confess that our souls are strengthened and refreshed in the Sacrament of the body and blood of Christ: we call the bread and wine in **our service heavenly food. We** acknowledge that we spiritually **eat** the flesh of Christ, and drink His blood. We declare that in that Sacrament we join Him, and He us, as drops of water that mingle in the sea, and that we are, in that awful hour, very members incorporate in the mystical body of the Son of God, —words well-nigh too deep to apprehend **or** to explain.

Mr. Hawker, holding, as has been shown, that mediation was distinct from intercession, admitted that the dead in Christ could pray for their brethren struggling in the warfare of life, as really and more effectually than they could when living. If the souls under the altar seen by St. John could cry out for vengeance on those upon earth, surely they could also ask for mercy to be shown them.

He thought that all the baptised had six sponsors, the three on earth and three in heaven. Those in heaven were the guardian angel of the child, the saint whose name the child bore, and the saint to whom the church was dedicated in which the baptism took place; and that, as it was the duty of earthly sponsors to look after and pray for their godchildren, so it was the privilege and pleasure of their heavenly patrons to watch and intercede for their welfare.

He did not see why Christians should not ask the prayers of those in bliss, as well as the prayers of those in contest; and he contended that this was a very different matter from Romish invocation of saints, that invested the blessed ones with all but Divine attributes, and which he utterly repudiated. He quoted Latimer, Bishop Montague, Thorndike, Bishop Forbes, in the seventeenth century; and Dean Field, and Morton, Bishop of Durham, etc., as holding precisely the same view as himself.

Of course his doctrines to some seem to be perilously high. But in the English Church there are various shades of dogmatism, and the faintest tinge to one whose views are colourless is a great advance. The slug at the bottom of the cabbage-stalk thinks the slug an inch up the stalk very high, and the slug on the stalk regards the slug on the leaf as perilously advanced, whilst the slug on the leaf considers the snail on the leaf-end as occupying an equivocal position.

Catholicism and Popery have really nothing necessarily in common. The first is a system of belief founded on the Incarnation, the advantages of which it applies to man through a sacramental system; while the latter is a system of ecclesiastical organisation, which has only accidentally been linked with Catholicism, but which is equally at home in the steppes of Tartary with Buddhism.

Popery is a centralisation in matter of Church **government:** it is autocracy. A man **may** be theoretically an Ultramontane without being even a Christian, for he may believe in a despotism. And a man may be **a Catholic in all** his views, **without** having the smallest sympathy with Popery. As a matter of fact, the most advanced men in the English Church are radically liberal in their views of Church government; and if they **strive** with one hand to restore forgotten doctrines, and reinstate public worship, with the other they do battle for the introduction of Constitutionalism into the organisation of the Church of England, the element of all others most opposed to Popery.

It is quite possible to distinguish Catholicism from Romanism. Romanism has developed a system—a miserable system of indulgences and dispensations on one side, and restraints on the other—all issuing from the throne of St. Peter, as an impure flood from a corrupt fountain, and which has sadly injured Christian morals. A student of history cannot fail to notice that the Papacy has been a blight on Christianity, robbing it of its regenerating and reforming **power, a** parasitic growth draining it of its life-blood,

He may love, with every fibre of his soul, the great sacramental system, the glorious Catholic verities, common to Constantinople and Rome, to Jerusalem and Moscow; but it is only to make him bitterly regret that they have been used as a vehicle for Romish cupidity, so as to make them odious in the eyes of Protestants. Holding Catholic doctrines, and enjoying Catholic practices, an English Churchman may be as far removed in temper of soul from Rome as any Irish Orangeman.

Mr. Hawker held the Blessed Virgin in great reverence. The ideal of womanhood touched his poetical instincts. Yet he checked his exuberant fancy, when dealing with this theme, by his conscience of what was right and fitting. He says, in a sermon on the text: "He stretched forth His hand towards His disciples, and said, Behold My mother and My brethren; for whosoever shall do the will of God, the same is My brother and sister and mother:" "His mother also, whom the angel had pronounced blessed among women, because on her knees the future Christ should lie, sought to usurp the influence of nature over the Son Divine. But to teach that although in the earth He was not all of the earth, and aware of the blind idolatry which future men would yield unto her who bare Him, and those to whom His Incarnation in their family gave superior name, Jesus publicly renounced all domestic claim to His particular regard. More than once did He remind Mary, His mother, that in His miraculous nature she did not partake; that in the functions of His Godhead she had nothing to do with him."

The Rev. W. Valentine, rector of Whixley, perhaps the most intimate friend Mr. Hawker had, writes to me of him thus:—

During the first six months of my residence at Chapel House, Morwenstow, September, 1863, to April, 1864, I and he invariably spent our evenings together; and although for ten weeks of that period I took the Sunday morning and evening duties at Stratton Church, during the illness of the vicar, I always rode round by Morwenstow vicarage on Sundays to spend an hour with him, at his urgent request, though it took me some miles out of my way over Stowe Hill and by Combe. I thus got to know Mr. Hawker thoroughly, more intimately perhaps, as to character and social habits, than any other friend ever did; and on two important points no one will ever shake my testimony, viz. (a) his desire to be buried by me beneath the shadow of his own beloved church, "That grey fane, the beacon of the Eternal Land"; and (b) his constant allusions to the Roman Catholics as "Romish Dissenters".

But Mr. Hawker was not a theologian, nor was he careful in the expression of his opinions. He spoke as he thought at the moment, and he thought as the impulse swayed him. Many of his most intimate friends, who met him constantly during the last years of his life, and to whom he opened his heart most fully, are firm in their conviction that he was a sincere member of the Church of England, believing thoroughly in her Divine mission and authority. But it is quite possible, that, in moments of excitement and disappointment, to others he may have expressed himself otherwise. He was the creature of impulse; and his mind was never very evenly balanced, nor did his judgment always reign paramount over his fancies.

Mr. Valentine writes in another letter to me:—

I have only one sermon to send you, but to *me* it is a deeply interesting one, as it was delivered more than once just over the spot where he told me so often to lay him; and I feel assured that whenever he preached it, his thoughts would wander onward to that coming day when he himself, as he contemplated, would form one of that last and vast assemblage which will be gathered in Morwenstow churchyard and church. Ever since I knew dear old Hawker, and for years before, he preached *extempore*. His habit was to take a prayer-book into the pulpit, and expound the Gospel for the day. He would read a verse or two, and then with a common lead pencil, which was ever suspended by a string from one of his coat-buttons, mark his resting-point. Having expounded the passage, he would read further, mark again, and expound. His clear, full voice was most mellifluous; and his language, whilst plain and homely, was highly poetical, and quite enchanting to listen to. He riveted one's whole attention. His pulpit MSS. are very rare, because, just before taking to *extempore* preaching, "basketsful" of his sermons were destroyed under the following circumstances, as he used to relate it to me: A celebrated firm of seedsmen advertised something remarkable in the way of carrots; and Mr. Hawker, who had long made this root his especial study, sent for some seed. He was recommended to sow it with some of the best ashes he could procure, and therefore brought out all his sermons one morning on to the vicarage lawn, set fire to the pile, and carefully collected the precious remains. The crop was an utter failure; but the cause thereof, on reflection was most palpable. He remembered that a few of old Dr. Hawker's sermons were lying amongst his own; and the conclusion forced upon him was, that his grandfather's heterodoxy had lost him his crop of carrots.

He refers to this destruction in another letter to Mr. Carnsew:—

DEC. 6, 1857. *My dear Sir*,—To-morrow I send for my last load of materials for building, the close of a long run of outlay extending through nearly thirty years. Bude, Whitstone, Trebarrow, Morwenstow, have been the scenes of my architecture. Anderson writes that he has bought a cottage of yours. I am glad of it for his wife's sake. I wrote to him offering a young pig of mine, and twelve MS. sermons, for a young boar of the same age; and, do you know, he has taken me at my word. So I am to send him my MSS. and to fetch the boar. Did I ever tell you that I once dressed a drill of turnips for experiment with sermon ashes (I had been burning a large lot), and it was a complete failure? Barren, all barren, like most modern discourses; not even posthumous energy.

The sermon that is spoken of by Mr. Valentine was on the general resurrection, and was preached at the "Revel," Midsummer Day.

The Revel or Village Feast is—in some places was—a great institution in Cornwall and West Devon, held on the day of the Saint to whom the church is dedicated.

One of his sermons which is remembered to this day was on the text, Gen. xxii. 5: "Abide ye here with the ass; and I and the lad will go yonder and worship, and come again to you."

He pointed out in this sermon how that in Morwenstow and many other villages, the church is situated at some distance from the congregation. At Okehampton the church is on a hill, and the town lies below it in the valley. At Brent-tor it is planted on the apex of a volcanic cone, rising out of a high table-land; and the cottages of which it is the parish church lie in combes far away, skirting the moor. At Morwenstow it stands above the sea, without a house near it save the vicarage and one little farm. This, said he, was no bit of mismanagement, but was done purposely, that those who went up to Jerusalem to worship might have time to compose their thoughts, and frame their souls aright for the holy services in which they were about to engage.

Is it a trouble to go so far? Does it cost many paces? Yea! but an angel counts the paces that lead to the house of God and records them all in heaven.

"Abide ye here with the ass," away from the hill of the Lord, from the place of sacrifice; tarry, dumb ass and hireling, whilst the son goes on under the guidance of his father. The poor hireling, not one of the family; the unbaptised, no son; and the coarse, brutal nature, the ass—they stay away; they have no inclination, no call to go up to the house of God. "Abide ye here with the ass; and I and the lad will go yonder and worship."

CHAPTER X

The First Mrs. Hawker—Her Influence over her Husband—Anxiety about her Health—His Fits of Depression—Letter on the Death of Sir Thomas D. Acland—Reads Novels to his Wife—His Visions—Mysticism—Death of his Wife—Unhappy Condition—Burning of his Papers—Meets with his Second Wife—The Unburied Dead—Birth of his Child—Ruinous Condition of his Church—Goes to London—Sickness—Goes to Boscastle—To Plymouth—His Death and Funeral—Conclusion.

MRS. HAWKER was a very accomplished and charming old lady, who thoroughly understood and appreciated her husband. She was a woman of a poetical, refined mind, with strong sense of humour, and sound judgment. The latter quality was of great advantage, as it was an element conspicuously absent in the composition of her husband.

She translated from the German, with great elegance, the story of Guido Goerres, the *Manger of the Holy Night;* and it was published by Burns in 1847. The verses in it were turned with grace and facility. Another of her books was *Follow Me*, a Morality from the German, published by Burns in 1844.

The author remembers this charming old lady now many years ago, then blind, very aged, with hair white as snow, full of cheerfulness and geniality, laughing over her husband's jokes, and drawing him out with a subtle skill to show himself to his best advantage. In his fits of depression she was invaluable to him, always at his side, encouraging him, directing his thoughts to pleasant topics, and bringing merriment back to the eye which had dulled with despondency.

ASH WEDNESDAY, 1853. *My dear Mrs. M.——,* — Among my acts of self-research to-day one has regarded you, the wife of one of the very few whom I would really call my friends. Since my days of sorrow came, and self-abasement, I have shrunk too much into myself, and too much regarded the breath that is in the nostrils of my fellows. But what have I not been made to suffer? But—and I have sworn it as a vow —if my God grants me the life of poor dear Charlotte, all shall be borne cheerfully. Beyond that horizon I have not a hope, a thought, a prayer. And now I feel relieved at having written this. It lifts a load to tell it to you, as I should long ago to your guileless husband had he been here to listen. But he is gone to be happier than we, and would wonder, if he read this, why I grieve. And then how basely have those who vaunted themselves as my friends dealt with me! All this I unfold to you for my relief. Do you please not to say a word about . . . or anything to vex or harass Charlotte. She is, I thank God, well and quiet. We hardly ever go out, save for exercise, in the parish. My thoughts go down in MS., of which I have drawers full. But I print no more.

The friend to whose widow he thus writes died in 1846. He then wrote to a relative this note of sympathy :—

Your letter has filled us with deep and sincere sorrow. We feared that our friend was sincerely ill, but we were not prepared for so immediate an accession of grief. That he was ready to be dissolved, I doubt not, and to be with Christ I am equally satisfied. He, already, I trust, prays for us all effectually.

There was ever a sad undertone in Mr. Hawker's character. He felt his isolation in mind from all around him. His best companions were the waves and clouds. He lived "the ever alone," as he calls himself in one of his letters, solitary in the Morwenstow ark, with only the sound of waters about him. "The Lord shut him in."

With all his brightness and vivacity, there was constantly "cropping up" a sad and serious vein, which showed itself sometimes in a curious fashion. "This is as life seems to you," he would say, as he bade his visitor look at the prospect through a pane of ruby-tinted glass, "all glowing and hopeful. And this is as I see it," he would add, turning to a pane of yellow, "grey and wintry and faded. But keep your ruby days as long as you can."

He wrote on 2nd Jan., 1868:—

Wheresoever you may be, this letter will follow you, and with it our best and most earnest prayers for your increased welfare of earthly and heavenly hopes in this and many succeeding New Years. How solemn a thing it is to stand before the gate of another year, and ask the oracles what will this ensuing cluster of the months unfold! But, if we knew, perhaps it would make life what a Pagan Greek called it, "a shuddering thing." We have had, through the approach to us of the Gulf Stream, with its atmospheric arch of warm and rarefied air, a sad succession of cyclones, or, as our homely phrase renders it, "shattering sou'westers," reminding us of what was said to be the Cornish wreckers' toast in bygone days:—

"A billowy sea and a shattering wind,
The cliffs before, and the gale behind,"

but, thank God, no wrecks yet on our iron shore.

The following letter was written to Mrs. Mills, daughter of Sir Thomas D. Acland, on the death of her father; a letter which will touch the hearts of many a "West Country man" who has loved his honoured name.

MORWENSTOW, July 27, 1861. *My dear Mrs. Mills,*—The knowledge of your great anguish at Killerton has only just reached us. How deeply we feel it, I need not tell: although long looked for, it smote me like a sudden blow. Yet we must not mourn "for him, but for ourselves and our children." "It shall come to pass, at eventide there shall be light." The good and faithful servant had borne the burden and the heat of the day; and at set of sun he laid him down and slept. My heart and my eyes are too full to write. May his God and our God bless and sustain yours and you! My poor dear wife, who is ill, offers you her faithful love; and I shall pray this night for him who is gone before, and for those who tarry yet a little while. I am, dear Mrs. Mills, yours faithfully and affectionately,

R. S. HAWKER.

During his wife's blindness and the gentle fading away of a well-spent, God-fearing life, nothing could be more unremitting than the attention of Mr. Hawker. He read to her a great part of the day, brought her all the news of the neighbourhood, strove in every way to make up to her for the deprivation of her sight.

He had a ten-guinea subscription to Mudie's Library, and whole boxes of novels arrived at the vicarage; these he diligently read to her as she sat, her arm-chair wheeled to the window out of which she could no more see, or by the fireside where the logs flickered.

But though he read with his lips and followed with

his eyes, his eager mind was far away in that wondrous dreamland where his mental life was spent. After he had diligently read through the three volumes of some popular novel, he was found to be ignorant of the plot, to know nothing of the characters, and to have no conception even of the names of hero and heroine. These stories interested him in no way: they related to a world of which he knew little, and cared less. Whilst he read, his mind was following some mystic weaving of a dance, in the air, of gulls and swallows; tracing parables in the flowers that dotted his sward; or musing over some text of Holy Scripture. To be on the face of his cliff, to sit hour by hour in his little hut of wreck-wood, with the boiling Atlantic before him, sunk in dream or meditation, was his delight. Or, kneeling in his gloomy chancel, poring over the sacred page, meditating, he would go off into strange trances, and see sights: Morwenna, gleaming before him with pale face, exquisitely beautiful, and golden hair, and deep blue eyes, telling him where she lay, drawing him on to chivalrous love, like Aslauga in Fouqué's exquisite tale. Or, he saw angels ascending and descending in his dark chancel, and heard "a noise of hymns."

>A gentle sound, an awful light!
>   Three angels bear the holy Grail.
>With folded feet, in stoles of white,
>   On sleeping wings they sail.
>
>Ah, blessed vision! blood of God!
>   My spirit beats her mortal bars,
>As down dark tides the glory slides,
>   And star-like mingles with the stars.

We have seen hitherto the sparkling merriment of his life; but this was the surging of the surface of a character that rolled on its mysterious, unfathomable way.

To him the spiritual world was intensely real: he had in him the makings of a mystic. The outward world, the carnal flesh, he looked upon with contempt, with almost the disgust of a Manichæan. The spiritual life was the real life: the earthly career was a passing, troubled dream, that teased the soul, and broke its contemplations. The true aim of man was to disentangle his soul from the sordid cares of earth, and to raise it on the wings of meditation and prayer to union with God. Consequently the true self is the spiritual man: this none but the spiritual man can understand. The vicar accommodated himself to ordinary society, but he did not belong to it. His spirit hovered high above in the thin, clear air, whilst his body and earthly mind laughed, and joked, and laboured, and sorrowed below. Trouble was the anguish of the soul recalling its prerogative. The fits of depression which came on him were the moments when the soul was asserting its true power, pining as the captive for its home and proper freedom.

It will be seen that nothing but his intense grasp of the doctrine of the Incarnation saved him from drifting into the wildest vagaries of mysticism.

He would never open out to any one who he thought was not spiritually minded.

A commonplace neighbouring parson, visiting him once, asked him what were his views and opinions.

Mr. Hawker drew him to the window. "There," said he, "is Hennacliff, there the Atlantic stretching to Labrador, there Morwenstow crag, here the church and graves: these are my views. As to my opinions, I keep them to myself."

The flame, after long flickering in the breast of his dearly loved wife, went out at length on 2nd Feb., 1863. She died at the age of eighty-one.

He had a grave—a double grave—made outside the chancel, beside the stone that marks where an ancient priest of Morwenstow lies, and placed over her a stone with this inscription:—

<blockquote>
HERE RESTS THE BODY OF

CHARLOTTE E. HAWKER,

FOR NEARLY FORTY YEARS THE WIFE OF ONE OF THE VICARS OF THIS CHURCH.

SHE DIED FEB. 2, 1863.

There is sprung up a light for the righteous, and joyful gladness for such as are true-hearted.
</blockquote>

The text had reference to her blindness.

At the bottom of the stone is a blank space left for his own name, and a place was made by his own orders at the side of his wife for his own body.

MORWENSTOW, Oct. 16, 1864. *My dear Mrs. M——*, — I have intended every day to make an effort, and go down to Bude to see you, and to thank you for all your kindness to me in my desolate abode; but I am quite unequal to the attempt. If you return next year, and you will come, you will find me, if I am alive, keeping watch and ward humbly and faithfully by the place where my dead wife still wears her ring in our quiet church. If I am gone, I know you will come and stand by the stone where we rest. My kindest love to Mr. M—— and your happy little children.

After the death of Mrs. Hawker, he fell into a condition of piteous depression. He moped about the cliffs, or in his study, and lost interest in everything. Sciatica added to his misery; and to relieve this he had recourse to opium.

He took it into his head that he could eat nothing but clotted cream. He therefore made his meals, breakfast, dinner and tea, of this. He became consequently exceedingly bilious, and his depression grew the greater.

He was sitting, crying like a child, one night over his papers, when there shot a spark from the fire among those strewn at his feet. He did not notice it particularly, but went to bed. After he had gone to sleep, his papers were in a flame: the flame communicated itself to a drawer full of MSS., which he had pulled out, and not thrust into its place again; and the house would probably have been burnt down, had not a Methodist minister seen the blaze through the window, as he happened to be on the hill opposite. He gave the alarm, the inmates of the vicarage were aroused, and the fire was arrested.

Probably much of his MS. poetry, and jottings of ideas passing through his head, were thus lost. "Oh, dear!" was his sad cry, "if Charlotte had been here this would never have happened."

The vicar had brain fever shortly afterwards, and was in danger; but he gradually recovered.

A friend tells me that during the time that he was a widower, the condition he was in was most sad. His drawing-room, which used to be his delight, full of old oak furniture, and curiosities from every corner

MORWENSTOW PARISH CHURCH.

ANCIENT FONT IN MORWENSTOW CHURCH.

"PARSON HAWKER," OF MORWENSTOW.

THE CHURCH AND VICARAGE, MORWENSTOW.

of the world, was undusted and neglected. The servants, no longer controlled by a mistress, probably did not attend properly to the comforts of the master.

However, a new interest grew up in his heart. It was fortunate that matters did not remain long in this condition. It was neither well nor wise that the old man should linger on the rest of his days without a "helpmeet for him," to attend to his comforts, be a companion in his solitude, and a solace in his fits of depression. The Eastern Church is very strong against the second marriage of priests. No man who has had a second wife is admitted by the orthodox communion to holy orders But Mr. Hawker was about, and very fortunately for his own comfort, in this matter to shake off the trammels of his Orientalism.

Previous to the death of his first wife, he had some good stories to tell of men, who, when the first wife was dead, forgot her speedily for a second. One belongs to the Cornish moors, and may therefore be here inserted.

A traveller was on his way over the great dorsal moorland that runs the length of Cornwall. He had lost his way. It was a time of autumn equinoctial storm. The day declined, and nothing was to be seen save sweeps of moor, broken only by huge masses of granite; not a church tower broke the horizon, not a dog barked from a distant farm.

After long and despairing wanderings in search of a road or house, the traveller was about to proceed to a pile of granite, and bury himself among the rocks for shelter during the night, when a sudden burst of revelry smote his ear from the other side of the hill. He hasted with beating heart in the direction whence came the sounds, and soon found a solitary house, in which all the inhabitants were making merry. He asked admission and a lodging for the night. He was invited in, and given a hearty welcome. The owner of the house had just been married, and brought home his bride. The house, therefore, could furnish him with plenty of food; saffron cakes abounded: but a bed was not to be had, as brothers and cousins had been invited, and the only place where the traveller could be accommodated was a garret. This was better than a bed on the moor, and the stormy sky for the roof; and he accepted the offer with eagerness.

After the festivities of the evening were over, he retired to his attic, and lay down on a bed of hay, shaken for him on the floor. But he could not sleep. The moon shone in through a pane of glass let into the roof, and rested on a curious old chest which was thrust away in a corner. Somehow or other, this chest engrossed his attention, and excited his imagination. It was of carved oak, and handsome. Why was it put away in a garret? What did it contain? He became agitated and nervous. He thought he heard a sigh issue from it. He sat up on the hay, and trembled. Still the moonbeam streaked the long black box.

Again his excited fancy made him believe he heard a sigh issue from it. Unable to endure suspense any longer, he stole across the floor to the side of the garret where stood the box, and with trembling hand he raised the lid. The moonbeam fell on the face of a dead woman, lying in her winding-sheet in the chest. He let the lid drop with a scream of fear, and fainted away. When he came to himself, the bride and bridegroom, brothers and cousins, surrounded him in the attic, in somewhat *dégagé* costume, as they had tumbled from their beds, in alarm at the shriek which had awakened them.

"What is it? What have you seen?" was asked on all sides.

"In that chest," gasped the traveller, "I saw a corpse!"

There was a pause. Slowly—for the mind of an agriculturist takes time to act — the bridegroom arrived at a satisfactory explanation. His face remained for three minutes clouded with thought, as he opened and explored the various chambers of memory. At length a gleam of satisfaction illumed his countenance, and he broke into a laugh and an explanation at once. "Lor', you needn't trouble yourself: its only my first wife as died last Christmas. You see, the moors were covered with snow, and the land frozen, so we couldn't take her to be buried at Camelford, and accordingly *we salted her in* till the thaw shu'd come; *and I'm darned if I hadn't forgotten all about her*, and the old gal's never been buried yet."

"So, you see," Mr. Hawker would say, when telling the story, "in Cornwall we do things differently from elsewhere. It is on record that the second wife is wedded before the first wife is buried."

There is a Devonshire version of this story told

of Dartmoor; but it wants the point of the Cornish tale.

The Rev. W. Valentine, vicar of Whixley in Yorkshire, bought Chapel House, in the parish, in the October of 1863, and, having obtained two years' leave of absence from the Bishop of Ripon, came there into residence. He brought with him, as governess to his children, a young Polish lady, Miss Kuczynski. Her father had been a Polish noble, educated at the Jesuit University of Wilna, who, having been mixed up with one of the periodical revolts against Russian domination, had been obliged to fly his native country and take refuge in England. He received a pension from the British Government, and office under the Master of the Rolls. He married a Miss Newton, and by her had two children, Stanislaus and Pauline.

On the death of Count Kuczynski, his widow married a Mr. Stevens, an American merchant. He lost greatly by the war between the Northern and Southern States, and Miss Kuczynski was obliged to enter the family of an English clergyman as governess to his children.

Mr. Hawker, as vicar of the parish in which Chapel stands, made the acquaintance of this lady of birth and education. A sunbeam shone into his dark, troubled life, and lighted it with hope. He was married to her in December, 1864, " by a concurrence of events manifestly providential," he wrote to a dear friend. " Her first position was in the family of Mr. Valentine, who so recently arrived in my parish of Morwenstow. There I saw and understood her character; but it was not her graceful **person and winning demeanour** that **so** impressed me, as her strong intellect, high principle and similitude **of** tastes with my own. **She** won **my** people before she won me; and it was a saying among my simple-hearted parishioners: 'Oh, if Miss Kuczynski would but be mistress **at** vicarage!' Her friends, as was natural, objected to the marriage; but I went to town, saw them, and returned hither Pauline's husband."

His marriage had a good effect on him **immediately.** He for a time gave up opium-eating. His spirits rose, and he seemed to be entirely, supremely happy.

In November, 1865, he **was given a daughter, to** be the light and joy of his eyes. **He says in a letter** dated 30th Nov., 1865:—

> **The kind interest you have taken in us** induces me to think **that you may be glad** to hear, that, just before **midnight on Monday, I was** given a daughter—a fair and gentle child, who **has not up to** this time uttered a single peevish sound. As is very natural, **I think her** one of the loveliest infants I ever took **in my** arms. **Both child and** mother **are going** on very well, **and the** happiness which **the** event has **brought to** my house is indeed a blessing. **The baby's name is to be** Morwenna Pauline.

A second daughter was afterwards given to him, Rosalind; and then a third, who was baptised Juliot, after a sister of St. Morwenna, who had **a cell and** founded a church near Boscastle. The arrival of these heaven-given treasures, however, filled the old man's mind with anxiety for the future. The earth **must** soon close over him; and he would leave a widow and three helpless orphans on the world, without being able to make any provision for them. This preyed on his mind during the last year or two of his life. It was a cloud which hung over him, and never was lifted off. As he walked, he moaned to himself. He saw no possibility of securing them a future of comfort and a home. He could not shake the thought off him: it haunted him day and night.

His church also was fallen into a piteous condition of disrepair: the wooden shingle wherewith he had roofed it some years before was rotten, and let in the water in streams. The pillars were green with lichen, the side of the tower bulged, and discoloured water oozed forth. A portion of the plaster of the ceiling fell; storms tore out the glass of his windows.

In 1872 he sent forth the following appeal to all his friends:—

Jesus said: "Ye have done it unto me!"

The ancient church of Morwenstow, on the northern shore of Cornwall, notwithstanding a large outlay of the present vicar, has fallen into dilapidation and disrepair. A great part of the oak shingle roof requires to be relaid. The walls must be painted anew, and the windows, benches and floor ought to be restored. To fulfil all these purposes, a sum amounting to at least £500 will be required. In the existing state of the Church-rate law, it would be inexpedient and ineffectual to rely on the local succour of the parishioners, although there is reason to confide that the usual levy of a penny in the pound per annum (sixteen pounds), now granted in aid of other resources, would never be withheld. But this church, from the interest attached to its extreme antiquity and its striking features of ecclesiastical attraction, is visited every year by one or two hundred strangers from distant places, and from Bude Haven in the immediate neighbourhood. It appears, therefore, to the vicar and his friends, that an appeal for the sympathy and the succour of all who value and appreciate the **solemn** beauty and the sacred associations of such **a scene** might happily be fraught with success. A committee, **to consist** of the vicar and churchwardens, **of** J. Tarratt, Esq., late of Chapel House, Morwenstow, and W. Rowe, Esq., solicitor, Stratton, will superintend the disposal of the contributions, under the control of **a** competent builder, and account to the subscribers for their outlay.

And the benediction of God the Trinity will assuredly requite every kindly heart and generous hand that shall help to restore this venerable sanctuary of the Tamar side.

A voluntary rate raised £32 ; and offertory, £2 2s. 10½d.; and he had donations **of** about £150 **from** various friends.

In 1874 he went to London for his health. He was very much broken then, suffering in his heart and from sciatica. At the same time he resolved to preach in such churches as were open to him, for the restoration fund of St. Morwenna's sanctuary.

He wrote to me on the subject :—

16 HARLEY ROAD, SOUTH HAMPSTEAD, April **20**, 1874. *My dear Sir,*—I am here in quest of medical aid for my wife and myself. I am so far better that I can preach, and I **am** trying to get offertories here for the restoration of my grand old Morwenstow Church. Only one has been granted me thus far—last night at St. Matthias, Brompton, where I won an evening offertory " with my sword and with my bow," twenty-two pounds eighteen shillings, whereas the average for **two** years at evensong has been under five pounds. But I find the great clergy shy to render me the loan of their pulpits. Do you know any one of them ? Can you help me ? And about St. Morwenna. Cannot **I see** your proof sheets of my *Saint's Life*, or can you in any way help me in the delivery of her legend to London ears ? At all events, do write. I seem

nearer to you here than at home. If you come up, do find us out. I write in haste.

Yours faithfully,
R. S. HAWKER.

The previous October he had written to me from his "sick-room, to which I have been confined with eczema for full two months." In November he wrote: "Ten days in bed helpless." I had been in correspondence with him about St. Morwenna *not* being identical with St. Modwenna; his answer was: "I have twice received supernatural intimation of her identity, by dream and suggestion." Such an answer was clearly not that of a man of well-balanced mind.

16 HARLEY ROAD, HAMPSTEAD, March 10, 1874. *My dear Mrs. M——*,—You may well be astonished at my address; but our journey hither was a matter of life or death to both of us, and so far I am the only gainer. Dr. Goodfellow, after a rigid scrutiny, has pronounced me free from any perilous organic disease, and is of opinion that with rest and a few simple remedies, "there is work in me yet". . . .

Yours faithfully,
R. S. HAWKER.

But the grand old man was breaking. There was pain of body, and much mental anxiety about his family. He could not sleep at night: his brain was constantly excited by his pecuniary troubles, and the sufferings he endured from his malady. By the advice of his doctor, I believe, it was that he had recourse to narcotics to allay the pain, and procure him rest at night. Mr. C. Hawker wrote to me:—

Towards the close of his life, my brother (I am grieved to state it) renewed a habit he had contracted on the death of his first wife, but had abandoned—of taking opium. This had a most injurious effect on his nerves: it violently excited him for a while, and then cast him into fits of the most profound depression. When under this influence he wrote and spoke in the wildest and most unreasonable manner, and said things which in moments of calmer judgment, I am sure, he bitterly deplored. He would at times work himself into the greatest excitement about the most trivial matters, over which he would laugh in his more serene moments.

Whilst Mr. Hawker was in London, he called one day on some very kind friends, who had a house in Bude, but were then in town. Mrs. M——, thinking that the old man would be troubled at being away from his books, very considerately offered to lend him any from her own library which he might take a fancy to read. But he said: "All I want is a reference Bible. If I have that I care for no other books." And he carried off a Bagster's Polyglot that lay on the table.

From London Mr. Hawker returned to Morwenstow, to fresh suffering, disappointment, and anxieties. I give a few of his last letters to one whom he regarded as his best friend.

MORWENSTOW, Sept. 22, 1874. *My dear Valentine,*—You brought to my house the solitary blessing of my life. My three daughters came to me through you, as God's instrument. I must write to you. You will not have many more letters from me. . . . My mind has been so racked and softened that I shall never be myself again. My health, too, is gone. My legs are healed, but the long drain has enfeebled me exceedingly. Money terrors, too, have reached a climax. I have so many claims upon me, that I cannot regard my home as sure, nor my roof certain to shelter my dear ones. On the school-building account I am responsible for seventy pounds odd, more than I

17

have collected from subscribers. . . . I have to pay the master twelve pounds ten shillings quarterly. But there is one thing more—the curate, whom I must have, for I cannot go on serving both churches as I do now, with daily service here. T——, and his mother, will give me one-half, or nearly his salary. But besides Dean Lodge there is no house that he can live in. Let him rent it until you sell it. I implore you, grant this last kindness to me whom you once called a friend. My heart is broken. It is a favour you will not have to grant me long, as my pausing pulse and my shuddering heart testify. Oh, God bless you!

Mr. Valentine came to Chapel House, Morwenstow, in October, 1874, and renewed his old warm friendship with the vicar. Had there been any change in the views of Mr. Hawker, it would certainly have been made known to his most intimate friend of many years. But Mr. Valentine found him the same in faith, though sadly failing in mental and bodily power.

Nov. 13, 1874. *My dear Valentine,*—You will be sorry to hear that over-anxieties and troubles are incessant. First of all, no curate. A Mr. H—— came down from Torquay. He had all but agreed to come, but when he saw Dean Lodge he declined. He thought it too far to walk to church. I have advertised in three papers, but only one applicant. I have invited him to come and see for himself, but he has not yet appeared or written. We are so remote and forlorn that unless a man be very *sincere and honest* there is no inducement. No sphere for strut or grimace, or other vanity. Another trouble that we have is scarlet and typhus fever both, in several parts of the parish. . . . And now I am compelled to remind you that you promised me this month your subscriptions to our charities. I want to pay the schoolmaster, this next week, his quarter's salary. This will make the adverse balance run to nearly fifty pounds against me. It is most ruinous. Upon the school-building account I am responsible for sixty-eight pounds beyond the subscriptions. . . .

What a life this is to lead in the flesh! Mine has been indeed a martyrdom.

Nov. 17, 1874. *My dear Valentine*,[1] . . . One part of your letter has troubled our earnest hope. If you would but fulfil your suggestion, and come to Dean Lodge, the advantages to me would be incalculable. You would not, I know, object to help me in the church once a Sunday. I cannot, by any effort, obtain a curate. The work—thrice a day on Sunday—is killing me, and your presence would soothe the dreadful depression into which I am sinking fast. Make any effort, I do entreat you, to come. The cry after your last appearance in church[2] was, that no sermon had been heard in church for a long time equal to yours: not very complimentary to me, but that I don't mind. Come! anything you want at Dean, that we have, you are most welcome to have from us. Your presence in the parish will be ample compensation. Come, I do entreat you, and gladden us by deciding at once, and telling us so. I shall have hope then of getting over the winter, which now I cannot realise. My great terror is that I have all but lost the power of sleep. I cannot rest in bed quietly above two or three hours. Now, it would be cruel to awaken hope, and crush it again. You shall have horses and carriage, and anything you want.

At Christmas he was very ill, and thought that life's last page was being turned, and that before the daisies reappeared in Morwenstow churchyard he would be resting in his long home.

But he got slowly better. On 28th April, 1875, he was still in trouble about a curate, and wrote to Mr. Valentine, begging him to allow him to take Dean Lodge, and make it a cottage for his curate. " Write

---

[1] Then returned to Yorkshire.
[2] In the previous month, October.

to me at once," he said, "to relieve my poor broken mind of one of the *pressures* which are now dragging it down. Pray write immediately, because my second letter must have apprised you how unable I am in my present shattered state. And mind, I rely on you for standing by me in these, my last trials."

In June Mr. Hawker went for change, with his wife and children, and a lady, the companion of Mrs. Hawker, who was staying with them, to Boscastle, to visit his brother at Penally.

Did any prevision of what would take place pass before his mind's eye ere he left his beloved Morwenstow? Had he any thought that he was taking his last look at the quiet combe, with its furze and heather slopes, the laughing, sparkling, blue sea that lashed the giant cliffs on which St. Morwenna had planted her foot, cross in hand? We cannot tell. It is certain that it had been all along his wish to lay him down to rest in his old church. The grave made for his wife was, by his orders, made double; a space was left on the stone for his name; and he often, at all events before his second marriage, spoke of his desire to be laid there, and made a friend promise, that, should he by accident die away from Morwenstow, he would fetch his body, and lay him there.

When he heard that it was illegal to be buried inside the church, he pointed out a place under the east wall of his chancel where he wished to be laid; but he hoped that, owing to the remoteness of Morwenstow, no difficulty would be raised about his being laid in the grave he had prepared for himself in the church where he had ministered so long.

However, later on, he often quoted St. Monica's last prayer: "Lay my body anywhere—only do not forget to remember me at the altar of God."

Is it to be wondered at, that now there are Morwenstow people who say, that, since his death, they have seen the old man standing at the head of the stone that covers his wife, looking mournfully at the blank space where he had hoped his name would be cut; and that others, who have not seen him, aver that they have heard his familiar sighs and moans from the same spot?

Whilst he was at Boscastle he was neither mentally nor bodily himself. His brother, Mr. Claud Hawker, wrote to me that he was often in a state approaching stupor. "When he came down here in August he was very ill, and certainly broken in his mind, nearly all the time he was here: he was often in a scarce-conscious state."

Whilst Mr. Hawker and family were staying at Penally, Mr. Claud Hawker fell ill, and it was necessary for them to move out of the house. Mr. Robert Hawker would have returned to Morwenstow, had not the curate been in the vicarage: then he wished to take lodgings at Boscastle, but was persuaded by Mrs. Hawker to go to Plymouth.

His brother wrote to me: "Robert came down to see me ill in bed. I was ill at the time; but I could see he was not like himself in any way, and it was no act of his to go to Plymouth. He declined to do so for some time, until at last, most reluctantly, and against his better judgment, he was persuaded to do so."

On the other hand, Miss E. Newton says that the visit to Plymouth was a planned thing, as Mr. Hawker was desirous of medical advice there.

They left on 29th June, and took lodgings in Lockyer Street, Plymouth. Mr. Robert S. Hawker was still very ill and failing.

The Rev. Prebendary Thynne, rector of Kilkhampton, a near and attached friend of sixteen years, was in Plymouth not long before the end, and saw the vicar of Morwenstow. He was then agitated because he had not been able to be present at the Bishop of Exeter's visitation at Stratton, fearing lest the bishop should take it as a slight. The rector of Kilkhampton quieted him by assuring him that the bishop knew how ill he was, and that he was away for change of air. Then he brightened up a little, but he was anything but himself.

The curate of Kilkhampton wrote to me: "Mr. Hawker complained that we had not invited him to a retreat held by one of the Cowley Missioners in the same month in which he died. Of course we knew that he could not have come, and so did not ask him. But surely his making a kind of grievance of it is hardly consistent with the idea that even at that time he was in heart a Roman Catholic."

On Sunday, 1st Aug., Mr. Hawker went with his wife to St. James Church, Plymouth, for morning service. The service was choral, and he much enjoyed it. Mrs. Hawker saw him home, and then went on to the Roman Catholic Cathedral, to high mass; and in the evening he accompanied her to benediction, and was pleased with the beauty of the service, which to him had all the attractions of novelty, as he had never travelled abroad, and so was unfamiliar with Roman Catholic ritual. The church was very solemn, and nicely cared for; and benediction is one of the most touching, popular and elastic of services.

He was so pleased, that he said he should be quite happy to spend a night in the church.

During the week he began to fail rapidly, and on Friday spent the greater part of the day on his bed. He suffered from great mental prostration. One evening he was got out of the house as far as to the Laira, a beautiful creek with the Saltram woods beyond, touching the water; but he was too weak in body and depressed in mind to go out for exercise again.

Feeling himself growing weaker, and, as Mrs. Hawker wrote to his niece, " with the truth really beginning to dawn upon him," he became nervously impatient to get away from Plymouth as speedily as possible, and to return to the home he loved, hallowed by the feet of St. Morwenna, and rendered dear to him by the associations of more than forty years.

But before he left Plymouth, when all had been ordered to be in readiness for departure, and notice had been given that the lodgings would be left the ensuing week, a curious occurrence took place. His beloved St. Cuthbert's stole was sent for from Morwenstow, and a biretta, a distinctively priest's cap, was borrowed for him—a thing he never wore himself—and he had himself photographed in cassock, surplice, stole and biretta, as a priest. It was his last conscious act; and it is certainly very inconsistent with the supposition that at the time he disbelieved in his Orders. This photograph was taken on Saturday, 7th Aug.: on Monday, 9th Aug., he was struck down with paralysis.

His action in this matter was the more extraordinary, as he had at one time manifested an extreme repugnance to having his likeness taken. He has told me himself that he would have inscribed on his tombstone: " Here lies the man who was never photographed." For a long time he stubbornly refused the most earnest requests to be taken; and his repugnance was only overcome, at last, by Mrs. Mills bringing over a photographer from Bude, in her carriage, to Morwenstow, and insisting on having him stand to be taken.[1]

It was the old man's last act, and it was a very emphatic and significant one. The photograph was taken on the very day on which Mrs. Hawker represented him as seeing that his end was drawing nigh. Every preparation was made for departure, the boxes were packed, and all was ready, on Monday; his impatience to be gone rapidly growing.

Mrs. Hawker wrote to his nephew at Whitstone, eight miles from Stratton, to say that they would lunch with him on Tuesday, the 10th, on their way back from Plymouth to Morwenstow, intending to drive the distance in the day.

---

[1] The photographs taken on this occasion were by Mr. Thorn of Bude Haven. The most admirable one is of Mr. Hawker standing in his porch to receive visitors. He was, however, afterwards taken by Mr. Thorn at Bude, with his wife and children. That of him in surplice and stole is by Mr. Hawke of Plymouth.

He never came, nor was the reason known till it was too late for his nephew to see him.

On Monday evening, when all was ready for departure on the morrow, about seven o'clock, Mrs. Hawker saw her husband's left hand turn dead, white and cold. Perceiving that he had a paralytic stroke, she sent immediately for a surgeon. On the morrow, Tuesday, the day on which the old man's face was to have been turned homewards, it became evident that his face was set to go towards a happier and an eternal home.

It was then clear that there was no return for him to Morwenstow; and the lodgings were taken on for another week, which would probably see the close of the scene.

On that evening Mrs. Hawker wrote to his sister, Mrs. Kingdon, a very aged lady at Holsworthy, to tell her that her brother had had a stroke, and that the medical attendant had "forbid him doing any duty if he goes back to Morwenstow. . . . Of course the knowledge that he can be no longer of use at Morwenstow is a terrible blow to his mind." She also requested Mrs. Kingdon to keep his sickness a profound secret from every one. At Whitstone he was in vain expected, day after day, for lunch. Nor were his brother and niece at Boscastle aware that his illness was serious, and that life was ebbing fast away, till all was over.

Mr. Claud Hawker informed me that even on that Tuesday, when he learned that he must not take duty again in his loved church, he was restless to be off, and would not have the things unpacked. On that day one of the arteries of the left arm with the pulse had stopped. On Wednesday the companion of Mrs. Hawker, who helped to nurse him, was satisfied that he knew her, and seemed to be pleased with her attentions. His wife ministered to him with the most devoted tenderness, and would allow no hired nurse near him, nor even one of the servants of the house to invade the room, so jealous is love of lavishing all its powers on the object of affection. On Thursday his pulse was weaker, and consciousness scarcely manifested itself. His solicitor from Stratton had been telegraphed for, and arrived on that day: he was informed by Mrs. Hawker that her husband was quite unconscious, and not fit to see any one. Understanding that there was no chance of Mr. Hawker recovering sufficiently to discuss final arrangements of money affairs, and that it was therefore useless to stay in Plymouth, he returned to Stratton.

Mrs. Hawker and her friend, finding themselves unable to raise the sick man in bed, sent for his servant-man from Morwenstow; and he arrived on Friday. His master recognised him, and gave tokens of pleasure at seeing him at his side. The same evening he knew the medical man who attended him, and said a word or two to him in a faint whisper; but his brain was in part paralysed, and he hovered between consciousness and torpor, like a flickering flame, or the state of a man between sleeping and waking.

On Saturday morning Mrs. Hawker informed him that she was going to send for the Roman Catholic

Canon Mansfield to see him. She believed that he seemed pleased; and, as so often happens shortly before death, a slight rally appeared to have taken place. According to her statement she sent for the priest at his request. Mrs. Hawker, herself, was not, however, received into the Roman Catholic communion till after his death.

During the day he murmured familiar psalms and the " Te Deum." [1]

In the evening at half-past eight o'clock he was visited. He was in a comatose condition; and, if able to recognise his visitor, it was only that the recognition might fade away instantaneously, and he lapsed again into a condition of torpor.

It was then clear that Mr. Hawker had not many hours to live. At ten o'clock at night Canon Mansfield was introduced into the dying man's chamber; and the sacraments of baptism, penance, extreme unction and communion, four in all, were administered in succession.

During the night his groans were very distressing, and seemed to indicate that he was in great suffering. At eight o'clock next morning he was lifted up in his bed to take a cup of tea, with bread sopped in it. A change passed over his face, and he was laid gently back on the pillow, when his spirit fled.

<pre>
            Youth, manhood, old age, past,
            Come to thy God at last!
</pre>

[1] Through the kindness of Mr. Hawker's relatives, I have been furnished with every letter that passed on the subject of his death, and reception into Roman communion. In not one of them is it asserted that he asked to have Canon Mansfield sent for: the last expression of a wish was, that he might go back to Morwenstow.

The funeral took place on Wednesday, 18th August. The body had been transferred to the Roman Catholic Cathedral the night before. At 10 A.M. a solemn requiem mass was sung by the Very Rev. Canon Woollet, the vicar-general of the titular diocese. Around the coffin were six lighted candles, and a profusion of flowers.

During the playing of the " Dead March in Saul," and the tolling of the church bell, the coffin was removed to the hearse, to be conveyed to the Plymouth cemetery. The coffin was of oak, with a plain brass cross on it, and bore the inscription :—

ROBERT STEPHEN HAWKER.

FOR FORTY-ONE YEARS VICAR OF MORWENSTOW,

WHO DIED IN THE CATHOLIC FAITH,

ON THE FEAST OF THE ASSUMPTION OF OUR BLESSED LADY,

1875.

REQUIESCAT IN PACE. AMEN.

It is far from my intention to enter into controversy over the last sad transaction in the life of him whose memoir I have written. The facts are as I have stated, and might have been made clearer had I been at liberty to use certain letters, which I have seen, but am not allowed to quote.

According to Roman Catholic doctrine, there is no salvation for those who die outside the Church, unless they have remained in ignorance of Catholic verities. No such plea could be urged in the case of Mr. Hawker; and therefore, from the point of view of a Romanist, his damnation was assured.

A Roman Catholic priest is bound by the rules of his Church, and in doubtful cases by the decisions of eminent canonists. The "Rituale Romanum" for the baptism of adults provides for the baptism of those who are unconscious, and even raving mad, on the near approach of death, if there have appeared in them, when conscious, a desire for baptism;[1] and the apparent satisfaction expressed by Mr. Hawker's face on Saturday morning was sufficient to express acquiescence, passive if not active. How far he was aware of what was proposed, with his brain partly paralysed, is open to question. However, in the case of such a sickness, the patient is regarded in the same light as an infant, and passive acquiescence is admitted as sufficient to justify the administration of the sacrament.

Dens, a great authority, in his *Theologia Moralis et Dogmatica*, says that in the case of those who are out of their mind, with no prospect of a lucid interval—which would, of course, include the period of unconsciousness before death—baptism may be administered, if there be reason to conjecture that the patient desired it when of sound mind. And, as

[1] *De Baptismo Adultorum:* "Amentes et furiosi non baptizentur, nisi tales a nativitate fuerint: tunc etiam de iis judicium faciendum est, quod de infantibus atque in fide Ecclesiæ baptizari possunt. Sed si dilucida habeant intervalla, dum mentis compotes sunt, baptizentur, si velint. Si vero antequam insanirent, suscipiendi Baptismi desiderium ostenderint, ac vitæ periculum immineat, *etiamsi non sint compotes mentis, baptizentur.* Idemque dicendum est de eo, qui *lethargo* aut phrenesi laborat, ut tantum vigilans et intelligens baptizetur, *nisi periculum mortis impendeat,* si in eo prius apparuerit Baptismi desiderium."

no proofs are laid down for testing the desire, the rule is a very elastic one.[1]

Billuart, however, asserts that, for the sacrament of penitence, full consciousness is necessary, as an act of penitence is an essential part of it; so that, though a man may be baptised who is insane or unconscious, such a man cannot be absolved. Marchantius, in his *Candelabrum Mysticum*, lays down that a man may be baptised when drunk, as well as when unconscious, or raving mad, if he had before shown a disposition to receive the sacrament.

Practically, no doubt, moved by desire to assure the salvation of the patient, Roman Catholic clergy will charitably trust to their being a disposition, on very slight grounds. The following instance will show this, communicated to me by a learned English divine: "Some time ago a lady wrote to me for counsel, on this ground. Her father-in-law, a very aged man, a Unitarian, had died whilst she was helping to nurse him, and had been unconscious for some days before his death. A very well-known and distinguished Roman Catholic wrote a letter to her, which she forwarded to me to read, blaming her very severely for not having seized the opportunity for baptising him, on the ground that he *might* have changed his views, and *might* have desired baptism, and that the sacrament, so administered, would have

---

[1] Dens, *Theologia Moralis et Dogmatica, Tract. de Sacramentis in Genere*, § 45: "De iis, qui quandoque habuerunt usum rationis, sed jam eo carent, judicanda est dispositio secundum voluntatem et dispositionem quam habuerunt sanæ mentis existentes. Observandum tamen, quod, si aliquando habeant lucida intervalla, tunc Sacramentum eis non sit ministrandum extra necessitatem, nisi dum mentis compotes sunt."

been his passport to heaven. She consulted me as to her blameworthiness, and as to whether she had, in fact, to reproach herself with a failure of duty. I replied in the negative, and stated that the purely mechanical view of the sacrament taken by her correspondent was, to say the least, highly untheological. I do not give the names, but you may cite me as having supplied you with this fact, which happened this year (1875)."

A case was brought before my notice also, of a man being baptised when dying in a condition of delirium tremens. To the English mind such a case is very shocking, but it is one provided for by Marchantius. In this case it was conjectured that the man had desired baptism into the Roman communion: he had previously been a member, though an unworthy one, of the English Church, and had shown no desire of secession.

I cannot dismiss this part of my subject without dealing briefly with an accusation made against Mr. Hawker by certain correspondents in the papers. They did not shrink from charging him with having been for many years a Roman Catholic at heart, only holding on his position of the Church of England for the sake of the loaves and fishes it offered him.

If I had considered there were grounds for this charge, his life would never have been written by me.

How far Mr. Hawker was a consenting party to the reception, how far he had gone towards contemplating such a change when incapacitated by paralysis from forming a decision, I cannot decide.

The testimony is conflicting. I hesitate to believe that it was his intention to leave the Church of England before he died. He was swayed this way or that by those with whom he found himself. He was vehement in one direction one day, as impetuous in another direction on the day following.

No one who knew Mr. Hawker intimately, not one of his nearest relatives, his closest friends to whom he opened his heart, can believe that he was a conscious hypocrite. If there was one quality which was conspicuous in his character it was his openness. He could not act a part, he could not retain unspoken a thought that passed through his brain, even when common judgment would have deemed concealment of the thought advisable. He was transparent as a Dartmoor stream; and all his thoughts, beliefs and prejudices lay clearly seen in his mind, as the quartz and mica and hornblende particles on the brook's white floor.

If there was one vice which, with his whole soul, he abhorred, it was treachery in its every form.

> Be true to Church, be kind to poor,
> O minister, for evermore!

were his lines cut by him over his vicarage door.

In 1873 or 1874 the rector of Kilkhampton was about to go to Exeter to preach an ordination service in its cathedral. The vicar of Morwenstow said to him: "Go, and bid the young men entering the holy ministry be honest, loyal, true." Is that the exhortation of a man conscious in his own heart that he is a traitor?

One day, not long ago, he was in Kilkhampton, and entered the house of an old man, a builder, there.

The old man said to him : " You know, Mr. Hawker, what names you have been called in your day. They have said you were a Roman Catholic."

"Hockeridge," answered Mr. Hawker, standing in the midst of the floor, and speaking with emphasis, " I am a priest of the Church, of the Church of God, of that Church which was hundreds of years in Cornwall before a Pope of Rome was thought of."

A clergyman in the diocese of London, who knew him well, thus writes :—

I think I never read any announcement with greater surprise than that the late vicar of Morwenstow had, shortly before his death, been "received" into the Church of Rome. Mr. Hawker and I were intimate friends for a number of years, and there were few matters connected either with himself or those near and dear to him on which he did not honour me with his confidence. It was just a year ago that I spent some days with him, shortly after his visit to London, to collect funds for the restoration of his interesting church, among the scenes he loved so well; and I feel perfectly assured, had he then meditated such a step, or had he so much as allowed it to assume a form in his mind, however indefinite, it would have been among the subjects of our converse. Nothing, however, was more contrary to the fact. I am certain that at that time not an idea of such a thing occurred to him. I received most confidential letters from him down to a short period before his death; and there is not a line in them which hints at any change in those opinions which had not only become part of himself, but which, as opportunity offered, he was accustomed to defend with no small amount either of logic or of learning. My friend was a man of profound learning, of very great knowledge of passing events, and able to estimate aright the present aspect of the Church and her difficulties. He was also a man of transparent honesty of purpose, of the nicest sense of honour, and of bold and fearless determination in the discharge of his duties. On two matters he was an enthusiast—the scenery and the early Christian history of his beloved Cornwall, and, which is more to my purpose, the position and rights of the Church of which he was, in my most solemn belief, a dutiful and faithful priest. He was never weary of asserting her claim as the Catholic Church of England, possessed of orders as good as those of any other branch of the Sacred Vine, and alone possessed of the mission which could make their exercise available. His very aspect was that of the master in Israel, conscious of his indubitable position, and whose mind was thoroughly made up on questions about which many other men either have no certain opinions, or at least have no such ground for holding them as that with which his learning and acuteness at once supplied him. Such was the late vicar of Morwenstow, one of the very last men in England to leave the Church of which he gloried to be a priest, of whose cause he was at all times the most unyielding defender, and in whose communion it was his hope and prayer to die.

Nevertheless I think it possible, that during the last year or two of his life, when failing mentally as well as bodily, and when labouring under the excitement or subsequent depression caused by the opium he ate to banish pain, he may have said, or written recklessly, words which are capable of being twisted into meaning a change of views. There can be little doubt that the taking of narcotics deadens the moral sense, the appreciation of Truth, and possibly, towards the end, Mr. Hawker may have had hankerings Romeward. But we must consider the man as he was when sound in body and in mind, and not when stupified by pain, and the medicines given to deaden the pain.[1] I have

[1] I have omitted from this edition some controversial matter that has ceased to be of interest.

laboured, above all things, in this book, to give a true picture of the man I describe: I have not painted an ideal portrait.

And now my work is done. I have written truthfully the life of this most remarkable man: I have taken care to " nothing extenuate, nor aught set down in malice." I cannot more worthily conclude my task than with the peroration of Mr. Hawker's visitation sermon, already quoted.

'The day is far spent, and the night is at hand: the hour cometh wherein no man can work. A little while, and all will be over.' 'Their love and their hatred, and their envy, will have perished; neither will they any longer have a name under the sun.' The thousand thoughts that thrill our souls this day, with the usual interests and the common sympathies of an earthly existence—of all these there will not, by and by, survive in the flesh a single throb. This, our beloved father in the Church, will have entered into the joy of his Lord, to prefer, perchance, in another region, affectionate supplications for us who survive and remain. We, who are found worthy, shall be gathered to a place and people where the strifes and the controversies of earth are unnoted and unknown. "Violence shall no more be heard in that land, wasting nor destruction within its borders; but they shall call the gates Salvation and the walls Praise. There the envy of Ephraim shall depart and the adversaries of Judah shall be cut off: Ephraim shall not envy Judah, and Judah shall not vex Ephraim."

Nevertheless all will not perish from the earth. That which hath done valiantly in the host will not glide away into a land where all things are forgotten. Although the sun may go down while it is yet day, it shall come to pass that at evening-tide there shall be light. Moses is dead, and Aaron is dead, and Hur is gathered to his fathers also; but, because of their righteous acts in the matter of Rephidim, their memorial and their name live and breathe among us for example and admonition still. So shall it be with this generation. He, our spiritual lord, whose living hands are lifted up in our midst to-day—he shall bequeath to his successors and to their children's children, the eloquent example and the kindling heritage of his own stout-hearted name. And we, the lowlier soldiers of the war—so that our succour hath been manifest and our zeal true—we shall achieve a share of humble remembrance as the duteous children of Aaron and of Hur.

They also, the faithful few, who have lapped the waters of dear old Oxford, and who were the little company appointed to go down upon the foe with the sword of the Lord and of Gideon, and to prevail—honour and everlasting remembrance for their fearless names! If, in their zeal, they have exceeded; if, in the dearth of sympathy and the increase of desolation, they should even yet more exceed—nay, but do Thou, O Lord God of Jeshurun, withstand them in that path, if they should forsake the house of the mother that bare them for the house of the stranger!

Still let it never be forgotten, that their voices and their volumes were the signals of the dawn that stirred the heart of a slumbering people with a shout for the mastery. Verily, they have their reward. They live already in the presence of future generations; and they are called, even now, by the voices yet unborn, the giants of those days, the mighty men that were of old, the men of renown!

Whosoever shall win the war, whatsoever victories may wait hereafter on the armies of the living God, it shall never fail from the memory and heart of England, who and what manner of men were they that, when the morning was yet spread upon the mountains, arose, and went down to the host, and brake the pitcher, and waved the lamp and blew the trumpet in the face of Midian!

God Almighty grant that they and their adversaries and we ourselves also, may look on each other's faces and be at rest, one day, in the city of God, among the innumerable company of angels, and the first-born whose names are written in heaven, and the spirits of just men made perfect, and Jesus the Mediator of the new covenant, through the blood of sprinkling that speaketh better things than that of Abel!

APPENDIX A

The Granville Letters in the Possession of Ezekiel Rous, Esq., Bideford

From	At	To	Date	At
The Countess of Bath	Tawstock	Barnard Grenville, Esq.	April 24, 1603	
Barnard Grenville, Esq.		My beloved sonne Bevill Grenvile	May 1, 1615	
John Grenvile	Lincoln's Inn	His brother Bevill Grenvile	July 18, 1621	
George Granville	Wear, near Doncaster	The Hon. Mr. Bernard Granville	Oct. 6, 1638	
Lady Francis Carteret	(London)	Mrs. Waddon	Feb. 14, 1715	Tonacombe.
Sir Beville Grenville	Laners (?)	Lady Grace, his wife	Jan. 6, 1642	
Lansdowne		Mr. Bevill Granville upon his entering into Holy Orders		
Sir Beville Grenville	Hayne	The Lady Grace Grenville	March 15, 1639	Stow.
Sir Beville Grenville	Cuttinbeake	Mrs. Grace Grenvile	Nov. 29, 1628	Stow.
Lady Grace Grenvile	Stow	Sir Bevill Grenvile	Nov. 23, 1641	
Barnard Grenvile		My beloved sonn Bevill Grenvile	March 21, 1617	
Thomas Drake		Bevill Grenvile, Esq.		
Barnard Grenvill	Keligarth	My beloved sonne Bevill Grenvile	Aug. 6, 1614	London.
Sir Beville Grenville		The wife of the Chancellor of the Diocese		
		My Co. Porter		

One letter from Sir Bevil to the Chancellor of the Diocese, to oblige the minister of Suttcombe to let the parish get a lecturer, as he is scarce able to read, utterly unable to preach, and what he speaks in the church can hardly be understood—one letter signed Clanricarde, another signed G. Talbot—a pass signed Jo. Coplestown.

APPENDIX A

GRANVILLE LETTERS.—*Continued.*

From	At	To	Date	At
Sir Beville Grenville	Stow	My Co. Ri. Prideaux	Feb. 8, 1634.	Maydeworthey, near Exon.
Barnard Grenville, Esq.		The Lady Grace Smith	Sept. 3, 1618	
Belville Grenville		His son Richard.		
Sir Beville Grenville		His son Richard.		
Richard Grenville, Esq.		My honoured father Sir Beville Grenville.		
Lady Grace Grenville	Stow	My loving sonne Richard Grenville	Feb. 10, 1638	Glocester Hall, in Oxford.
Sir Beville Grenville		His father		
Sir James Bagg		Mr. Richard Estcott		
Sir Beville Grenville		Mr. Byrd.		
Sir Beville Grenville (?)		Sir William Wray.		
Sir Beville Grenville		Mr. Oldesworth.		
Sir Beville Grenville		Mr. Coriton.		
Sir Beville Grenville	Stow	Mr. Oldesworth	Jan. 18, 1627.	
Sir Beville Grenville	Stow	My Co. Rous[1]	March 20, 1625.	
Sir Beville Grenville (?)		Mr. Pollard.		
Sir Beville Grenville		Sir William Waller.		
Sir Beville Grenville		Sir William Waller.		
Sir Beville Grenville		Sir Nicholas Stanning.		

[1] In this letter occurs the expression: "Since I did engage myself by my word, which I value above all worldly wealth, and will not breake it for an empire".

APPENDIX A

GRANVILLE LETTERS.—Continued.

From	At	To	Date	At
Sir Beville Grenville		Mr. Rouse.		
Sir Beville Grenville		My Co. Arundell.		
Sir Beville Grenville	Bydeford	To my best friend, Mrs. Grace Grenville[1]	March 29, 1636	Stow.
Sir Beville Grenville		Sir John Trelawney.		
Sir Beville Grenville		Mr. Wheare.		
Sir Beville Grenville		Mr. Wheare.		
Sir Beville Grenville		His son Richard.		
Sir Beville Grenville		Mr. Rashleigh.		
Sir Beville Grenville		My Co. Harris of Haine.		
Sir Beville Grenville		His brother.		
Sir Beville Grenville		His brother.		
Sir Beville Grenville		Mr. Arscott.		
Lady Grace Grenville		To the Lady Jane Grenville.		
Damaris Arscott		The Right Worshipful Sir John Grenville.		
William Grosse	Morwenstow	For my honoured brother Sir John Grenville.	Dec. 26, 1656	Stow.
J. Thornehill			July 6, 1656	London.
Sir Beville Grenville	Liskeard	The Lady Grace Grenville	Jan. 19, 1642	Stow.
Sir Beville Grenville		The Lady Grace Grenville	Feb. 26, 1642	
Lady Grace Grenville	Stowe	Sir Beville Grenville.		

[1] In this letter occurs the expression: "Let me hear a Saturday night whither the picture came home safe, and did scape the wett". This seems to refer to his portrait of same date, now in possession of Rev. W. Waddon Martyn.

GRANVILLE LETTERS.—*Continued.*

FROM	AT	TO	DATE	AT
Lady Grace Grenville	Madford	Mrs. Bevill Grenville	July 4, 1625	London.
Lady Grace Grenville	. .	Mrs. Bevill Grenville	Aug. 20, 1625	. .
Sir Beville Grenville	. .	His son Richard	. .	. .
Robert Cary	Clovelly	For the Right Hon. Earl of Bath	March 29, 1671	Stow.
Sir Beville Grenville (?)	. .	Mrs. Acland	. .	. .
Sir Beville Grenville	Stow	(?)	Aug. 23, 1627	. .
Sir Beville Grenville	Bodmin	Mr. Webber	. .	. .
Sir Beville Grenville	Stow	Lady Grace Grenville	March 25, 1640	. .
Lady Grace Grenville	Stow	Sir Beville Grenville	Dec. 1, 1641	London.
George Granville[1]	. .	William Henry, Earl of Bath, etc.	Sept. 4, 1711	The Camp in Flanders.

[1] This letter ends with the following sentences : " 'To fear God, and honour the King,' were injunctions so closely tack'd together that they seem to make but one and the same command ; a man may as well pretend to be a good Christian without fearing God as a good subject without honouring the King". " 'Deo, Patriæ, et Amicis,' was your great-grandfather, Sir Bevil's motto—in three (? these) words he has added to his example a rule, which in following you can never err in any duty of life. The brightest courage and the gentlest disposition is part of Lord Clarendon's character of him ; so much of him you have begun to show us already ; and the best wish I can make for you is to resemble him as much in all but his untimely fate."

APPENDIX B

SERMON BY REV. R. S. HAWKER

PREACHED AT LAUNCESTON, 1865

Lo, I am with you always, even unto the end of the world (MATT. xxviii. 20).

THE election of the Jewish people from among the nations had fulfilled its promised end. Their fortunes had displayed the alliance between transgression and punishment, obedience and reward, in the temporal dispensations of God; and suggested an analogy between these and the spiritual allotments of a state future and afar. They had treasured up, with a reverence approaching to superstition, the literal language of the old inspiration, the human echo of the voice of the Lord. But the national custody of prophetic evidence and typical illustration was no longer demanded from those guardians of the oracles of God. Prediction had been fixed and identified by event, and type had expired in substantive fulfilment. The ritual also of the old covenant was one of fugitive and local designation. The enactments of their civil code anticipated miraculous support; and, had this been vouchsafed to many nations, miracle, instead of an interruption in the harmony of nature, would have been in the common order of events. The observance, again, of their ceremonial law, restricted to one temple and a single altar, was impracticable to all save those in the vicinity of that particular land; many, indeed, were merely possible under peculiar adaptations of climate, manners and governments. Even the solemn recognition of the old morality embodied in the Scripture of Moses, and made imperative by the signature of God; inasmuch as it exacted utter obedience, and yet indicated no ceremonial atonement for defect, was another argument of a mutable creed. The impress of change, the character of incompletion, were traceable on every feature of the ancient faith. The spirit of their religion, as well as the voice of prophecy, announced that the sceptre must depart from Judah, and a new covenant arrive for the house of Israel. It was not thus with the succeeding revelation. When the fulness of time was come (that is to say, when the experiment of ages had ascertained the Gentile world that the sagacity of man was inadequate to the counsels of God), and when the long exhibition of a symbolic ritual by the chosen Israelites had conveyed significant illustration of the future and final faith, God sent His Son. Then was brought to light the wisdom and coherence of the one vast plan. The history of man was discovered to be a record of his departure from a state of original righteousness (after the intervention of a preparatory religion) and eternal existence, and his restoration thereto by a single Redeemer for all his race. For this end, the Word, that is to say, the Revealer, was made flesh. That second impersonation of the sacred Trinity "took our manhood into God". The Godhead did not descend, as of old, in partial inspiration, nor were its issues restrictive and particular to angel or prophet; but, because the scheme about to be developed was to be the religion of humanity, its Author identified Himself with human nature, and became, in His own expressive language, the Son of man. He announced, in the simple solemnity of truth, the majestic errand of His birth—to save sinners; repealed, by a mere declaration, every previous ritual, and substituted one catholic worship for the future earth. Now, the elements of durability were blended with every branch of this new revelation. Firstly, unlike the old covenant, it had no kingdom of this world, it depended on no peculiar system of political rule, interfered not with any civil right, but submitted to every ordinance of man as supreme to itself. The Christian faith was obviously ment to cohere with the political constitution of any country and all lands; to be the established religion of republic or monarchy according to the original laws, or any fundamental compact between ruler and realm; as, for example, this our Church of England received solemn recognition as a public establishment, and had assurance of the future protection of her liberties and privileges unharmed, in the Charter of King John. The new ceremonial usages again were as watchfully calculated for stability, as the forms of the old law had been pregnant with change. The simplicity of baptism—that rite of all nations—was invested with a sacramental mystery, and constituted the regenerative and introductory rite of a vast religion.

One sacrifice, and that to be offered not again, was exhibited upon Mount Calvary, that last **altar of** earthly oblations; and the sources of redemption were thenceforth complete. **The memory of** this scene was to be perpetuated, and its benefits symbolised and conveyed, by an intelligible solemnity, common to all countries, and attainable wheresoever two or three were gathered together in His name. The moral law proceeding on the perpetuity of natural **obligation entered of** necessity into the stipulations of the new covenant. But it was no longer fettered in operation by a literal Decalogue; no longer repulsive from its stern demand for uncompromising obedience. Its enactments were transferred by the Founder of Christianity into the general and enlarged principles of human action, and defect in its observance supplied by an atonement laid up or invested in the heavens. But not only was this alteration of **doctrine** and ceremony made from transitory to eternal: the law being changed, there arrived of necessity a change in the priesthood also. The temporary functions of the race of Aaron were superseded by the ordination of a solemn body of men, whose spiritual lineage and clerical **succession should be as** perpetual as the creed they promulgated.

The scene recalled by our text is that of the shore of Genesareth, whereon stood the arisen Lord, with the eleven **men.** Thence the sons of Zebedee, and others among them, had departed at His mere command from their occupation of the waters, and **had** become the followers of His path of instruction in Judæa, and Samaria, and Galilee. They had seen the supernatural passage of His life in wonder and in sign. They had gradually imbibed the doctrines of His mouth; for them He had given unto the olive and the vine the voice of instruction, and hung, as it were, a parable on every bow. From the cross of shame, indeed, they had shrunk in shuddering dismay. But then, faith revived with His resurrection and they were permitted to identify His arisen body. And now they beheld Him on that accustomed spot, the apparent Conqueror of death, from whose grasp He had returned, the Author of that second life, the breath which He breathed into his new-founded Church; the evident Lord of—in His own declaration—all power in heaven and on earth.

In the first ordination of Christian antiquity, the Son of God invested with His last authority the apostles of His choice: "Go ye into all the world, and proclaim the gladening message into every creature. Make disciples in all nations by baptism unto the religion and worship of the Father, the Son, and the Holy Ghost."

Such was the tenor of that awful commission which they had to undertake and discharge. It was conferred at that hour on none beside, imparted with no lavish distribution to a multitude of disciples, but restricted to the blessed company of apostles; and by implication to those whom they in after-time might designate and ordain, save that the supernatural interference of the same Lord in the vocation of particular apostles might and did afterwards occur.

Who is sufficient for these things? must have been the conscious, though unuttered, question of every apostolic heart at that hour of awe. The fishermen of Bethsaida to arise from their nets to convert the nations! Unknown Galilæans to compel the homage of distant and enlightened cities to the Crucified! The Searcher of hearts, aware of their natural diffidence and usual fear, therefore gave them assurance that the purifying and instructing Spirit He had promised should descend upon them at Jerusalem, and that miracle and sign should attend their ministerial path; and then, to banish the apprehension and awaken the courage of His succeeding servants, he uttered to those representatives of the Christian clergy the consolation of our text—a catholic promise to a catholic Church—"Lo, I am with you always, even unto the end of the world." Amply was that pledge redeemed, that promise fulfilled! After not many days, urged onward by the impulse of the descended Spirit, upheld by the conscious presence of their invisible Lord, the apostles, from the guest-chamber of Jerusalem proceeded on their difficult path. Peril and hostility were on every side. On the one hand, the Jews, haughty and stubborn, clung to the altars of Abraham, Isaac and Jacob, and would not have "that man to reign over them." On the other hand, the Gentiles, absorbed in the indulgence of a luxuriant superstition, were unlikely to forego the gods of their idolatry, and elect from among the various formularies of worship the adoration of Jesus of Nazareth. Yet mightily grew the word of the Lord, and prevailed. Not only were Jewish converts counted in vast multitudes beneath the eloquence of St. Peter and St. John, but, in Gentile countries, a tent-maker of Tarsus obtained much people in every city. The mantle of the apostles descended on early martyrs and succeeding saints, until, not four centuries after the ascension of its Lord, the yoke of Christianity was on the neck of men having authority. A vast empire was docile to its tenets, and a conqueror was found to inscribe on his banner the symbol of human redemption, the wood of shame.

These, it may be urged, were days of miracle and sign. They were so; but it was only because prodigy and supernatural proof were the chief exigencies of those times. The supply of grace—by which word I understand aidance Divine imparted to human endeavour—was not intended to be uniform or redundant, but "by measure." Thus the display of the co-operation declared in our text, and the contribution of the Holy Ghost, to the structure and stability of the apostolic Church, these were to be accorded in rigid proportion to time and circumstance and local need. When that Church, built upon the rock of a pure confession, and reared by the succeeding hands of apostles and saints, had survived the wrath of early persecution, and baffled the malice of Pagan antiquity, then, in the next section of her history, heresy and schisms within her walls tried her foundations, and assayed her strength. In this peril He was with her always—vouchsafed other manifestations of His presence and His power. Wise and courageous champions "for the faith once delivered to the saints" appeared on the scene, clad with faculty and function obviously from on high. The warfare of controversy produced the exposition of error and the triumph of truth. Those sound statements of the Triune Mystery and the attributes of the Second Person therein, which we confess in our Nicene and Athanasian formularies, were documents deduced from those Arian and Sabellian dissensions which they were embodied to refute. The suggestions of Pelagianism, again, in the succeeding era, tended to the more accurate definition of Scriptural doctrine on the union of Divine with human agency in the conduct of man; and the experiment of centuries afforded ample comment on the text of the apostle, that "heresies must needs be, in order that the orthodox might appear." True it is that in the following times, under Papal encroachment, a long period of lowering superstition was permitted to threaten the primitive doctrine and distort the liturgical simplicity of the Church of Christ; yet even then the fire of the apostolic lips was not wholly quenched. The sudden impulse given to the human mind by the appeal of Luther, proved that the elements of early faith yet endured—that the former spirit was breathing still, and awaited only that summons to respond to the call. The success of that German monk, and the other lowly instruments whereby a vast work was wrought exhibited another interference of that supernatural succour promised by our text. The fortunes of our Church of England, since that reformation, have been somewhat given to change. Once her sanctuaries have been usurped, and often her walls assailed. Evil men have "gone round about our Sion, and told the towers thereof, and marked well her bulwarks," but with hostile intent. The present days are not without their danger! Still we hitherto remain. Still we have the promise of the text sounding in our ears. Still have we the contribution of our own endeavours to sustain the spiritual fabric whereto we belong. The circumstances that originate with ourselves to impair our ecclesiastical validity appear to be, firstly, a spirit of concession. The right hand of paternity is too often extended, when the glove over

Edom, the gauntlet of defiance, should be cast down, and the sword of the Spirit grasped to combat and refute. Dissent may be inseparable from religious freedom, as prejudice and error are congenital with the human mind. But the wanderers from our discipline and doctrine forget that they have voluntarily destroyed their identity with the flock; freely abandoned the pasture and refuge of the true fold; and have wilfully resigned all inheritance in its spiritual safety and in the secular advantage which may thereto accidently belong. If, then, through some narrow gate of misconception or error they have "**gone from** us because they were not of us," they cannot, in **honesty,** look that it should be widened for their readmittance, when that return, too, is with unfavourable design towards us and ours. Far be it from me to display unnecessary hostility towards any sect or denomination of men! but if, as I conceive, it be in supposition, that, by some compromise of doctrine or ceremony on our part, future stability may accrue to **this** Church of England, let us remember that Divine co-operation is not proposed to unworthy means, and that recorded experiment hath shown that it were even better that the Ark of God should tremble than that the hand of Uzzah should sustain its strength.

One other source of future insecurity may be apprehended from the growth of vanity in theological opinion and private interpretation among the members of our own body. For example, it is matter of lamentation, that the terms "orthodox" and "**evangelical**" should have attained contrasted **usage in a Church** whose appellations, like her doctrines, should be catholic and one. As in the perilous time of the early Corinthian Church, the existence of divisions in practice **extorted** the indignant expostulations of St. Paul, so, in these days of danger, it behooves every sincere friend to ecclesi**astical order, to** deprecate the exhibition of internal diversity, either on questionable doctrine or custom indifferent, to the surrounding foe. Better it were that those energies which are dissipated on the shibboleths of party, were applied, in unison, to the vindication and honour of the general Church! The theory of ministerial operation might appear to be, that every apostolic officer of Christ should combine, with the intrepid discharge of his own duty, a corporate anxiety for the common weal; that each of us should convey his personal stability as a contribution to the strength of our spiritual structure, and regard the graces of individual ministry as instrumental to the decoration of a general edifice, built upon the foundation of the apostles and prophets, Jesus Christ himself being the chief Cornerstone. To this end, the solemnity of that function which the apostolic clergy have to discharge is in itself argument and exhortation. Unto them was transferred the especial guardianship and authoritative exposition of the oracles of God. By them alone the Founder of their faith gave promise to infuse sacramental advantage into the souls of men. The pledge and reward, the privileges and hopes, of Christian Scripture, regard that Universal Church wherein they hold pastoral rank from the Chief Shepherd, to bind and loose, shut and enclose in his earthly fold. The constant remembrance of these things might both kindle zeal and repress presumption; for, though the office be "but a little lower than the angels," how can we forget that it is intrusted to frail and erring men? The train of thought suggested by a retrospect of these remarks is, that the erection of our enduring Church was always the hopeful predestination—the original intent of God; that three periods of revelation absorb the spiritual history of man: the simple worship of the patriarchal times; that rudiment of religion, the particular, but mutable and transitory, covenant of Moses; and the catholic faith which we confess. In this last inspiration, all doctrine and usage, stationary and complete, are final; and we approach in this concluding dispensation the threshold of eternity; and the text has announced the prophecy of the Revealer, that the official existence of its ministers shall expire only with the close of time. Local illustration of this durability is extant in our own ecclesiastical records. What changes have glided over the land since these towers of the past were set upon our hills, the beacons of the eternity whereto they lead! What alternations of poverty and wealth, of apprehension and hope, have visited those who have served at their altars! times of vigour and decay! And yet we have assembled this day to exhibit our adoration to the one true God, and Jesus Christ whom He hath sent, in this surviving sanctuary " grey with His name "; but the voice of history, that prophet of the past, affords us full assurance of hope for the future continuance of our beloved Church. Vicissitudes may approach, but not destruction; external attack, but no intrinsic change! Whatsoever the hand of sacrilege may perpetrate on the temporal fortunes of the Church of England, these are accessory but not essential to her spiritual existence. Howsoever she may be despoiled of her earthly revenues, though silver and gold she had none, there would be much, apostolic and sacramental, that men must seek at her hands; and with the memory of Him who uttered the consolation of the text, we confide, that, while England shall bear that name, in the imagery of the Psalmist, " The sparrow will find her a home, and the swallow a nest where she may lay her young, even thine altars, O Lord of Hosts, my King and my God!" Because He will be with us in the control and guidance of human events, for all power is given unto Him in heaven and on earth; with us in the general anxiety of His providence and the particular interference of His aid, since the Chief Shepherd must keep the watches of the night over His earthly fold; with us in the issues common and ministerial of His most Holy Spirit, which is in continual procession from the Father and the Son—Lo! He is with us always, even unto the end of the world!

www.ingramcontent.com/pod-product-compliance
Lightning Source LLC
Chambersburg PA
CBHW030817230426
43667CB00008B/1257